ANGELS
Their Purpose and
Your Responsibility

Dirk Waren

ANGELS: Their Purpose and Your Responsibility

Copyright © 2017 by Dirk Waren

All rights reserved. No original part of this book may be reproduced or transmitted in any form or by any means, electronic or mechanical, including photocopying, recording, or by any information storage and retrieval system, without the written permission of the Publisher, except where permitted by law.

Unless otherwise indicated, all Scripture quotations are taken from the Holy Bible, New International Version®. NIV®. Copyright © 1973, 1978, 1984, 2011 by the International Bible Society. Used by permission of Zondervan Bible Publishers.

Many NIV citations are from the 2011 Revised edition.

Passages marked "NASB" are taken from the New American Study Bible. Copyright © 1977 by The Lockman Foundation.

Passages marked "KJV" are taken from the King James Version of the Bible.

Passages marked "NKJV" are taken from the New King James Version®. Copyright © 1979, 1980, 1982 by Thomas Nelson Inc.

Other translations cited in the text are listed in the **Bibliography**.

All underlining and italics in scriptural citations are added by the author.

Pronominal references to Deity in this work are not always capitalized.

Cover art and Ark of the Covenant illustration by KEEII.

ISBN: 978-0692936320
PUBLISHED BY SOARING EAGLE PRESS
Youngstown

Printed in the United States of America

Are not all angels ministering spirits sent to serve those who will inherit salvation?

~ Ephesians 4:13

CONTENTS

Introduction   11

1   What are Angels? What's their Purpose?   13
     Fallen Angels   14
     The Difference between the Holy Spirit and Angelic Spirits   15
     Be Aware of Angels and Partake of their Services, but
         DON'T Worship Them   16
     Angels are Created Beings who Witnessed the Creation   18
     Angels are Watchers   19
     The Population of Angels   20
     Angels are Praise & Worship Warriors   20
     Angels Don't Procreate   21
     What is an Archangel?   22
     Michael, Gabriel and Lucifer   24
     Angelic Hierarchies   28
     Angelic Varieties (Seraphim, Cherubim, Living Creatures, etc.)   29
     How Exactly Will We "Judge Angels"?   33
     Other Facts or Insights about Angels   33

2   DON'T Overemphasize Fallen Angels!   35
     We Have 'em Outnumbered!   37
     Twelve Legions of Angels   38
     "Those who are with us are more than those who are with them"   39
     Cults Tend to Start with Some Kind of Angelic Visitation   39
     Focus on the Victor, the LORD, not the Loser   39

3   How to Enlist the Help of Angels   41
     The Purpose of Angels is to Serve You, Watch Over You
         and Protect You   42
     "His Angels Concerning You"   44
     "...To Guard You in all Your Ways"   46
     Pray for the Help of Angels or Simply Speak in Faith?   47

4   The Power of Your Words   49
     WORDS have the Power of Life and Death   52
     Words have THE POWER OF LIFE   53
     Words have THE POWER OF DEATH   54
     God's Word is His Will; Your Word is Your Will   56

5	**Angels are Listening!**	**57**
	"Keep this Book of the Law always on Your Lips"	*59*
	"Forget Not All His Benefits"	*60*
	Forget Not the Benefit of Angels!	*61*
	Confessing the Word, or Not, is Transferred to the Angels	*62*
	Saved by an Angel in the Fiery Furnace!	*63*
	Daniel Saved by an Angel in the Lion's Den	*66*
	Was this "Angel" the Pre-Incarnate Christ?	*67*
	What about Cases of God-Approved Martyrdom?	*68*
6	**What Goes on Behind the Scenes?**	**70**
	"According to Your Faith will it be Done to You"	*70*
	Speaking God's Word increases Faith	*72*
	Speaking & Believing for Negative Things	*73*
	Good and Bad Angels "Released" through Your Words	*74*
	Do Unbelievers have Angels Assigned to Them?	*76*
	The Power of the Tongue and Your RESPONSIBILITY	*77*
	Prayer "Releases" Angels to Serve You and Others	*79*
	My Example in Praying for People	*83*
	Praying for Governing Authorities	*84*
	What Goes on Behind the Scenes: The Bottom Line	*84*
	Spiritual Attacks for Righteousness' Sake	*84*
	Distinguishing SITs, MITs and DITs	*88*
7	**Who is "*The* Angel of the LORD"?**	**91**
	The First Appearance of The Angel of the LORD	*91*
	The Angel of the LORD Appears to Moses in the Burning Bush	*93*
	The Angel of the LORD Appears to Gideon	*94*
	The Angel of the LORD Appears to the Parents of Samson	*95*
	Jacob Wrestles with God	*95*
	The Commander of the Army of the LORD	*97*
	Understanding God's Name—YHWH	*99*
	If Christ is "The Angel of the LORD" is He an Angel?	*102*
	Father God Speaks to People through the Son,	
	<u>*who Created all Things*</u>*!*	*103*
	Jesus Christ: Superior to Angels	*105*
	What Does it Mean that Jesus is God's "Firstborn"	*107*
	Angels Worship Jesus	*109*
	'Wouldn't Calling Jesus "The Angel of the LORD"	
	Mislead Some People?'	*110*
	The Angel of the LORD in the New Testament	*112*
	The Angel of the LORD distinguished from an Angel of the LORD	*114*
	Jesus Christ—Mighty LORD, Not Milksop	*115*
8	**DON'T Vex Angels!**	**118**
	Don't Provoke The Angel of the LORD	*121*
	"Do Not Rebel Against Him"	*123*

	What Happened to the Israelites are Examples for Us	*125*
	More on the Application of 1 Corinthians 10:6-11	*128*
	Who is "the Destroying Angel"?	*129*
	Believers are "Saved" from <u>the LORD</u>'s Wrath	*132*
	"Kiss the Son, Lest... You Perish in the Way"	*135*
	Examples of The Angel of the LORD Destroying	*136*
	The LORD Utilized the Help of Destroying Angels	*141*
	Christ the Destroyer?	*143*
	Angels are Assigned to You to Help You Enter Your "Promised Land"	*144*
9	**Understanding Fallen Angels (Evil Spirits)**	**146**
	Unclean (Filthy) Spirits	*147*
	Evil Spirits are Demons	*149*
	Satan was a "Cherub" who Fell from Heaven	*149*
	The Devil & His Angels Dwell in the Underworld	*151*
	Addressing Two Alternative Views	*152*
	Hierarchies and Territories of Evil Spirits	*153*
	Why Do Demons Desire to Possess People (and Sometimes Even Animals)?	*154*
	The Prime Directive of Evil Spirits	*155*
	How Do You Prevent Demonic Oppression or Possession?	*157*
	Evil Spirits are Attracted to "Dry Places"	*160*
	The "Put Off" / "Put On" Principle	*161*
	Evil Spirits getting attached to Kids or Youths	*162*
10	**The Nephilim and the "Sons of God"**	**163**
	Why Did the Nephilim Copulate with Women?	*166*
	Were the Nephilim in the Promised Land?	*168*
11	**The Chief "Enemy" Angel**	**169**
	Slanderer, Liar, Murderer	*170*
	Lucifer: Before he became "the Enemy"	*171*
	"Anointed Guardian Cherub"	*175*
	"You were Perfect in Your Ways"	*175*
	Lucifer's Fall	*176*
	Lucifer's Pride wouldn't allow Him to Serve God or People	*179*
	Humankind's Slavery to Satan	*181*
	The Fall of Humanity	*183*
	Satan's "Power of Suggestion"	*187*
	The Consequences of Sin	*187*
	The Ramifications of Satan's Rule	*189*
12	**The Liberation of Humanity & Creation**	**190**
	"All the World's a Stage"	*191*

	God's Plan of Redemption for Humanity	*192*
	The First Adam and the Great Wall	*194*
	The Second Adam Demolishes the Great Wall	*198*
13	**The Restoration of All Things**	**203**
	STAGE ONE: Spiritual Regeneration through the Gospel	*204*
	STAGE TWO: The Rapture	*205*
	STAGE THREE: Christ's Millennial Reign on Earth	*206*
	God's Purpose for the Millennium	*207*
	STAGE FOUR: The Eternal New Heavens and New Earth	*208*
	Creation Itself "Waits in Eager Expectation"	*209*
14	**The DEFEAT of Satan & his Losers**	**211**
	What if You Don't Believe?	*212*
	Satan & his Loser Angels are Disarmed and Defeated!	*213*
15	**Demons vs. Jesus Christ—No Contest!**	**215**
16	**Exorcism and the Believer's Authority**	**218**
	The Exorcism of Anneliese Michel	*218*
	Observations	*219*
	A Real-Life Experience with Demonic Possession	*220*
	Further Commentary on the Film	*221*
	The Believer's Authority	*221*
	Jesus Christ is the Genuine "Lion" while Satan is a Counterfeit	*223*
	Walking in the Amazing Authority of Jesus Christ	*224*
	Rise Up and Walk in Your Authority!	*226*
	Dealing with "Spirits of Infirmities"	*228*
17	**How to Deflect Demonic Spirits**	**233**
	Human Nature and Spiritual Influence	*234*
	How to Distinguish Spiritual Thoughts from Fleshly Thoughts	*235*
	Managing the Soil of Your Heart	*237*
	Demons Work with People through their Flesh	*239*
	How Does Satan "fill a Person's Heart"?	*241*
	How did Satan fill Judas' Heart?	*242*
	Can Believers be Possessed?	*246*
	Satanic Head Games	*247*
	The Sword of the Spirit and the Law of Displacement	*249*
18	**How to Deflect Demonic Spirits II**	**252**
	Examples of Demonic Head Games	*252*
	Two Real-Life Stories	*254*
	How the Enemy Blinds People's Minds	*257*
	Noémas—Mindsets, Ideologies	*258*

	How to Prevent Demonic Oppression and Possession	*261*
	Resist the devil and he will flee from you	*261*
	Draw Near to God	*262*
	Purify Your Heart	*265*
	'You Kids Stay Off Drugs!'	*269*
	Are there Spirits of Certain Sins, like Lust?	*270*
19	**The Armor & Weaponry of God**	**273**
	Differentiating the Shield of Faith and Sword of the Spirit	*284*
	"Putting On" the Armor of God on Any Given Day	*287*
	An Erroneous Reaction to the Armor & Arms of God	*289*
	A Personal Example	*290*
20	**Do You Know What You're Fighting For?**	**291**
	Jesus Christ was Your *Substitutionary Curse*	*292*
	The Five General Curses of the Law	*293*
	The "Hour When Darkness Reigns"	*294*
	When Satan Attacks He Uses One of the Five General Curses	*295*
	Handing an Unrepentant Believer Over to Satan	*301*
	God Motivates People through the Attraction of Blessings	*302*
	The New Covenant is Superior to the Old Covenant	*303*
	Spiritual Laws Work in Conjunction with Natural Laws	*305*
	Financial Blessing is determined by Season, Calling & Environmental Context	*307*
	What is "Prosperity," Anyway?	*309*
	Objections to the Blessing of Health/Healing	*310*
	Don't be Like Job's "Friends"!	*312*
	The Five Main Blessings of Your Covenant	*313*
	The Blessing of a Meaningful Life with God-Given Purpose	*314*
	The Enemy WILL attack these God-Given Blessings	*315*
	Master the Ten Curses and Contrasting Blessings	*317*
	You Must Fight the Good Fight of Faith for Your Rights!	*318*
	'What about Hebrews 11:39?'	*319*
21	**Christ is *Our* Ark of the Covenant**	**322**
	The Ark of the Covenant	*322*
	The Total Sinfulness of Humanity	*324*
	The Christ Symbolism of the Ark	*325*
	The Ark of the Covenant was Lost	*325*
	Why isn't the Ark Mentioned in the New Testament?	*326*
Closing Word & Benediction		**327**

Appendix A	Angels and Gender	329
Appendix B	Were Angels "Created in the Image of God"?	337
Bibliography		343

Introduction

The human race seems to be fascinated by angels. Why else do we observe references to these spiritual beings almost everywhere? Angels are in our movies, our books, our songs, our lyrics, our conversations, our graveyards, our ornaments, our greeting cards, our décor and other forms of art, like paintings and album covers.

Speaking of art, Solomon had the Holy Temple in Jerusalem decorated with cherubim, including the walls (1 Kings 6:23-29). Moreover, the lid to the sacred Ark of the Covenant had two gold-sculptured angels facing each other; and it was between these artistic cherubim that the LORD's presence would dwell on Earth during the Old Covenant.[1]

This is all fine and dandy, but are angels *real*? Do they *really* exist and dwell in the invisible spiritual realm? And, if so, what is their purpose? *Why* do they exist? Furthermore, do we have control over their

---

[1] See **Chapter 21** for a couple mind-blowing revelations on the Ark.

activity in some way? In other words, do our actions or *in*actions determine what they do or don't do? Also, can angels appear in the physical realm as people? And what about *dark* angels; that is, evil spirits or demons? What's the Bible say?

Please notice that the question is "What's *the Bible* say?" and not "What's my sect say?" That's because this book is not concerned with what a particular ministry or denomination teaches on angels, but rather what the Bible itself says. In other words, this is a decidedly *non-sectarian* Scripture-focused look at the subject.

ANGELS combines longer chapters that are dense with info with shorter ones which drive home simpler points. While this book was written to be read front-to-back you're welcome to jump around to get what *you* want out of it. Just use the CONTENTS page to zero-in on the topic that interests you. If you come to a section or chapter that doesn't interest you, just jump to the next one. Cross-referencing is provided for your convenience, as are proof texts. Speaking of which, I'm a stickler for proof texts because they place the relevant data at your fingertips. I encourage you to have a Bible handy so you can look up the texts yourself.

Some important points are *re*emphasized now and then in subsequent chapters because **1.** I don't assume that a reader has read the other chapters and **2.** I consider the point in question to be indispensable to the body of Christ at this juncture. So I'm not being redundant, I'm just driving something home that *needs* driven home. The 1st century apostles practiced this, so I'm in good company (2 Peter 1:12-13).

If something is brought up and isn't elaborated on to your content, it's likely because it's detailed more fully elsewhere in the book.

Like most biblical topics, angelology is a complex subject and so the answers aren't always simple or clear cut. Sometimes an answer depends on various criteria and balancing numerous passages, which is mandatory for "rightly dividing" God's Word. Sometimes we're compelled to speculate based on the biblical data at hand.

Join me now as we dig into the Holy Scriptures to mine them for answers. I think you'll be amazed at what the Bible says about angels and linking topics. Moreover, I believe this study will thoroughly enrich your spiritual walk, as it has mine.

Chapter 1

What are Angels? What's their Purpose?

This chapter could also be called *Angels: The Basics* because we're going to establish the basics about these spiritual beings—good *and* evil ones—and then branch out in the ensuing chapters.

The first thing we need to do is define the term. The word 'angel' is *angelos (ANG-el-os)* in the biblical Greek[2] and *malak (mal-AWK)* in Hebrew, both of which simply mean "a **messenger**." While the messenger in question *could* be human (1 Kings 19:2), it typically refers to a supernatural courier conveying news or directives from God to people.

Further insight can be observed in this fundamental description of angels:

> **Are not all angels ministering spirits sent to serve those who will inherit salvation?**
> **Hebrews 1:14**

---

[2] Biblical Greek is *koiné* Greek, meaning "the common dialect" of the Greek language in the 1st century. *(Koiné is pronounced KOY-nay).*

As you can see, angels are defined as "ministering *spirits*." They are not people, nor are they people who have become angels; they are *spiritual* beings distinct from humanity.

Angels are described as *"ministering* spirits," which means they are given to serve. Whom do they serve? Their Creator first and foremost, but the verse specifies that they are "sent [by God] to serve those who will inherit salvation." This means people because we're the ones who are to inherit salvation. As such, angels are serving spirits who serve the LORD and are commissioned to minister to people, whether by conveying news and instructions or helping us in some other manner, like provision in time of need (1 Kings 19:5-7), ministry when we physically expire (Luke 16:22), fighting demonic spirits on our behalf (Daniel 10:12-13) and, of course, protection.

A good example of the latter can be observed in this psalm:

> **[11] For he [God] will command his angels**
>   **concerning you**
>   **to <u>guard you in all your ways</u>;**
> **[12] they will lift you up in their hands,**
>   **so that you will not strike your foot**
>   **against a stone.**
> **[13] You will tread on the lion and the cobra;**
>   **you will trample the great lion and the serpent.**
>   **Psalm 91:11-13**

So angels are supernatural servants of the LORD whose purpose is to *serve* God by *serving* people. With this understanding, let's briefly consider…

Fallen Angels

The fact that angels are ministering spirits sent to serve people shows why Satan & his fallen angels do **the precise opposite**—they constantly try to hinder & oppress people, especially God's people. One of their main objectives, of course, is to keep those who are lost from eternal salvation.

The rebellion and fall from Heaven of Satan & his filthy angels occurred sometime *after* the creation of the Universe and human beings, yet *before* the devil's temptation of Eve, which means sometime between Genesis 1:31 and Genesis 3:1.[3] This time period could involve many years, plenty of time for Satan's harebrained coup attempt and their subsequent ousting from Heaven (Luke 10:18).

The reason this is important to our topic is because it shows Satan's rebellion occurring relatively soon after the creation of human beings. Could it be that one of the main reasons these angels rebelled was because they were jealous of God's new creation—people—the only physical beings created in God's image? Could it be that they didn't want to spend their lives serving humans, as angels were mandated? Is it likely that their envy was further stirred when they caught wind of the fact that people were expressly created to be *co-heirs* with Christ, seated *with Him* at the right hand of the Father?[4] Does two plus two equal four?

The bottom line is: **There are angels who work for us and fallen angels—demons—who work against us.** Evil spirits are not ministering *for* you; they're ministering *against* you.

Satan's rebellion, by the way, shows that angels possess freewill, just as people do.

We'll look at fallen angels in more detail as we progress, starting with **Chapter 9**.

The Difference between the Holy Spirit and Angelic Spirits

The Holy Spirit is God[5] who *indwells* the spiritually reborn believer. This makes every genuine Christian a "temple" of God (1 Corinthians 6:19). The Holy Spirit's function is to help, counsel, teach, comfort and lead believers (John 14:26 & 16:13).

---

[3] This is the young Earth perspective, which I believe is the most biblically faithful position on the age of the Earth/Universe. Gap theorists, who embrace the old Earth model, place the fall of Lucifer & his angels sometime between Genesis 1:1 and 1:2.

[4] See Romans 8:17, Hebrews 1:13 and Ephesians 2:6.

[5] See Matthew 28:19, 2 Corinthians 13:14 and Ephesians 4:4-6.

Angels, by contrast, do not dwell in you or lead you. They are here to minister for you, that is, *serve* you in one capacity or another.

It is the Holy Spirit's job to "guide you into all truth" (John 16:13), which is why Romans 8:14 says "those who are led by the Spirit of God are the children of God." Notice that it does *not* say "those who are led by angels are the children of God." Why? Because angels aren't here to lead us, the Holy Spirit is. Angels are here to *serve* us.

Their service includes conveying divine messages, which is why angels are also called "messengers." However, angels do not *teach* us spiritual truth (reality) as the Holy Spirit does. It's the Holy Spirit—*God*—who provides revelation knowledge.

You could say that the Holy Spirit ministers *to* believers whereas angels minister *for* us. If I lay hands on you and pray I'm ministering *to* you whereas if I catch you when you fall I'm ministering *for* you. Just the same, when the Holy Spirit gives you a revelation He's ministering to you whereas when angels help you escape a trap they're ministering for you, like when an angel helped Peter escape from prison (Acts 12:5-10).

A pastor gave a testimony of how the LORD saved him from certain death while serving as a missionary. He was about to put his luggage on a plane at a small airport in the bush when he discerned a voice telling him not to do it. He obeyed and the plane crashed on takeoff. In his testimony he wrongly attributed this voice to his guardian angel. No, it was the Holy Spirit, who indwelt him and guided him. *If* he had entered the plane and was miraculously saved when it crashed then that could be attributed to guardian angels. Do you see the difference?

Be Aware of Angels and Partake of their Services, but DON'T Worship Them

Because angels are supernatural beings they're fascinating creatures and we should appreciate them and take advantage of their services, but we must not entertain any temptation to worship them. 'Worship' is *proskuneó (pros-koo-NAY-oh)* in the Greek, which literally means "to acknowledge and adore by kissing the ground in prostration." The apostle John was tempted to do this twice with an angel while he was receiving the revelation of Jesus Christ imprisoned on the Island of Patmos. Notice what this angel says to John on these occasions:

> **So I fell at his feet to worship to him. But he told me, "<u>Do not do that</u>! <u>I am a fellow servant with you and your brothers</u> who rely on the testimony of Jesus. <u>Worship God!</u>"**
>
> **Revelation 19:10**

> **But he said to me, "<u>Don't do that</u>! <u>I am a fellow servant with you and with your fellow prophets and with all who keep the words of this scroll. Worship God!</u>"**
>
> **Revelation 22:9**

It's important to understand this because the Bible warns us that **the worship of angels stems from an "unspiritual mind" and it is a key element of those who try to mislead believers** (Colossians 2:18). Cults thus put undue emphasis on either heavenly angels or fallen spirits. Do not be misled by these false teachers. Let your worship be reserved for God alone, as this particular angel instructed John.

These verses, by the way, explain why angels so seldom make themselves visible to people and, when they do, they often masquerade as humans (Hebrews 13:2). This also might explain the rather generic descriptions of angels in the Bible, at least "common angels" anyway. It's just too tempting for us in our current state to be so awed by celestial beings that we naturally respond with worship, as John does above. If this great apostle was inclined to worship an angel who appeared to him, how much more so believers of lower stature?

The angel's responses show that these spiritual beings are adamant about our attention being focused on the Lord, their 'employer,' not them. They prefer to stay in the background and let the Mighty Christ have the throne. As created beings, they know their rightful place and their purpose: To worship and serve the Creator, not be worshipped themselves.

Lastly, notice how this heavenly angel described himself in each of his responses to John: He said "I am **a fellow servant with you**". We must get ahold of this fact: **Angels are "ministering spirits"**—*serving spirits*—**sent by God** (their 'Boss') **to serve people.** People, by contrast, do not serve angels; they serve us. In fact, we are mandated to judge angels one day, which we'll address at the end of this chapter.

Angels are Created Beings who Witnessed the Creation of the Earth

Scripture shows that angels were created by Christ:

> **The Son is the image of the invisible God, the firstborn over all creation.** [16] **For <u>by him all things were created</u>: <u>things in heaven and on earth, visible and invisible</u>, whether thrones or powers or rulers or authorities; all things have been created through him and for him.**
>
> **Colossians 1:15-16**

It was implied earlier that angels were present when God created the Heavens and the Earth. We see evidence of this in the LORD's humbling response to Job:

> [3] **Brace yourself like a man;**
>   **I will question you,**
>   **and you shall answer me.**
> [4] **"<u>Where were you when I laid the earth's foundation</u>?**
>   **Tell me, if you understand.**
> [5] **Who marked off its dimensions? Surely you know!**
>   **Who stretched a measuring line across it?**
> [6] **On what were its footings set,**
>   **or who laid its cornerstone—**
> [7] **<u>while the morning stars sang together</u>**
>   **and <u>all the angels shouted for joy</u>?**
>
> **Job 38:3-7**

This is a form of Hebrew poetry called synonymous parallelism where the second part of the verse restates the same thought as the first in different words. With this understanding, notice that verse 7 refers to angels as "morning stars." Keep this in mind for future reference.

The point is that angels *already existed* when the LORD created the Earth and Universe. They celebrated God's awe-inspiring work with great joy—singing and shouting.

Angels are Watchers

Angels not only observed the formation of the physical Universe and all things in it, they've been watching events on Earth ever since; at least some of them anyway. This is akin to sports fans at a big game or spectators in an ancient Roman arena. The apostle Paul put it like this: "For it seems to me that God has put us apostles on display at the end of the procession, like those condemned to die in the arena. We have been made a spectacle to the whole universe, to angels as well as to human beings" (1 Corinthians 4:9).

Our cats like to gaze out our windows and so Carol & I dub the windows "cat TV." You could say that the Earth is "angel TV." Angels are watching us and seem to be fascinated by us; Christ pointed out that they celebrate when someone turns from sin to God (Luke 15:7,10).

The fact that at least some angels are watchers can be observed in Daniel 4 where the Chaldean Aramaic word *iyr (eer)* is used to describe them; the word means "a watcher; i.e. an angel as guardian" (verses 13, 17 & 23). This doesn't mean watcher in a merely passive sense, as *iyr* stems from an action-oriented Hebrew word that means "on the watch." One of their jobs is likely to record events, including our words. A minister testified that she was able to see in the spiritual realm on one occasion and saw an angel nearby chronicling the conversations. Why would an angel chronicle words? Because Christ said we'll be acquitted or condemned by them (Matthew 12:37) and this can't happen if they're not somehow recorded.

Later this chapter we'll observe how cherubim and "living creatures" are described as being "covered with eyes." This is likely a figurative statement which perhaps suggests that watcher angels are of the cherub and living creature variety.

Lastly, while watcher angels observe and document what's unfolding on Earth and take action to the degree that we allow them (more on this in **Chapter 4** and **5**), they're not God and therefore they don't know everything that's going to happen; for instance, they don't know the specific day or hour of Christ's return (Matthew 24:35-36).

The Population of Angels

The Bible doesn't provide an exact count of these celestial beings, although in John's heavenly vision he saw "many angels numbering thousands upon thousands, and ten thousand times ten thousand" encircling God's throne (Revelation 5:11). This coincides with a vision Daniel had (Daniel 7:10). That's over 100 million angels! Of course, this indefinite figure doesn't take into account the billions of angels assigned to minister to people *on Earth* nor the fallen angels who fell from Heaven with Satan nor the angels elsewhere in Heaven. It's simply a testimony of the myriad angels functioning around God's throne in Heaven.

In any case, the passage offers a magnificent picture of the activity in God's presence and suggests the number of angels to be incomprehensible. But, while the population of angels may be incredibly vast, it *is* a definite number; we just don't know what it is.

Angels are Praise & Worshipers

Speaking of Revelation 5:11, the passage goes on to show the multitudes of angels praising & worshiping the Almighty (verse 12). The "four living creatures" that John saw around the throne are a form of angel and they're also depicted worshiping God (Revelation 4:8); not to mention many other angels (Revelation 7:11-12).

Someone might ask: Why are these angels praising the LORD so much? Why would God need or want so much adulation? Actually, it's not a matter of the Almighty being insecure and *needing* praise in a fleshly sense; rather, worship is simply the natural response to God's stunning magnificence. Think about it in terms of watching great musicians, athletes or artists: We are so marveled by their talents we react with enthusiastic applause or shouts, sometimes even jumping up & down. You can times this to the nth degree when encountering the Most High. After all, who's greater—the created or the Creator?

When Christ was born in a stable in Bethlehem an angel appeared to some shepherds in a field nearby to inform them of this awesome event (Luke 2:8-15). They were terrified by the sighting, as is usual in Scripture, but the angel encouraged them not to be afraid and told them where to find the amazing baby. Then this happened: "Suddenly a great company of the heavenly host [angels] appeared with the angel, **praising God** and saying, '**Glory to God in the highest**, and on earth peace to men on whom his favor rests' " (verses 13-14).

Praising God is obviously a priority for angels and one of their favorite activities. It's healthy to celebrate & adulate the LORD, not just for angels, but all creation (Psalm 103:20-22 & Psalm 148).[6]

Angels Don't Procreate

Christ pointed out in Luke 20:34-36 that angels don't marry, which means they don't copulate and therefore don't procreate. So their population is a set figure, unless God were to create more.

This doesn't necessarily mean, however, that angels *can't* copulate; just that they don't marry and therefore don't have sex. This doesn't necessarily apply to the fallen angels, of course, as they are in rebellion against the Creator. In fact, a group of them manifested in the physical realm for the very purpose of having sexual relations with women and procreating, which gave birth to the giant Nephilim *(NEF-ah-lim)*, as detailed in Genesis 6. We'll examine this fascinating topic in **Chapter 10**.

By the way, Jesus said that angels don't marry; he *didn't* say that there are only male angels nor did he say that angels are asexual. We'll explore whether or not there are female angels in **Appendix A**.

---

[6] For more on the importance of praise & worship see the section *Draw Near to God* in **Chapter 18**, specifically the part on *Hallowed be Your Name*.

Neither do the Scriptures ever say that "all of the angels were created simultaneously," as I read a couple ministers teach. While this may be likely, it's not specifically stated. What we do know is that angels already existed when the Earth & Universe were created. We also know they possess intrinsic immortality, which means they *can't* die, even if they're fallen (Luke 20:34-36). Such immortality is only available to *people* who are redeemed (2 Timothy 1:10 & Romans 2:7).

What is an Archangel?

The prefix 'arch' is a Greek term meaning "of the first order, chief." So an archangel is a *ruling* angel. This word only appears twice in Scripture:

> **But even <u>the archangel Michael</u>, when he was disputing with the devil about the body of Moses, did not himself dare to condemn him for slander but said, "The Lord rebuke you!"**
>
> **Jude 1:9**

> **For the Lord himself will come down from heaven, with a loud command, with the voice of <u>the archangel</u> and with the trumpet call of God, and the dead in Christ will rise first.**
>
> **1 Thessalonians 4:16**

The first passage shows that Michael is the **ruling angel** in the LORD's service. While the second passage doesn't mention Michael by name, we can safely conclude that it refers to Michael because the verse is addressing the resurrection of the dead and other passages cite Michael as the chief angel in charge of this endeavor (Jude 1:9 & Daniel 12:1-3). Scripture interprets Scripture.

Although it's possible that Michael is the only ruling angel, a couple of things point to the likelihood of more archangels subordinate to Michael. For one, notice how an angel speaking to Daniel describes Michael in this passage:

> "Do not be afraid, Daniel. Since the first day that you set your mind to gain understanding and to humble yourself before your God, your words were heard, and <u>I have come in response to them</u>. [13] But <u>the prince of the Persian kingdom resisted me twenty-one days</u>. Then <u>Michael, one of the chief princes</u>, came to help me, because I was detained there with the king of Persia.
> **Daniel 10:12-13**

This anonymous angel informs Daniel that he came in response to his prayers immediately but was detained for 21 days because the "prince of the Persian kingdom" resisted him. This "prince" was obviously a high-ranking evil spirit that ruled over Persia at the time. The messenger angel was only able to break free from this wicked spirit with the assistance of Michael. This shows that Michael is mightier than common angels, as well as fallen angels who rule over whole nations, which is befitting a chief angel or archangel.

Anyway, notice that the nameless angel describes Michael as "*one of* the chief princes," which means *one of* the ruling angels.

Jewish tradition says that there are seven archangels, and this passage implies it:

> And I saw <u>the seven angels who stand before God</u>, and seven trumpets were given to them.
> **Revelation 8:2**

It stands to reason that these seven angels are chief angels—archangels—in light of the fact that they're standing before God. Think of it in terms of top generals who get direct instructions from their king or president.

I'm not going to list the names of the seven archangels from Hebraic tradition because it's irrelevant in a study based purely on Scripture. However, the top two archangels on this list are cited in the Bible—Michael and Gabriel. Being the only two *heavenly* angels cited by name in the Bible, we know this marks Michael and Gabriel as special. In light of this, plus the fact that Michael is called an archangel—a ruling angel—and *"one of* the chief princes," it's safe to conclude that Gabriel is also a chief angel.

The only other angel cited by name is Lucifer, but he foolishly rebelled against God due to pride and was thus banished from Heaven.

Michael, Gabriel and Lucifer

Being the only three angels cited by name in Scripture, let's consider each of them and their heavenly duties:

Michael. As noted above, Michael is an archangel—the only angel specifically referred to as such—and is described by a subordinate angel as "one of the chief princes." 'Chief' in the Hebrew is *rishon (ree-SHOHN)*, which means "first." And 'prince' is *sar (SAR)*, meaning chieftain, ruler, official, captain, prince. So "chief prince" (*rishon sar*) can be defined as first ruler or top official. Furthermore, Michael is also described in Daniel as a "great prince" (Daniel 12:1). 'Prince' is the same Hebrew word as above whereas 'great' is *gadol (gaw-DOHL)*, which simply means "great." Thus Michael isn't just a ruling angel, he's a *great* ruling angel—the *top* one. So, while there may likely be seven archangels, Michael is the top one.

Is it any wonder, then, that Michael will lead the fight against Satan and his angels when they strike one last time against the Almighty?

> Then war broke out in heaven. <u>Michael and his angels</u> <u>fought against the dragon</u>, and <u>the dragon and his angels fought back.</u> ⁸But he was not strong enough, and they lost their place in heaven. ⁹The great dragon was hurled down—that ancient serpent called the devil, or Satan, who leads the whole world astray. He was hurled to the earth, and his angels with him.
>
> **Revelation 12:7-9**

This prophetic passage is actually a double reference. There are often double references in Bible prophecy, which simply means that the prophecy has both a more immediate application and a far-flung one, whether past or future. The context of this particular prophecy in the book of Revelation shows that it refers to the devil's last ditch effort against his Creator during the mid-point of the future seven-year Tribulation, which fails. However, this is *also* a flashback to the devil's original rebellion in Heaven and his embarrassing ouster, along with "his angels" who joined his harebrained scheme. We'll look at this further in **Chapter 9** and <u>11</u>.

In any case, Michael is listed as the top heavenly angel in command of fighting and defeating the enemy. "The dragon" (i.e. the devil) and his loser angels are "not strong enough" and thus lose "their place in heaven" and are "hurled to the earth."

This, plus the fact that Michael helped an unnamed angel get a message to Daniel by defeating the demonic "king of Persia" (Daniel 10:13) shows that Michael is a warrior angel—the top one, in fact. You could say that he's the 5 Star General of angels.

He's also in charge of the resurrection of the dead, as pointed out earlier.

Michael's name, by the way, means "Who is like God?" which fittingly honors the LORD.

Speaking of which, Michael is decidedly *submitted* to the LORD (Jude 1:9), but this doesn't negate Michael's mightiness in the least, as testified by the above passages. This is important to grasp because wives are instructed to submit to their husbands in Scripture (Ephesians 5:22), which is interestingly related to the hierarchal ranks of angels and their submission to authority:

> **That is why a wife ought to have a symbol of authority on her head, <u>because of the angels</u>.**
> **1 Corinthians 11:10**

As such, a wife submitting to her husband does not negate her greatness or glory in the least. Chew on that.

Gabriel. This angel's name literally means "God is my strength" (literally "God is my strong man"), but could also be rendered "devoted to God" or "hero of God." All are fitting for this mighty angel. In the Bible Gabriel is shown delivering important messages to three different individuals:

1. Daniel (Daniel 8:15-17 & 9:21-23)
2. Zechariah (Luke 1:8-20)
3. Mary, the mother of Jesus (Luke 1:26–38)

On the latter two occasions he announces the births of John the Baptist and Jesus Christ. As such, Gabriel is **the angel of annunciation**—God's angel who announces special events or messages. He's therefore likely the angel who will proclaim the gospel of Christ during the Tribulation, as shown here:

> Then I saw <u>another angel flying in midair, and he had the eternal gospel to proclaim to those who live on the earth</u>—to every nation, tribe, language and people. [7] He said in a loud voice, "Fear God and give him glory, because the hour of his judgment has come. Worship him who made the heavens, the earth, the sea and the springs of water."
> **Revelation 14:6-7**

The angel is described as "flying in midair," which shows that he has the power of flight and therefore *perhaps* wings of some sort.

When Gabriel came to Zechariah to proclaim the pregnancy of his wife, Elizabeth, and the forthcoming birth of John, Zechariah foolishly responded with unbelief. Notice Gabriel's stern response:

> "I am Gabriel. <u>I stand in the presence of God</u>, and I have been sent to speak to you and to tell you this good news. [20] And now you will be silent and not able to speak until the day this happens, because you did not believe my words, which will come true at their appointed time."   **Luke 1:19-20**

Gabriel describes himself as one who stands in the very presence of God. Is this not reminiscent of the seven angels standing before God in John's vision (Revelation 8:2)? This suggests that Gabriel is a chief angel—an archangel—although Michael is the top ruling angel.

Lucifer. This is the angel who pompously rebelled in Heaven and thus lost his position, falling to the Earth in defeat. Technically he fell to the "underworld," which is the spiritual dimension that undergirds the Earth and Universe. He was fittingly renamed Satan, which means "adversary" or "the enemy," as well as devil, which means "slanderer."

'Lucifer,' by contrast, means "shining one" or "light-bearer." He was a top cherub in Heaven, obviously an archangel and presumably in charge of worship. But he rebelled when people were created because he was envious of their nature as the only beings created in God's image intended to be co-heirs with Christ. Not to mention he didn't want to *serve* them, as angels are commissioned to do. Then there's his utter arrogance in craving a position above the Almighty.

I say Lucifer was "obviously an archangel" because he misled a third of the angels in his imprudent revolt and they fell from Heaven with him. You can't mis*lead* others unless you're leading them in the first place, which shows that Lucifer was a *leading* angel; and a leading angel is an archangel.

Here's something to consider: There are only three angels *named* in Scripture and one of these, Lucifer, misled a third of the angels and they were kicked out of Heaven with him. Who leads the other two-thirds who weren't banished from Heaven? Who else but Michael and Gabriel, the only other two angels cited by name?

We'll look at the devil in more detail in **Chapter 9** and, particularly, **Chapter 11**.

One last thing about archangels: This verse suggests that archangels periodically report to God, including Satan:

> **One day the angels came to present themselves before the LORD, and Satan also came with them.**
>
> **Job 1:6**

Which angels came to report to the LORD? Obviously not every angel in existence and unlikely common angels. So this must refer to the ruling angels—the archangels—presenting themselves to God to give account. Job 2:1 shows this happening again, which suggests that it's a periodic obligation, much like supervisors reporting to managers.

These verses illustrate the sovereignty of God: Even Satan, the fallen "god of this world" has to give account to the Almighty. The passages could thus be read as such: "the ruling angels came to present themselves before the LORD, and even the disgraced archangel Satan came with them."

Angelic Hierarchies

The fact that there are archangels—*ruling* angels—shows that there are angelic hierarchies, just as there are hierarchies in the natural, such as in families, businesses, companies, governments, militaries, assemblies and sects. With this understanding, let's take another look at a passage, which suggests the hierarchy of angels:

> **The Son is the image of the invisible God, the firstborn over all creation.** [16] **For by him all things were created: things in heaven and on earth, visible and invisible, whether <u>thrones</u> or <u>powers</u> or <u>rulers</u> or <u>authorities</u>; all things have been created through him and for him.**
> **Colossians 1:15-16**

This reveals that there are subordinate authorities under Christ, and they are hierarchal in nature. Hierarchies are leadership divisions. Think of it in terms of militaries where there's a chain of command. The chain starts with 5 Star generals, then subordinate officers (lower generals, colonels, majors, captains, lieutenants), and, finally, non-commissioned officers.

While hierarchies sometimes have a negative connotation they're necessary for order in any group. It doesn't mean that those in the group aren't equal in the sense of intrinsic worth as living beings; it just means that some in the group are in leadership positions and therefore have more power and thus more responsibility, which makes them more important.

Angelic Varieties

The Bible also shows that there are varieties of angels. Here are the types cited:

Seraphim *(SAIR-ah-fim)*. Isaiah 6:1-7 describes one of Isaiah's visions where seraphim flew above the throne of God. This is different from cherubim, who dwell around it. Seraphim (or seraphs) are described as having six wings, two of which are used for flying. The other two sets are used to cover their faces and feet. Their faces were likely covered to protect them from God's glory since they were so close to the throne. Their feet were probably covered because feet were considered unclean in Hebrew culture.

In any case, a seraph *(SAIR-uhf)* is depicted in the prophet's vision holding a live coal with tongs, taken from the heavenly altar, which the angel uses to touch Isaiah's lips for purification. We observe that the seraph has hands.

Seraphim are only depicted by name this one time in Scripture. The Hebrew word means "fiery ones," likely an allusion to their burning love, readily willing to minister to the LORD or whomever. As such, they're sometimes called the "ones of love" because their name may be derived from the Hebrew root for "love." All this points to the idea that they're personal attendants of God. The Hebrew *saraph (saw-RAWF)* is ironically used five other times in the Old Testament in reference to "fiery serpents" or "flying serpents."

The seraphim in Isaiah's vision are shown constantly glorifying and praising God, saying: "Holy, holy, holy is the LORD Almighty; the whole earth is full of his glory." Using the same word three times to describe someone or something in Hebrew culture meant that the person or thing was utterly like the word. As such, the LORD is intrinsically holy; that is, absolutely pure, unlike fallen angels, which are unclean, impure or filthy.

Cherubim *(CHAIR-ah-bim)*. In modern culture cherubs are typically depicted as pudgy children with wings, akin to Cupid in classical mythology. Scripture, however, describes them much differently. Cherubim are an order of mighty angelic beings. The Hebrew term is probably related to the Akkadian *karabu*, meaning "great, powerful, mighty." They are first mentioned in the Bible as angels whom the LORD assigns to guard the Garden of Eden after Adam & Eve fell and were expelled (Genesis 3:24).

Cherubim are associated with God's holy presence and thus the LORD's glory. God instructed that the pure gold cover of the Ark of the Covenant be made with two cherubim facing each other, their wings spread upward overshadowing the Ark (Exodus 25:17-22). It was between these gold-sculptured cherubs that the LORD's very presence would dwell on Earth during the Old Covenant period (Psalm 80:1 & 99:1). While this refers to the earthly Ark, it was a reflection of the heavenly reality: The LORD is enthroned in Heaven guarded by mighty cherubim on either side.

What's more, David described the LORD as mounting cherubim and flying to help him in a life-threatening situation (Psalm 18:10 & 2 Samuel 22:11). "LORD" in this context refers to the pre-incarnate Christ, also known as *The* Angel of the LORD, which we'll address in **Chapter 7**. While David *may* have been speaking somewhat figuratively, it nevertheless shows the Mighty Christ utilizing the services of cherubim to save his servant.

Ezekiel had an incredible vision that explains how the LORD "mounted the cherubim and flew": God sat on a throne which rested on a huge platform that looked like sparkling ice. Underneath the platform were four living creatures—cherubim—who propelled the platform with the aid of four giant wheels within intersecting wheels (Ezekiel 1). While the passage doesn't identify these "living creatures" as cherubim, the prophet does so in another vision in Ezekiel 10 (see verses 15 & 20 in particular). If you Google "Ezekiel's vision" you can view several awe-inspiring depictions of this Divine craft from different artists. This is how the LORD travels by "mounting the cherubim."

Speaking of these two visions, Ezekiel provides the most detailed description of cherubim: Unlike the seraphim, they only have four wings—two covering their bodies and two for flying. They have the form of human beings with the appearance of burning coals or torches; and they're said to be covered with eyes (Ezekiel 1:18 & 10:12). They have arms & hands, but their feet are likened to hooves. Curiously, they have four different faces on each side of their heads—like that of a man on the front, a lion on the right, an ox on the left, and also an eagle. God gave them four faces perhaps to represent supremacy over the Earth and atmosphere: Humankind is declared the ruler over creation (Genesis 1:26); the lion is the proverbial "king of beasts"; the ox is the most powerful & useful domesticated animal; and the eagle rules the skies.

While Ezekiel's description seems to change a bit in his later vision with the ox-like face switching to that of a cherub (Ezekiel 10:14), verse 22 verifies that he was simply referring to one of the four faces of the *cherub*, which his earlier vision confirmed as looking like an ox. In any case, just as humans, lions, oxen and eagles represent the greatest of their respective domain in the earthly realm, so the cherub is the greatest of angels in the celestial realm.

I should add that there's no reason to think that every cherub looks like the ones Ezekiel described. After all, there's a wide range of appearance in the varieties of people, right? Not all Caucasians, Africans, Asians and Australoids look alike; nor do all cherubim. The gold-sculptured ones on the Ark of the Covenant, for instance, only had one face and, evidently, two wings rather than four (Exodus 25:17-20).

Let's also remember that Ezekiel was describing amazing otherworldly things from a 6th century BC mindset. It would be akin to a primitive native from the remotest parts of the Earth seeing a modern city for the first time and trying to describe skyscrapers and the like.

Also keep in mind that, with visions, the line between the literal and the symbolic is sometimes blurred. For instance, are the cherubs that Ezekiel saw literally covered with eyes or is this simply figurative of the fact that they're "watchers," as denoted earlier? Do they really have four different faces or is this also emblematic? Could they perhaps be wearing helmets with decorated faces on each side?

The hermeneutical rule is to take the Scriptures literally wherein at all possible and only figuratively when symbolism is apparent or highly suspected for one reason or another; in which case we should look for the obvious truth the symbolism intends to convey.

Living Creatures. John chronicles "four living creatures" around God's throne in Heaven that share characteristics of both the seraphim and cherubim (Revelation 4:6-9). Interestingly, Ezekiel described the four cherubim he saw as "four living creatures" (Ezekiel 1:5,13) and, like them, the living creatures in John's vision are said to have faces reminiscent of a man, lion, ox and eagle, except that they only have one face each, as opposed to four. Is this how they really appear or are they wearing symbolic helmets of some sort? They are also covered with eyes, which suggests they are watchers, like cherubim. But, like the seraphim in Isaiah's vision, they have six wings and constantly say, "Holy, holy, holy is the Lord God Almighty." So the four living creatures are modified versions of seraphim and cherubim.

Since the four faces of the living creatures are analogous to earthly beings that are the greatest in their category—human, lion, ox and eagle—it is thought that the four living creatures *represent* creation worshiping the Creator.

Common Angels. When heavenly angels are cited in Scripture they are most often referred to simply as angels and are not designated as seraphs, cherubs or living creatures. While they *may* be one of these, the Bible doesn't distinguish this. Furthermore, they are typically described in terms of young men with shining faces wearing white, gleaming garments (e.g. Matthew 28:2-3, Mark 16:5, Luke 24:4 & Daniel 10:5-6). You'll note that there is no reference to wings in such passages, which supports the idea that not all angels have wings. While this *may* mean that these angels didn't have wings, it could also simply mean that their wings weren't mentioned, just as their hands & feet aren't cited. Or perhaps the way common angels appear to fallen humans *isn't* exactly as they look in the spiritual realm.

In any case, are these angels a fourth classification? Whether they are or not, it's only appropriate that we distinguish them, which is why I dub them "common angels."

And what of archangels, that is, ruling angels? Are they a separate species of angel or are they just angels that have acquired leadership status—whether seraphim, cherubim, living creatures or (maybe) common angels? I would say the latter in light of the fact that Lucifer was referred to as a cherub before his fall. Speaking of which, it *could* be argued that all archangels are cherubim since, as noted above, cherubim are the "great, powerful, mighty" angels associated with God's presence. This is not to say, of course, that all cherubim are archangels.

Consider human rulers throughout history, whether monarchs, dictators, presidents or prime ministers—are they a wholly different type of human being or are they simply people of varying races and socio-economic levels who attained ruling status one way or another? This is why I didn't list archangels as one of the *varieties* of angels, but rather distinguished them as chiefs in the hierarchy of angels.

How Exactly Will We "Judge Angels"?

It was pointed out earlier that we don't serve angels; rather they are commissioned to serve us. In fact, we're called to judge angels. This can be observed in a rhetorical question that Paul asked the believers at Corinth:

> **Do you not know that we will judge angels? How much more the things of this life!**
> **1 Corinthians 6:3**

What does it mean that we will judge angels? Answer: Since believers are co-heirs with Christ and we "will reign for ever and ever" with Him (Romans 8:17 & Revelation 22:5), we will have the authority to judge angels. This makes sense in light of the fact that the job of these celestial beings is to serve us. It should be added that judging angels would include *governing* them since the Greek word for 'judge' can mean "to rule or govern." As such, angels will serve us in the eternal age of the new Heavens and new Earth as we govern them (2 Peter 3:13).

An alternative interpretation is that we shall judge fallen angels, but this is unlikely since their judgment is already set (Matthew 25:41).

Other Facts or Insights about Angels

➤ Since angels are spiritual beings they are not ordinarily visible to the human eye.

- If they are seen, it's allowed by God for a particular purpose (Luke 2:8-15). In such cases they either reveal themselves to certain people with God's permission or the LORD allows them to be seen.
- When this occurs, they often appear simply as normal human beings (Hebrews 13:2). This obviously isn't their real appearance because when people see angels in their true form (presumably as they appear in the spirit realm) they are either awed by them or terrified (Revelation 19:10 & Luke 1:11-12).
- Unlike God, angels are neither omniscient (know everything) nor omnipresent (present everywhere at the same time).
- The scriptural description of seraphim, cherubim and living creatures shows that they have wings. Since Lucifer was a cherub before his fall we assume that he also had wings, which suggests Satan has them. The scant evidence also points to Gabriel having wings, as noted earlier. While Michael is never described as having wings we assume that he does since he's the *chief* angel. How could he be the top angel if he didn't at least have the talents of his subordinates? While common angels aren't said to have wings, it doesn't say they don't either. Yet, here's an alternative possibility: Perhaps angels described as having "wings" is mere symbolism for the fact that they possess the power of flight.
- Jacob had a dream where he saw a stairway (or ladder) going up to Heaven with angels ascending and descending. This illustrates the incessant activity of angels going back-and-forth from Heaven to Earth in the LORD's service (Genesis 28:12).
- Someone argued that angels don't need wings if they can use this stairway. No, all it means is that they utilize this traveling convenience to go back-and-forth from one realm to another. It doesn't mean they don't have wings or cannot fly.
- Angels going back & forth from Heaven to Earth obviously refers to angels delivering messages or carrying out other services and then returning (Daniel 10:12). Perhaps angels relieve those on Earth so they can go back to the presence of God and "recharge" before returning to duty. Remember, God *is* the Fountain of Life (Psalm 36:9).

Chapter 2

DON'T Overemphasize Fallen Angels!

Some ministers & Christians speak as if there's a demon behind every bush. The problem with this is that they're putting so much emphasis on a defeated foe that it becomes a veritable *testimony to* the devil & his filthy spirits. In essence, they're *praising* the kingdom of darkness (!). But notice what the Bible says about our enemy:

> **And having <u>disarmed</u> the powers and authorities, he [Christ] made a public spectacle of them, triumphing over them by the cross.**
> **Colossians 2:15**

The Mighty Christ *disarmed* the kingdom of darkness, by making "a public spectacle" of these fallen angels through his death and resurrection. The phrase "a public spectacle" is likely figurative, but it literally refers to a victory parade where a conquering army would parade their defeated enemies through the streets to the cheers & jeers of the exuberant crowds. God's Word is telling us that this is essentially what happened to the devil & his loser minions through the Messiah's death & resurrection. Notice how another translation puts it:

> He <u>**stripped the rulers and authorities [of their power]**</u> **and made a public spectacle of them as he celebrated his victory in Christ.**
> **Colossians 2:15** (God's Word)

Get ahold of the fact that Satan & his wicked spirits are *stripped* of their authority and power when it comes to spiritually-regenerated believers. If you're a reborn follower of Christ this means YOU. **We should only speak of the kingdom of darkness in terms of their defeat.** We must not speak as if we're testifying to the great things the enemy is doing, but rather proclaim them to be defeated foes because that's what the Word of God says they are! Since Christ already won the victory we must not fight as if we're fighting the battle over again; instead, we simply **enforce the victory**.

As far as there being "a demon behind every bush," keep in mind that the devil was only able to mislead about one-third of the angels, as pointed out last chapter. Yes, the Bible describes Satan as the "god of this world" and so his minions are causing havoc on the Earth (2 Corinthians 4:4), **BUT** they're *stripped* of their authority and power when it comes to believers who are born-again of the seed of Christ. 'Seed' is "sperm" in the Greek and therefore believers are born of the sperm of Christ, spiritually speaking (1 John 3:9)! As such, we're *co-heirs* with Christ through spiritual rebirth (Romans 8:17)! [7]

---

[7] I make several references in this book to believers being spiritually born of *Christ's* seed. This is based on 1 Peter 1:23, which says that believers are "born again, not of perishable seed, but of imperishable, <u>through the living and enduring word of God</u>." Since Jesus *is* the living Word of God (John 1:1-4) we may soundly conclude that we are born-again of *Christ's* seed. This is supported by the word 'Christian,' which means "belonging to the party of Christ (the Anointed One)" or, as I heard it put, "little Christs" (aka "little anointed ones"). However, I can also see the argument for us being born-again of the *Father's* seed since Jesus & Paul instructed us to address Him as "Father" (Matthew 6:9

It's imperative that you get a hold of this if you want to walk in victory. We are "more than conquerors" through the Mighty Conqueror (Romans 8:37)! Jesus already did the hard part—defeating the enemy—all we have to do is "fight the good fight of faith" by conducting spiritual warfare and standing in faith (1 Timothy 6:12). "Spiritual warfare," by the way, simply means overcoming demonic attacks via the spiritual tools that God has provided us. You've been given authority and power to overcome all the power of the enemy (Luke 10:19). 'Authority' means the *right* to rule whereas 'power' means the *ability* to rule. You have both over the kingdom of darkness. Speak like it; act like it!

The New Testament declares that "greater is He who is in you than he who is in the world" (1 John 4:4). The Holy Spirit (God) who is in you is greater than the defeated one who's in the world; that is, the devil & his filthy spirits. Make this your confession and testimony. Say: "Greater is God, who's in me through the Holy Spirit, than the devil & his wicked minions who are in the world!" Remember, words have the power of life and death (Proverbs 18:21). Speak life, not death!

We Have 'em Outnumbered!

There will always be believers foolishly misled by "deceitful spirits and the teachings of demons" (1 Timothy 4:1). This is unfortunately true, but it doesn't have to be **YOU**. That's why grasping what the Bible says about angels is so important; and that's why I wrote this book. The body of Christ worldwide needs to grasp the angels of God in our midst. There are also evil spirits and there is a devil, but **we have 'em out-powered *and* out-numbered**! Remember, Lucifer only misled a fraction of the angels to join in his asinine insurgence.

Consider the example of Elisha & his assistant when the king of Aram sent an army with horses & chariots to capture the prophet in Dothan. The king's forces surrounded the city at night and look what happened the next morning:

& Romans 8:15-16) and we are "*co*-heirs *with* Christ" (Romans 8:17). The bottom line is that 1 John 3:9 says we're born of "God's seed (sperm)" and both the Father and the Son are God and they're one (John 10:30 & 14:9). So, whether Christ's seed or the Father's seed, we're born of *God's* seed. Amen?

> **When the servant of the man of God got up and went out early the next morning, an army with horses and chariots had surrounded the city. "Oh no, my lord! What shall we do?" the servant asked.**
> ¹⁶ **"Don't be afraid," the prophet answered. "<u>Those who are with us are more than those who are with them</u>."**
> ¹⁷ **And Elisha prayed, "Open his eyes, Lord, so that he may see." Then <u>the Lord opened the servant's eyes</u>, and he looked and saw <u>the hills full of horses and chariots of fire all around Elisha</u>.**
> **2 Kings 6:15-17**

The servant's eyes were opened to see in the spiritual realm and he thus saw the hills full of angelic horses and chariots of fire. With these invisible angelic legions on their side, Elisha & his servant had the imposing Arameans outnumbered!

Twelve Legions of Angels

Or consider Jesus' words to Peter in the Garden of Gethsemane where he was threatened with arrest after Judas' betrayal. Peter tried to defend the Lord with his sword, but Jesus stopped him saying, "Are you not aware that I can call on My Father, and He will at once put at my disposal more than twelve legions of angels?" (Matthew 26:53).

Jesus *had* to submit to this unjust arrest because it was God's will and it corresponded to prophecy, but he said it was within his authority to pray for the assistance of twelve legions of angels, if necessary. A Roman legion at the time of Christ amounted to 5,120 soldiers; so twelve legions of angels would be about 61,500 angels. Just keep in mind that Jesus said "more than" twelve legions of angels.

"Those who are with us are more than those who are with them"

Remember Elisha's assuring words to his servant: "Those who are with us are more than those who are with them." This is a fact; get ahold of it!

On top of this, the Bible emphatically declares—as noted above—that "the one who is in you [the Holy Spirit] is greater than the one who is in the world [the devil and his loser followers]" (1 John 4:4). Let's get excited about the good spirits of God, including the Holy Spirit who's *in* us, and not be so concerned about the *defeated* filthy spirits.

The bottom line is this: There are angels working for us and they outnumber the demons working against us, but let's not get out of balance by overemphasizing either or, worse, allow ourselves to be seduced into the "worship of angels" (Colossians 2:18).

Cults Tend to Start with Some Kind of Angelic Visitation

If you've ever studied cults or false religions you know that many of them started with an angelic visitation. A good example is Mormonism with the angel Moroni, who started visiting Joseph Smith in the early 1800s. While this "Moroni" was an angel, he was obviously a *fallen* angel.

Another good example is Islam, which originated when Muhammad was visited by an angel masquerading as Gabriel in a cave near Mecca. Again, this was a *fallen* angel.

Needless to say, let's keep our eyes on the LORD, the author and finisher of our faith (Hebrews 12:2) and not get sidetracked by an unhealthy overemphasis on angels, fallen or otherwise. Amen?

Focus on the Victor, the LORD, not the Loser

It was imperative to include this chapter as early as possible in this book because I wanted to make sure no one takes the material and gets off balance, particularly the info on spiritual warfare in the second half. Let me give an example of what I mean: A pastor got in the habit of opening his services with the statement "Satan, I bind you in the name of Jesus." The problem with this is that the very first words out of his mouth were directed toward the ultimate loser. Why not rather open the services praising God? Like: "Praise the LORD!! God is good, amen?" To which the believers would respond with a hearty "Amen!!" Doing this would send the enemy fleeing in terror more so than a verbal "Satan, I bind you."

Consider a pitch black room: How do you remove the darkness? Do you enter the room and rebuke the darkness? No, you simply turn on the lights. It's the same principle in the spirit. Instead of ranting & raving against the devil and his defeated minions "turn on the lights" by praising the Victor, the LORD. Praise ushers in God's manifest presence and, when the LORD arrives on the scene, the enemy flees. This can be observed in this psalm:

> [1] **I will give thanks to you, Lord, with all my heart;**
> **I will tell of all your wonderful deeds.**
> [2] **I will be glad and rejoice in you;**
> **I will sing the praises of your name, O Most High.**
> [3] **<u>My enemies turn back;</u>**
> **<u>they stumble and perish before you.</u>**
> **Psalm 9:1-3**

In the first two verses David focuses on thanking & praising the Most High and thus, in the third verse, his enemies turn back, stumbling and perishing before God's mighty presence.

We'll look at the importance of praise & worship as a spiritual weapon against the enemy in **Chapter 18**.[8]

---

[8] In the section *Draw Near to God*, particularly the part on *Hallowed be Your Name*.

Chapter 3

How to Enlist the Help of Angels

In the previous chapter we saw that Christ said, "Are you not aware that I can call on my Father, and he will at once put at my disposal more than twelve legions of angels?" (Matthew 26:53). This shows that the Messiah *could* pray for the assistance of angels, if necessary.

Like Jesus, believers can pray for the help of angels when needed. "But Jesus was the Son of God," someone might contend. True, but the Bible says that spiritually-regenerated believers are *children* of God because **we've been born of the seed of Christ**, which is 'sperm' in the Greek (1 John 3:2,9). This brings up a powerful verse:

> Now if <u>we are children</u>, then we are <u>heirs—heirs of God</u> and <u>co-heirs with Christ</u>, if indeed we share in his sufferings in order that we may also share in his glory.
>
> **Romans 8:17**

We *are* children of God through spiritual rebirth via the seed of Christ and are thus "heirs of God and co-heirs with Christ." This means that we share in the inheritance of our heavenly Father *with* the chief heir, Jesus Christ.

As co-heirs with Christ we can pray for and call down angels, if necessary, but doing so takes *faith*—that is, belief—because everything that's available in our covenant with God is *by* faith (Hebrews 11:6 & Mark 11:22-24). How do we develop faith? Through exposure to truth and revelation by the Spirit of truth. 'Truth' is reality, the way it really is; it's the opposite of *un*reality, aka lies, which is the main weapon the "father of lies" uses to mislead people. The main source of truth, of course, is the written "word of truth" (2 Timothy 2:15 & John 17:17).

As such, in order to have the faith Christ had for calling on angels we're going to have to expose ourselves to what God's Word says about these spiritual beings. The more we do this, the more faith we'll have concerning them and this explains the purpose of this book: To expose the body of Christ to the reality of angels so we can benefit from their services since their very purpose is to "serve those who will inherit salvation" (Hebrews 1:14). So keep reading and you'll be blessed!

The Purpose of Angels is to Serve You, Watch Over You and Protect You

Speaking of Hebrews 1:14, since this verse is key to understanding angels, let's read it again:

> **Are not all angels <u>ministering spirits</u> sent to <u>serve</u> those who will inherit salvation?**
> **Hebrews 1:14**

Angels are "**ministering** spirits." The Greek for "ministering" is *leitourgikos (lih-toorg-ik-OS)*, meaning "given to serving." This is observed in the second part of the verse: Angels are sent by God "to **serve** those who will inherit salvation," that is, you and me. 'Serve' here is a different Greek word. It's *diakonia (dee-ak-on-EE-ah)*, which literally means serving in the sense of waiting on someone's table. So

Angels are here to serve us and help us; *they're waiting at our tables every day, 24/7.* Get ahold of this!

With this in mind, notice what this psalm says concerning how angels *can* serve us:

> ⁹ <u>**If you say, "The LORD is my refuge,"**</u>
>   **and you <u>make the Most High your dwelling</u>,**
> ¹⁰ **no harm will overtake you,**
>   **no disaster will come near your tent.**
> ¹¹ **For <u>he will command his angels concerning you</u>**
>   <u>**to guard you in all your ways**</u>**;**
> ¹² <u>**they will lift you up in their hands,**</u>
>   <u>**so that you will not strike your foot against a stone.**</u>
> ¹³ **You will tread on the lion and the cobra;**
>   **you will trample the great lion and the serpent.**
>   **Psalm 91:9-13**

If you *say* "the Lord is my refuge" and make God your dwelling, the LORD "will command **his angels concerning you** to *guard* you *in all your ways*" (verses 9 & 11). This is powerful! 'Guard' in the Hebrew is *shamar (shaw-MAR)*, which means "to watch over, preserve and protect." God will command his angels "concerning you" to watch over you, preserve you and protect you "in all your ways," which literally means all your paths in life.

But notice that there are *conditions* to partaking of this awesome promise: Verse 9 shows that it's necessary to **1.** *say* "the LORD is my refuge" and **2.** make God your dwelling. Let's consider both:

1. To *say* the LORD is your refuge is a positive faith confession, which is important because "the tongue has the power of life and death" (Proverbs 18:21) and the very course of your life is linked to what you do with your tongue, whether good or bad (James 3:2-6). So the fulfillment of verse 11 is partially linked to your speaking in positive faith.

    I should add that the saying "The LORD is my refuge" is not a magical phrase, like "Open Sesame." It's simply a general statement of faith concerning God's protection. As such, you could say a similar faith statement, like "God will protect me" or "God will deliver me," and it's just as effective.

2. To make God your dwelling simply means to abide in the LORD according to the terms of your covenant. You see, God works with people through covenants; a "covenant" is an *agreement* or *contract* in modern vernacular. New Testament believers walk in the *superior* New Covenant (Hebrews 8:6-7) where the terms are "faith working in love," which the Amplified Bible translates as faith being *activated* by love (Galatians 5:6).

Why is faith so important? Because "without faith it is impossible to please God" (Hebrews 11:6).

How is faith activated by love? By the fact that love is the supreme virtue (Colossians 3:14) and therefore fulfilling the first and second greatest commands automatically fulfills *all* the moral Law (Matthew 22:36-40). These two laws have three applications: LOVE GOD and LOVE PEOPLE as you LOVE YOURSELF.

Anyone who does this abides in the Lord and "makes the Most High [his or her] dwelling."

Since faith *works by* love it's important to walk in love (1 Corinthians 13:4-7) because, if you walk *out* of love, you walk out of faith and thus your faith won't be effective. I'm not heaping condo on you here, but rather encouraging you to keep brushed up on your love walk (which includes walking in *tough* love when appropriate), not to mention "keep in repentance" when you miss it (Matthew/Luke 3:8 & 1 John 1:8-9).

We'll look at this in more detail in **Chapter 20**.[9]

"His Angels <u>Concerning You</u>"

The devil quoted this verse—Psalm 91:11—to the Mighty Christ when tempting Him in the wilderness. Let's look at this occasion:

---

[9] In the section *The New Covenant is Superior to the Old Covenant*.

> Then the devil took him to the holy city and had him stand on the highest point of the temple. ⁶ "If you are the Son of God," he said, "throw yourself down. For it is written:
>
> " 'He will command <u>his angels concerning you</u>, and they will lift you up in their hands, so that you will not strike your foot against a stone.' "
>
> ⁷ Jesus answered him, "It is also written: 'Do not put the Lord your God to the test.' "
>
> Matthew 4:5-7

The Greek word for "concerning you" is *peri (per-EE)*, which means "about, concerning, around." The point is that every person has angels consigned to him/her personally. They're the angels that are "about" them and "around" them. Why are they around the person? Because angels by definition are "ministering spirits sent to serve those who will inherit salvation" and they cannot very well do this if they're not there to do it.

An interesting aside is that these angels won't just automatically protect the person; the Sovereign God has to command them and this is **in response to** the person fulfilling the aforementioned conditions of Psalm 91:9: If you **1.** make a positive faith declaration using the power of your tongue, like "The LORD is my refuge" (or something similar, such as "God will protect me," "God will deliver me," etc.), and **2.** "make the LORD your dwelling" *then* God will command His angels concerning you to guard you in all your ways. And angels naturally obey the voice of the LORD (Psalm 103:20). We'll expound on this next chapter.

Something Jesus said also shows that each person has angels dispatched to him or her:

> "See that you do not despise one of these little ones. For I tell you that <u>their angels in heaven</u> always see the face of my Father in heaven."
>
> Matthew 18:10

The Lord was referring to children and this shows that children have heavenly angels assigned to them.

Similarly, Christian assemblies are assigned angels to watch over the fellowship and to serve it (Revelation 1:20). Thus each of the seven churches of Asia Minor that Christ addresses in Revelation 2-3 is shown to have an angel consigned to it. Speaking of which, I heard a couple of ministers insist that these angels actually refer to the pastors of these churches. No, if Christ meant the pastor He would have said "pastor" (or the equivalent "shepherd" or "bishop").

Here are a few additional things to consider concerning angels assigned to specific people and ministries:

- It's unlikely that a single angel is assigned to a person or ministry, although one angel would obviously be in charge of the "operation."
- As noted at the end of **Chapter 1**, it stands to reason that angels periodically relieve others in order to return to Heaven and "recharge" or what have you (Genesis 28:12).
- Some people—like apostles, prophets, evangelists, pastors and teachers (Ephesians 4:11-13)—have higher callings and therefore greater responsibilities than the average person and, as such, would require *more* angels for service & protection; and likely *stronger* angels. As they say: "Higher levels, bigger devils."

"...To Guard You in all Your Ways"

When you fulfill the conditions of Psalm 91:9 the LORD will command his angels concerning you "to guard you in all your ways" (verse 11). This literally means **in any path you take in life**; which obviously doesn't include evil paths, like sneaking out on your spouse to commit adultery. To think that God's angels will protect you when you willfully break covenant by walking in outright wickedness is arrogant presumption, to say the least. The Book of Wisdom warns against this:

> **The integrity of the upright guides them, but the unfaithful are destroyed by their duplicity.**
>
> **Proverbs 11:3**

A good example of this is Ted Haggard who founded a megachurch in 1984, started a veritable sect, and was the leader of the National Association of Evangelicals from 2003-2006. He was the prized darling of Evangelicals and Charismatics alike. But it all came crashing down in a blaze of shame in November, 2006, when a serious scandal broke out to which he initially denied the allegations, but later confessed.

I don't mean any offense to this brother, by the way; I'm just citing this occasion as a well-known example of what happens when a person fails to walk in integrity and is duplicitous. I've messed up in lesser ways in the past and had to suffer the ramifications as well; you probably have too. Praise God that Ted was willing to honestly 'fess up and move on with his life. I wish him nothing but the best.

With the obvious exception of evil paths,[10] God will command his angels to guard you in all your ways. Whether you turn to the right or the left, God will be with you, and his angels will watch over you (Isaiah 30:21 & Genesis 28:15). Make this your positive confession—personalize it and shout it from the rooftops, so to speak. Fear will flee from you as you progress forward and fulfill the LORD's will.

Pray for the Help of Angels or Simply Speak in Faith?

As noted earlier, Christ said that he *could* pray to the Father and God would send myriad angels to help him (Matthew 26:53). Yet we never actually see him do this in the Scriptures. What we do see is Jesus miraculously escaping time after time when his life was in danger, presumably with the assistance of angels. Here are four examples:

➢ When the people of Nazareth tried to murder him by throwing him off a cliff (Luke 4:28-30).
➢ When hostile Jews attempted to seize him (John 7:30,44).

---

[10] Yet even in cases where someone foolishly or ignorantly takes a wrong path the LORD mercifully offers a generous period of grace (Luke 13:5-9). I've experienced this and I'm sure you have as well. My point is that we shouldn't be *presumptuous* about God's mercy when stubbornly choosing evil paths.

- When the offended religionists tried to kill him by stoning (John 8:59).
- When a murderous group tried to seize him in Solomon's Colonnade (John 10:31,39).

The only time Jesus allowed himself to fall into the hands of his enemies was in the Garden of Gethsemane when it was actually *God's will* for him to be arrested and crucified as our substitutionary death. This is an example of what Peter called "suffering according to God's will" (1 Peter 4:19). Other than this occasion, the Messiah refused to suffer at the hands of hostile people, aka those with harmful intent, which includes criminals. Rather he escaped, obviously with the aid of angels.

Yet we don't observe him praying for the assistance of angels, so how did they aid him on these four occasions? Simple: Jesus fulfilled the conditions of Psalm 91:9-11:

1. He spoke in faith concerning God's supernatural protection, and *believed* it.
2. He abided in the LORD by walking according to the terms of his covenant.

Jesus was our example. So this is all we need to do in order for angels to guard us in all our ways and save us when our lives are threatened. I'm not saying you *can't* pray for the service of angels—do so if led—I'm just saying that it automatically happens when you simply comply with these two conditions, as it did with Yeshua.[11]

I want to close this chapter by stressing that angels *want* to be involved in your life—in your home, in your work and in your ministry, which is your service for the Lord, small or great. They *want* to be involved in any project you take on, as directed of the Spirit. Why? Because they're "*ministering* spirits" that God has placed about you to help you and serve you in whatever you do. Needless to say, take advantage of this blessing!

Now let's get a little more specific about how to do this…

---

[11] Yeshua is the Hebraic form of the Greek Jesus, meaning "God saves."

Chapter 4

The Power of Your Words

Angels are ministering spirits sent to serve the people they're assigned to, but what is it they respond to? Notice what this passage says:

> **Praise the Lord, you his angels,**
> **you mighty ones who do his bidding,**
> **who obey his word.**
>
> **Psalm 103:20**

Angels don't just obey the bidding of the LORD, they obey His word period. Here's a more literal translation of the verse:

> **Bless the LORD, you His angels,**
> **Mighty in strength, who perform His word,**
> **Obeying <u>the voice</u> of His word!**
>
> **Psalm 103:20** (NASB)

The purpose of angels is to **perform God's Word**. You could say that their occupation is to obey the voice of God's Word. The Hebrew word for voice is *qol (kohl)*, which means "sound, voice." That's what angels obey—the sound or voice of the Word of God. But does your Bible make any sounds of itself? Does any passage make a sound when you read it or study it? No, it only makes sound *if* you **speak it**! That's why it's so important that you get the power of your tongue into play and start speaking the Word of God in faith, particularly the promises of God that apply to the New Testament believer. And, remember, **all the promises of God are "yes" in Christ** (2 Corinthians 1:20). This means that, if you're in covenant with God through Christ— i.e. you are "*in* Christ"—you can claim by faith any general promise of God you find in the Scriptures that strikes a chord in your spirit!

As an example, take the promises of divine protection of Psalm 34. When facing some type of human attack you can claim by faith verses 7, 17, 19-20 & 22, all of which promise God's deliverance when suffering severe persecution. We'll look at these verses in more detail next chapter.

Why is it that a person speaking God's Word in faith is so powerful, literally unleashing the angels to perform it? Because **people are the only beings God has created who are created in His likeness and called to be co-heirs with Christ**:

> **So God created mankind <u>in his own image</u>,**
> **<u>in the image of God</u> he created them;**
> **male and female he created them.**
> **Genesis 1:27**

The LORD created the Heavens and the Earth simply by speaking them into existence (Genesis 1). People are created in God's image and thus have this power as well. Of course, our words only have power corresponding to our faith, as Christ pointed out:

> "Have faith in God," Jesus answered. ²³ "Truly I tell you, if anyone says to this mountain, 'Go, throw yourself into the sea,' and <u>does not doubt in their heart but believes that what they say will happen, it will be done for them</u>."
>
> **Mark 11:22-23**

The Douay-Rheims Bible translates verse 22 as "Have the faith of God." We need to walk in faith as God walks in faith. We are the only physical beings created in His likeness and thus we're called to **imitate our Creator**:

> **Therefore, be <u>imitators of God</u>, as dearly loved children.**
>
> **Ephesians 5:1**

Many Christians don't realize this, but we are called to **imitate God!** And we can do it because we're *children* of God, born of the seed of Christ; we just have to learn how to live out of our new nature.

With this understanding let's return to Mark 11 above: Jesus goes on to say in verse 23: "Truly I tell you, <u>if anyone says</u> to this mountain, 'Go, throw yourself into the sea,' and does not doubt in their heart but believes that what they say will happen, it will be done for them." First of all, he says "if *anyone* says." He doesn't even specify that the person has to be a Christian. This applies to *anyone* created in God's likeness, how much more so those born-anew of the seed of Christ? (See 1 Peter 1:23).

He continues: "if anyone says to *this* mountain." Obviously there was a mountain nearby and Jesus used it to illustrate his point. "If anyone *says* to this mountain, 'Go, throw yourself into the sea,' and does not doubt in their heart but believes that what they *say* will happen, it will be done for them." This is an example of hyperbole, which is exaggeration for effect. The "mountain" is figurative, not literal. If there is, say, an obstacle in your way you can utilize the power of words spoken in faith and remove that obstacle. But—and this is an important "but"—you have to *believe* that what you *say* will happen and not doubt in your heart.

Jesus doesn't go into the precise mechanics of how this works, just that it works. But, in view of the other passages in this study, it's safe to say that the angels assigned to you respond to your words spoken in faith because **1.** they are assigned to you, **2.** it's their very purpose to serve you, and **3.** you are created in the likeness of God and are co-heirs with Christ. Thus they are released to help you in your situation… or they're released to *not* help you in the event that you speak words of death, doubt and unbelief and act accordingly.

On that note, let's do a quick brush-up on what the Bible teaches about the power of words:

WORDS have the Power of Life and Death

Proverbs 4:24 instructs: "keep corrupt talk far from your lips." The root Hebrew word for 'corrupt' is *luz (looz)*, which means "to turn aside or depart from what is right or good." To practice this verse you must realize the power of your tongue:

> **The tongue has the power of <u>life and death</u>,**
> **and those who love it will eat its fruit.**
> **Proverbs 18:21**

The "fruit" of the tongue is good, but only "those who **love it** will eat its fruit." This means that only those who realize and value the tongue's power—and therefore use it accordingly—will partake of its fruit.

You must get a hold of the fact that **your tongue is a powerful gift from God**, which has the potential to bless or destroy. Only those who realize the incredible value of the tongue will experience **the fruit** it has to offer.

Exactly how powerful is the tongue? The Bible likens it to the small rudder of a large ship that steers the vessel wherever the pilot wants it to go (James 3:2-6). Think about it: The **very course of your life** is linked to what you do with your tongue; or what you *don't* do.

This is so because your words are either **creative forces** or **destructive forces**. Let's look at examples of both.

Words have THE POWER OF LIFE

The Earth & Universe were **created** at God's command (Hebrews 11:3). You were created in God's likeness and therefore your words have creative power as well. Consider a few examples:

God promised Abram countless offspring (Genesis 15:5), but Abram was still childless 24 years later at the age of 91. While people lived longer back then (Abraham, for example, lived to be 175 years-old) 91 was still relatively mature and certainly uncommonly aged for having a child. In light of this, the LORD needed to get Abram's tongue into play in order to bring this miracle to pass:

- So God changed his name to Abraham, which means "father of a multitude" (17:3-5).
- Abraham and everyone near him were then 'forced' to speak of Abraham as "father of a multitude" every time they simply referred to him. For instance: "Father of a Multitude, please pass me the salt" or "Hi, Father of a Multitude, how are you doing today?" The more Abraham spoke this faith proclamation, as well as hear others speak it, the more he *believed* it in his heart and thus the promise came to pass (Romans 4:18).

Another example is the Old Covenant priestly blessing, which *blessed* people. The priests would bless people and God would in turn bless the people. Here's how the blessing went:

The Lord said to Moses, [23] **"Tell Aaron and his sons, 'This is how you are to bless the Israelites. Say to them:**

> ²⁴ ' "The Lord bless you
> and keep you;
> ²⁵ the Lord make his face shine on you
> and be gracious to you;
> ²⁶ the Lord turn his face toward you
> and give you peace." '
>
> ²⁷ "So they will put my name on the Israelites, and I will bless them."
>
> **Numbers 6:22-27**

To 'bless' simply means to speak positive words that have a productive impact. This explains why Jesus blessed children on occasion (Mark 10:13,16).

Another example of the positive impact of words was covered earlier this chapter: Christ stressed that your words, combined with belief, can remove obstacles (Mark 11:22-23).

Words have THE POWER OF DEATH

To 'curse' means to speak negative words that have a destructive impact. The Bible likens the tongue to a sword that can harm people, including oneself (Proverbs 12:18 & Psalm 64:3). Consider these examples:

An influential person—such as a parent, relative, teacher or coach—tells a girl that she's "fat," which she then takes to heart and eventually becomes anorexic.

Sadly, parents curse their very own children; the kids take their evil words to heart and so the words essentially become a **deadly prophecy** in their lives.

- Thankfully, underserved curses have no power over you, **unless you allow it**: "an undeserved curse *does not* come to rest" (Proverbs 26:2).

- You can counteract curses by speaking blessings over yourself. For instance, you can take 1 Peter 2:9, personalize it, and say: "**I am a part of a chosen people**, a **royal priesthood**, a **holy nation**, **God's special possession**, that I may declare the praises of Him who called me out of darkness into his wonderful light." Speak such blessings with fervor! Do it regularly.

Even worse, people speak curses *over themselves:* e.g. "I'm so clumsy," "I always get sick during flu season," "I *can't* do it"—"*I can't,*" "*I can't,*" "*I can't,*" "*I can't.*" Because they speak it and start believing it the words come to pass.

- **Never** speak ill of yourself, your worth, your work or your goals. If you do, you are cursing your own life, which could become a self-fulfilling prophecy.
- **If you say anything enough you'll eventually believe it**; and as a person thinks or believes in their heart, so they *are* (Proverbs 23:7 KJV, Proverbs 27:19 & Matthew 12:34-35).
- Your words **advertise** who you are and **where you are going**, like **signposts**.
- Reject the **victim vocabulary**—"I was abused" or "I don't have an education." Instead, seek the Lord for inner healing with the assistance of mature believers; and *get* educated in the areas that interest you, formally or informally. One of the most successful filmmakers of our time, James Cameron, didn't go to film school. He studied filmmaking on his own while working odd jobs and got experience by getting gigs on sets. He worked his way up as he increased in knowledge & skill.
- It is better to not speak at all than speak doubt, unbelief, negativity or curses.

We are to bless others (Romans 12:14), but *sometimes* cursing may be in order, like when Jesus **cursed** the fig tree, as a lesson for the disciples (Mark 11:12-14, 20-21) or when Paul cursed *Elymas (el-OO-mass)* the sorcerer (Acts 13:8-12).

Here's a powerful passage to chew on:

> **From the fruit of their lips people are filled with good things, as surely as the works of their hands reward them.**
>
> **Proverbs 12:14**

God's Word is *His* Will; Your Word is *Your* Will

Now that you have a better understanding of the power of your words, consider this little nugget: God's Word is His will. They are essentially one-and-the-same. Human beings are created in God's likeness and thus your word is your will. If your word isn't your will then why would you give voice to it?

Why do angels obey the voice of God? Because what God speaks *is* His will. Would not angels assigned to *us*—the only physical beings created in God's likeness—take our words as our will and respond accordingly?

Think about it.

Chapter 5

Angels are Listening!

Obviously our words are very important and we disregard what the Bible says on the power of the tongue to our own peril.

One reason our words are so crucial is that the angels around us are listening and respond to our words spoken in faith because we're created in the likeness of God. Yes, God commands his angels what to do, as shown in Psalm 91:11, but verse 9 shows that this is **in response to**: **1.** our *speaking* a positive confession based on the promises of our covenant—e.g. "the LORD is my refuge (shelter, protection)"—and **2.** abiding in the Lord according to our covenant. This passage offers further insight:

> **Praise the Lord, you his angels,**
> **you mighty ones who do his bidding,**
> **who obey his word.**
>
> **Psalm 103:20**

As you can see, **angels obey God's word. It's what they do**. Are you speaking according to God's Word? If not, get in the habit of speaking it in faith.

If you're not familiar enough with the Bible to speak it in faith then get in the practice of reading it daily. Do a Google search for some reading programs and try out a few until you develop one that fits your life. Choose a version of the Bible that you find readable, like the NIV (Nearly Infallible Version[12]). Since you're under the *New* Covenant and not the *Old* Covenant, I suggest getting to know the New Testament first before delving deeply into the Old Testament (with the exception of Psalms and Proverbs). Why? Because it's imperative that you understand *your* covenant with God before familiarizing yourself with the inferior covenant that the Israelites had with the LORD. This will keep you from confusing the two and tripping into the pitfall of sterile religiosity, like the Pharisees did (John 5:39-40).

Angels are ministering spirits sent to serve you and so the angels assigned to you are around you 24/7 listening to your words. If your words are in accordance with God's Word and you *believe* in your heart then the angels assigned to you will be released to obey—helping to bring to pass God's Word spoken in faith. You're a human and human beings are the only beings created in God's image called to be co-heirs with Christ.

However, if your words are in *opposition* to the Word of God then they obviously won't act. They'll be bound by your doubting, negative, destructive words. And if your angels are hindered from helping you, what kind of spirits do you think will take advantage of the situation? *Evil* spirits!

Why do you think Jesus gave such weight to our words? Notice:

> "But I tell you that <u>everyone will have to give account on the Day of Judgment for every empty word they have spoken</u>. [37] For by your words you will be <u>acquitted</u>, and by your words you will be <u>condemned</u>."
>
> **Matthew 12:36-37**

---

[12] Just kidding. ☺

Wow! Our words are being recorded and will be brought up when we stand before God. Believers will give an account of their lives at the Judgment Seat of Christ (2 Corinthians 5:10-11 & Romans 14:10,12) whereas unbelievers will be judged at the Great White Throne Judgment (Revelation 20:11-15). Either way, our words are being recorded and will either acquit us or condemn us! Christ said so. Why? Because words have the power of life or death! In fact, your very salvation is dependent upon your words spoken in accordance with what you believe in your heart. See Romans 10:9-10 if you find that incredulous.

The bottom line is this: The way we move-to-action angels assigned to us is by speaking in line with the Word of God. Speaking *contrary* to God's word will bind them up and prevent them from fulfilling their purpose, which is to serve us in the sense of waiting on our tables. Needless to say, **don't speak fear, worry, doubt and unbelief; speak in accordance with the Word of God!**[13]

"Keep this Book of the Law always on Your Lips"

This provides insight to God's instruction to Joshua after Moses' death when Joshua was about to lead the Israelites into the Promised Land of Canaan to conquer it:

> **<u>Keep this Book of the Law always on your lips</u>; meditate on it day and night, so that you may be careful to do everything written in it. <u>Then you will be prosperous and successful</u>.**
>
> **Joshua 1:8**

---

[13] Venting, on the other hand, is healthy and has its place. The Bible thus instructs us to cast all our anxieties and cares on to God (Psalm 55:22 & 1 Peter 5:7). This means to literally **go to the LORD in prayer and hurl your burdens on Him**. Why cast your cares on the LORD? Because we can't handle them. **Just as we must remove physical waste from our bodies so we must remove emotional waste.** No wonder venting is strongly encouraged in the Bible (Psalm 62:8) and we observe example after example of it (Psalm 142:1-3 & Jeremiah 20:7-18).

"The Book of the Law" refers to the first five books of the Old Testament, which was God's revealed Word at the time. Obviously part of the reason the LORD instructed Joshua to constantly keep the Word of the Law on his lips was so that he'd be careful to "do everything written in it." However, in light of what we know about angels from the rest of Scripture, speaking in line with God's Word would move the angels assigned to the Israelites to serve them, which is their very purpose. As such, Joshua and the Hebrews would be "prosperous and successful."

"Forget Not All His Benefits"

Observe the first five verses of this awesome Psalm:

> **¹ Praise the LORD, my soul;**
> **all my inmost being, praise his holy name.**
> **² Praise the LORD, my soul,**
> **and <u>forget not all his benefits</u>—**
> **³ who forgives all your sins**
> **and heals all your diseases,**
> **⁴ who redeems your life from the pit**
> **and crowns you with love and compassion,**
> **⁵ who satisfies your desires with good things**
> **so that your youth is renewed like the eagle's.**
>
> **Psalm 103:1-5**

David praises the LORD and tells his soul—his very *self*—to "forget not all his benefits." He then lists several benefits of being in covenant with God:

1. The LORD forgives sins when we humbly confess (1 John 1:9).
2. He heals *all* our diseases.
3. He redeems our lives from "the pit," a biblical synonym for death and, in this context, *premature* death.
4. He crowns us with love and compassion.
5. He satisfies our desires with good things.
6. So that our youth—our vigor—is renewed like the eagles.

At least some of these benefits would require the service of angels and angels only obey God's Word. So, if you want these benefits flowing in your life on a regular basis, be sure to speak in line with the Word of God. **You must remove doubt, fear, worry, unbelief and negativity from your lips! Speak scriptural words of faith that release the angels consigned to you to serve you accordingly!**

Forget Not the Benefit of Angels!

Speaking of "forgetting not all his benefits," the body of Christ in general has forgotten the benefit of angels and their services. Until first studying this subject several years ago I never heard one sermon in my life on the purpose and benefit of angels—not one! That's incredible when you consider I was almost three decades old in the Lord when I finally looked into the topic.

The purpose of this book is for the worldwide body of Christ to rediscover this benefit.

I encourage you to store up God's Word in your heart through study, memorization and positive confession until you're so full of it that you speak the Word of God (or speak *according to* the Word of God) in faith at the drop of a hat. This corresponds to something Jesus said:

> **"If you abide in Me, and <u>My words abide in you</u>, ask whatever you wish, <u>and it will be done for you</u>."**
>
> **John 15:7** (NASB)

The Greek for "abide" means to 'stay.' All true believers *stay* in the Lord. Just the same, "Let the word of Christ richly dwell *within* you" (Colossians 3:16 NASB). Why? Because, as Christ said:

> **For <u>the mouth speaks what the heart is full of</u>. [35] A good man brings good things out of the good stored up in him, and an evil man brings evil things out of the evil stored up in him.**
>
> **Matthew 12:34-35**

If your heart is full of God's Word, and hence the Word of God is *abiding* in you, you'll automatically speak accordingly. When you fulfill these two conditions—staying in the Lord and allowing his Word to abide in you—Jesus promises: "ask whatever you wish, and it will be done for you." Now, let me ask you: How is it that whatever you righteously ask for is done for you? Does the LORD come down from Heaven and do it? No, God enlists the services of angels to serve you accordingly. That, after all, is their function—to serve those who are to inherit salvation—*us*.

Confessing the Word, or Not, is Transferred to the Angels

Here's an interesting statement that Christ made:

> "And I say to you, everyone who <u>confesses Me</u> before men, <u>the Son of Man will confess him also before the angels of God</u>; ⁹ but he who <u>denies Me</u> before men <u>will be denied before the angels of God</u>.
> **Luke 12:8-9** (NASB)

This obviously means that, whether we confess or deny Jesus Christ before people on Earth, the Lord will do the same before the hosts of Heaven when we stand before the LORD at the Judgment Seat of Christ (2 Corinthians 5:10-11) or the Great White Throne Judgment (Revelation 20:11-15). Each one of us will stand at one or the other depending on whether we're a believer or unbeliever. This interpretation is verified by a similar passage in Matthew's gospel:

> "Whoever acknowledges me before others, I will also acknowledge before my Father in heaven. ³³ But whoever disowns me before others, I will disown before my Father in heaven."
> **Matthew 10:32-33**

Both verses are stand-alone statements that we can take at face value, but there's a principle here that we can extract: Jesus is the living Word of God (John 1:1) and, whether we confess the Word of God or deny the Word of God, it will be transmitted to the angels in Heaven and Father God.

Jesus is the living Word of God and therefore he's *"the* truth" (John 14:6). The written Word of God is also "truth" (2 Timothy 2:15). 'Truth' in the Greek is *alétheia (ah-LAY-thee-ah)*, which means "reality; the way it really is." When we confess the Living Word—reality—it is transmitted to the angels and our heavenly Father. If we deny the Living Word—reality—it is likewise transmitted to the angels and Father God. Don't you think the same principle is at play when we confess or deny the *written* Word of God, which is also reality?

Make no mistake, whether you confess the Word of God or deny the Word of God it affects the angels concerning you. Remember, angels are "the mighty ones" who do God's bidding and "obey his Word" (Psalm 103:20). If you ignore God's Word or, worse, deny it, the angels about you will be hindered from fulfilling their mandate—to serve you—because there's no Word of God for them to obey.

In the vacuum evil spirits will take advantage of the situation; and more so if your words are in *contradiction* to God's Word, such as words of doubt, fear, worry and general negativity (e.g. "I *can't* do it," "We're screwed" or "God's not gonna come through *this* time").

Needless to say, learn to "loose" your angels and allow them to serve you by speaking God's Word in faith.

Saved by an Angel in the Fiery Furnace!

A good example of this principle can be found in the book of Daniel when King Nebuchadnezzar erected a 90' image of gold and commanded the people of his empire to fall down and worship the colossal idol at the appropriate time. Those who refused faced death by incineration in a blazing furnace.

Three extraordinary Hebrews—Shadrach, Meshach and Abednego[14]—were administers in Babylon during Judah's exile and they refused to worship the image. Their enemies reported this to the King and so Nebuchadnezzar had them brought before him where he threatened them with death via the fiery furnace if they failed to comply with the edict. Observe their response:

> **Shadrach, Meshach and Abednego replied to him, "King Nebuchadnezzar, we do not need to defend ourselves before you in this matter. ¹⁷ If we are thrown into the blazing furnace, <u>the God we serve is able to deliver us from it</u>, and <u>he will deliver us</u> from Your Majesty's hand. ¹⁸ But even if he does not, we want you to know, Your Majesty, that we will not serve your gods or worship the image of gold you have set up."**
>
> **Daniel 3:16-18**

They were obviously respectful to the pagan monarch, but they took a bold stand against his edict because obeying it conflicted with their God-given Law; specifically, the first two of the Ten Commandments (Exodus 20:1-17 & Deuteronomy 5:4-21). This is a good example of *justified* civil disobedience. An excellent example in the New Testament is when the apostles refused to obey the Sanhedrin's order to *not* preach the message of Christ (Acts 5:27-32).

Notice what the three Hebrews publicly confessed before Nebuchadnezzar: "If we are thrown into the blazing furnace, the God we serve is able to deliver us from it, and *he will deliver us*." They were speaking in faith in accordance with their covenant, which promised them protection as they walked in obedience (Deuteronomy 20:4 & 28:1-7).

Thus the infuriated king commanded that they be tied-up and thrown into the blazing furnace. Yet, once this was done, Nebuchadnezzar saw them *alive* in the furnace, along with someone else

---

[14] I heard Miles McPherson—a *black* pastor—refer to them as "Shadrach, Meshach and a bad negro" (lol).

whom he described as a "son of the gods" (Daniel 3:19-25). This was such an incredible testimony to him that he referred to the Hebrews as "servants of the Most High God" and called them out of the furnace.

Nebuchadnezzar then said:

> **"Praise be to the God of Shadrach, Meshach and Abednego, <u>who has sent his angel and rescued his servants</u>!"**
>
> **Daniel 3:28**

Shadrach, Meshach and Abednego were saved by an angel sent by God. Keep in mind that angels are "the mighty ones" who do God's bidding and "obey his Word" (Psalm 103:20). What Word did this mighty angel obey? The three Hebrews' confession of faith that was in accordance with the revelation of God and their covenant.

By contrast, if they had spoken words of doubt that *contradicted* God's Word then it would've prevented the angel from saving them. Why? Because angels only respond to God's Word. They *cannot* and *will not* assist those who speak contrary to it. This is why it's so important that you learn to speak in accordance with the Word of God.

Now, you might be wondering about something the three Hebrews added to their confession of faith when they stood before the king:

> **"But <u>even if he does not</u> [deliver us], we want you to know, Your Majesty, that we will not serve your gods or worship the image of gold you have set up."**
>
> **Daniel 3:18**

This isn't doubt, but simple defiance in the face of pompous ungodliness. It's an example of godly bratty-ness! It's also an example of bold willingness to face martyrdom, *if* it were the LORD's will, which they may not have specifically known. We'll look at cases of God-approved martyrdom momentarily.

Daniel Saved by an Angel in the Lion's Den

A similar example can be observed three chapters later where Daniel is the protagonist. On this occasion the prophet refused to obey a decree that King Darius put into effect at the pressure of Daniel's enemies. The decree was to pray to no god except the king for a month. Daniel refused to obey this law, of course, which is another example of justified civil disobedience. Naturally, his enemies wasted no time in reporting this to the king (Daniel 6:10-13).

As with Shadrach, Meshach & Abednego and King Nebuchadnezzar, Daniel was brought before Darius where he still refused to obey the edict. So the king was forced to have Daniel executed by being thrown into a den of lions (verses 13-16). The main difference in these two stories is that, unlike the three Hebrews, Daniel had the monarch's favor and thus the king didn't *want* to execute him. He obviously respected the prophet, but was forced to throw him to the lions because of the edict.

After a sleepless night the king went to the den to see what happened to Daniel and was astonished to find him still alive in the lions' lair. How could he possibly still be alive? Daniel informed him:

> "My God sent <u>his angel</u>, and <u>he shut the mouths of the lions</u>. They have not hurt me, because I was found innocent in his sight. Nor have I ever done any wrong before you, Your Majesty."
>
> ²³ The king was overjoyed and gave orders to lift Daniel out of the den. And when Daniel was lifted from the den, no wound was found on him, <u>because he had trusted in his God</u>.
>
> ²⁴ At the king's command, the men who had falsely accused Daniel were brought in and thrown into the lions' den, along with their wives and children. And before they reached the floor of the den, the lions overpowered them and crushed all their bones.
>
> **Daniel 6:22-24**

While it's unfortunate that the wives & children of Daniel's enemies had to perish with them this was simply a reality in Babylon's brutal patriarchal society where wives and kids were considered property.

But this doesn't take away from the fact that Daniel was saved from the lions via an "angel" because "he had trusted in his God," which means that he stood in faith according to the promises of his covenant.

Was this "Angel" the Pre-Incarnate Christ?

Was the "angel" who saved the three Hebrews in the fiery furnace and the "angel" who saved Daniel in the Lions' den an angel or was it Jesus Christ in pre-incarnate form?

There are clear examples of Yeshua[15] making pre-incarnate appearances in the Old Testament, such as these three:

1. The "man" Jacob wrestled all night (Genesis 32:24,28 & 35:1).
2. The magnificent Commander of the Army of the LORD who appeared to Joshua (Joshua 5:13-15).
3. The "Angel of the LORD" who appeared to Gideon (Judges 6:11,14).

While Christ did make pre-incarnate appearances to people on several occasions, there's no verification that the "angel" who delivered Shadrach, Meshach & Abednego or Daniel was Christ. This "angel" *may* have been, but—again—it's not verified in either passage, so it's best to just go by what the account says—they were saved by a mighty angel.

But, whether it was an angel who saved them or Yeshua, the principle is the same: Those in covenant with the Almighty will be assisted by heavenly beings based on faithfully speaking and acting in line with the Word of God according to their covenant.

---

[15] Yeshua is the Hebraic form of the Greek Jesus, meaning "God saves."

What about Cases of God-Approved Martyrdom?

These two examples of miraculous deliverance from fatal persecution understandably raise the question: What about situations where people are martyred for their faith? *Could* they have been delivered, as were the three Hebrews and Daniel?

It all comes down to the Sovereign LORD's will on any given occasion. It *is* God's general will that His children be delivered from life-threatening persecution, and the Bible contains promises to this effect:

> **The angel of the LORD encamps around those**
> **who fear him,**
> **and he delivers them.**
>
> **Psalm 34:7**

> **The righteous cry out, and the LORD hears them;**
> **he delivers them from all their troubles.**
>
> **Psalm 34:17**

> **The righteous person may have many troubles,**
> **but the LORD delivers him from them all;**
> **he protects all his bones,**
> **not one of them will be broken.**
>
> **Psalm 34:19-20**

> **The LORD will rescue his servants;**
> **no one who takes refuge in him will be**
> **condemned.**
>
> **Psalm 34:22**

There are scores of promises like these in the Bible—both Old Testament and New Testament—and they are all "yes" **in Christ** (2 Corinthians 1:20). In other words, the New Covenant believer can claim them by faith and be delivered from any severe persecution, just like the three Hebrews and Daniel were. Keep in mind though that the LORD didn't deliver them until *after* they were thrown into the fiery furnace and the lions' den respectively. Furthermore, they didn't turn away from God when the going got tough. It was a test of their faith to see if it was genuine or not (1 Peter 1:6-7). Thankfully, their faith was sincere and they were rescued.

However, there are occasions where it *is* God's will that a person die for the cause of Christ. The martyrdom of Stephen is a good example. His death resulted in the mass scattering of believers and thus the spreading of the Word of God in that part of the world (Acts 7:54-8:4). Yet Stephen's martyrdom offers us an important insight: Just before Stephen was apprehended and stoned, the account points out that he was full of the Spirit and saw Heaven "open up," palpably viewing the glory of the Father with Christ at his right hand.

This reveals that God will give those He calls to die for their faith the grace to handle it. If you're in a situation where you're facing severe persecution and you don't discern the Holy Spirit leading you to martyrdom then it's obviously *not* God's will that you be martyred. In this event, stand on the promises of God's Word and the LORD will deliver you, just as he did with Shadrach, Meshach & Abednego and Daniel.

Unfortunately, some Christians are either biblically ignorant or have a martyrdom complex and so have unnecessarily died under persecution when, actually, it was God's will to deliver them.

We'll look into this subject in more detail next chapter.

Chapter 6

What Goes On Behind the Scenes?

With everything we now know about angels, let's consider the possibilities of what goes on "behind the scenes" in regard to angelic spirits, good and bad.

"According to Your Faith will it be Done to You"

In **Chapter 4** we saw how Christ emphasized the power of speaking in faith rooted in belief in the heart. He said we can move 'mountains' with this principle (Mark 11:22-23). And this explains Jesus' typical responses to people who experienced miracles through Him. For instance, when two blind men sought healing the Lord asked if they *believed* they would receive their healing through Him and they said "yes," to which he replied: "**According to your faith let it be done to you**" (Matthew 9:27-30).

The Messiah made similar statements when others received miracles (e.g. Matthew 8:13 & 9:22). These people spoke in faith with their mouths as they believed in their hearts and thus received the miracle they needed. *You* need to get a hold of this principle if *you* want to experience *your* miracle from the Lord!

This was briefly pointed out last chapter, but—if you're a believer—you already walked in this principle when you received the miracle of salvation. The Bible shows us precisely *how* a person is saved:

> **If you <u>declare with your mouth</u>, "Jesus is Lord," and <u>believe in your heart</u> that God raised him from the dead, you will be saved. For it is <u>with your heart that you believe</u> and are justified, and it is <u>with your mouth that you profess your faith</u> and are saved.**
>
> **Romans 10:9-10**

As you can see, you received eternal salvation by **1.** declaring with your mouth and **2.** believing in your heart that Christ is Lord and was raised from the dead for your justification. You can use this very same principle to receive any miracle—**declaring with your mouth** and **believing in your heart**.

You might say: "This is wonderful, but I'm having a hard time *believing* for my miracle." Then I suggest meditating more on the promises of God's Word, which is the basis of your faith. As Romans 10 goes on to say: "**faith cometh by hearing**, and hearing by **the word of God**" (verse 17 KJV).

Your faith will increase the more you speak in faith that for which you are believing, which is why David said:

> [13] **<u>With my lips I recount</u>**
>   **all the laws that come from your**
>   **mouth.**
> [14] **I rejoice in following your statutes**
>   **as one rejoices in great riches.**
> [15] **<u>I meditate on your precepts</u>**
>   **and <u>consider</u> your ways.**

> [16] **I delight in your decrees;**
> **<u>I will not neglect your word</u>.**
>
> **Psalm 119:13-16**

This was one of David's key secrets for being such a man of faith — "a man after God's own heart" [16]: He regularly and enthusiastically meditated on God's Word, recounting it with his mouth. The Hebrew for "meditate" is *siach (SEE-akh)*, which means to muse over and speak out loud. Meditating on God's Word in this manner naturally built David up in faith; and he acted accordingly. He thus slew the 9½ foot tall Goliath and became one of the greatest kings of Israel. David was so exceptional that, even though he lived 3000 years ago, people talk about his great exploits all over the world to this day, like right now.

Speaking God's Word increases Faith

The definition of *siach* shows that meditation isn't just musing over God's Word; it also involves speaking it out loud. If you're having trouble believing for a particular miracle, I encourage you to increase speaking the applicable Word of God in faith. The more you speak it the more you'll believe it; and it will ultimately manifest. Jesus alluded to this here:

> **For assuredly, I say to you, whoever <u>says</u> to this mountain, 'Be removed and be cast into the sea,' and does not doubt in his heart, but <u>believes</u> that those things he <u>says</u> will be done, he will have whatever he <u>says</u>.**
>
> **Mark 11:23** (NKJV)

Observe how the Lord emphasized **speaking** three times as much as **believing**. Why? Because the more you speak something the more you'll believe it. This works for the positive *and* the negative. Speaking of which, let's look at…

---

[16] See 1 Samuel 13:14 and Acts 13:22.

Speaking & Believing for Negative Things

Carol and I were hanging out with a couple recently and we noticed how the wife kept talking in negative terms; often about negative things like physical ailments, cancer and the possibility of dying. While she was likely ignorant of what she was doing, she was nevertheless speaking and believing for negative things utilizing the power of her tongue. Is it any wonder that she had ongoing problems with depression?

In the above verse Christ said that *"whoever"* says to this 'mountain' and believes in their heart shall have what they speak. Notice that Jesus didn't even specify that the person is in covenant with God. In other words, **this powerful principle works for anyone who uses it**, regardless of whether they're a believer or not.

This explains why the pagan Goliath used this principle when he faced David. The intimidating giant eyed the shepherd teen with contempt and *said* he was going to kill him and feed him to the vultures; David essentially said the same thing to Goliath (1 Samuel 17:43-47). They *both* used the principle of declaring by faith with their mouths and believing in their hearts in order to gain what they wanted—victory. This potent principle works across the board for whosoever takes advantage of it. This is why you'll read of it in secular self-improvement books.

So why did David have the victory on this occasion and not Goliath? The latter was a renowned champion with a long string of victories, so why didn't this principle work for him this time? Because David was in covenant with the Almighty and Goliath wasn't. In fact, David confirmed this when facing the giant: "You come against me with sword and spear and javelin, but I come against you in the name of the Lord Almighty, the God of the armies of Israel, whom you have defied" (1 Samuel 17:45). David no doubt experienced fear, but overcame it by speaking in bold faith according to the promise of his covenant. Courage is not the absence of fear, but rather stubbornly doing what you have to do in faith *despite* any fear you might experience.

You could say that being in covenant with the LORD gave David the edge and thus he had the victory.

If this powerful scriptural principle works for the positive for "whosoever" implements it, does it also work for the negative? Of course. This is why the Bible says the tongue has the power of life *and death* (Proverbs 18:21). Your words don't just have the power of life; they also have the power of death. If you speak negative things often enough you'll eventually believe them in your heart and they'll come to pass to the degree that you believe, one way or another.

I observed an excellent example of this on a TV show about unsolved mysteries. A teenage girl, who was about 17 years-old, got it in her head that she was going to somehow be "taken" and therefore wouldn't be around much longer. Her mother and sister heard her say this repeatedly over the course of a couple years. Then one day she went to the corner store to purchase a romance novel and she mysteriously disappeared. The evidence pointed to forcible apprehension and, sadly, her body was later found, molested. They were still trying to find the killer when the show aired.

How can this strange story possibly be explained? How did this girl "get it in her head" that she was going to be "taken" one day and never return? No doubt an evil spirit whispered this negative idea in her ear, so to speak, until she took hold of it and started speaking it. The more she spoke it to herself & others the more she *believed* it. And thus one day it came to fruition. Remember what Jesus said: "**According to your faith let it be done to you.**" Unfortunately, this girl had faith for negative things.

Good and Bad Angels "Released" through Your Words

What goes on "behind the scenes" in a scenario like this? We know that the angels assigned to us respond to the voice of God's Word:

> **Bless the LORD, O you <u>his angels</u>,**
> **you mighty ones <u>who do his word</u>,**
> **<u>obeying the voice of his word</u>!**
> **Psalm 103:20** (ESV)

God's written Word has no voice unless we speak it. When the Holy Spirit conveys a word to you in your spirit—whether you discern it as an impression, desire or inner voice—it also has no voice unless you speak it. Even if a New Testament prophet[17] speaks a divine word over you and it's confirmed in your spirit, that word has no ongoing voice in your life unless you agree with it and declare it. Whatever the case, when we *speak* the promises of God in faith we give voice to God's Word and this releases the angels to assist in carrying out whatever miracle for which we're believing. This is their very purpose—"to *serve* those who will inherit salvation," i.e. people (Hebrews 1:14).

However, if you don't speak according to God's Word then your angels cannot obey the voice of the Word because you're not giving voice to it. They are thus hindered—*prevented*—from fulfilling their purpose and you won't partake of their benefit.

Now consider this: If the purpose of godly angels is to serve people and obey the voice of God's Word, then fallen angels do the precise opposite—instead of serving people for their benefit they oppress people for their detriment! If heavenly angels respond to the voice of God's Word then evil angels respond to the voice of that which *contradicts* God's truth! In other words, they get *excited* about words that rebel against the LORD and His will; it *inspires* them!

---

[17] The function of New Testament prophets is vastly different from the function of Old Testament prophets due to the great differences of the two covenants. The primary purpose of the Old Testament prophet was to lead and guide Israel through the Word of the LORD and, unsurprisingly, a lot of their words became Holy Scripture, which we know today as the Old Testament. For this reason, the words of a prophet had to be 100% accurate. If their words were proven to be false, they were to no longer be regarded as prophets and, in fact, were to be put to death (Deuteronomy 18:20-22).

The New Testament prophet is different. The gift of prophecy was not given to the body of Christ for the purpose of leading and guiding God's people, as was the case in the Old Testament. Why? Because believers are born-again spiritually and have the Holy Spirit *within them* for this very purpose (John16:13). Since it's the Holy Spirit's job to guide believers in the New Testament era we don't need the gift of prophecy for this function. So when a prophet prophesies over you and says you're to do this or that and go here or there, don't receive it unless the Spirit has *already* been leading you in this direction. In other words, prophecies in the New Testament are to *confirm* what the Holy Spirit has *already* been leading you to do.

Now let's apply this data to the aforementioned girl and her tragic end: She got it in her head through the lies of an evil spirit that she was going to somehow be "taken" and never return home, meaning she would likely be killed. She took ahold of this idea, started speaking it to herself and others, and eventually believed it. The angels assigned to her were essentially bound up from helping and, instead, filthy spirits were released to bring to pass that for which she spoke and believed! These wicked spirts searched around the area for the 'right' sociopath and inspired him to go to that particular store at the very time she would be there; and when the girl showed up he took advantage of the situation.

Truly, our words have the power of life and death!

Like this unfortunate girl, I got something negative in my head when I was a teenager. The thought struck me that I was going to die by the time I was 26. I proceeded to dwell on it now and then, and consequently started sharing it with others. I may have only shared it a handful of times but, nevertheless, I was using this principle of speaking & believing for the negative, just as the girl in the story. Thankfully, I turned to the LORD when I was 20 and He soon taught me about the power of the tongue combined with believing in the heart. So I repented of speaking a curse over my life. At 53 years of age, as of this writing, I've more than *doubled* the time limit the enemy tried to put on my life!

Do *Un*believers have Angels Assigned to Them?

At this point a question springs up: Do unbelievers have angels assigned to them? For instance, did the girl who was apprehended and murdered have angels assigned to her, regardless of whether or not she was a believer? (If she was a believer, she was obviously ignorant of the power of her words combined with faith in the heart). How about me and my similar story—were there angels assigned to me before I accepted the gospel?

In **Chapter 3** we saw a few passages that suggest this (Psalm 91:11 & Matthew 4:6). In Matthew 18:10 Christ spoke of children and "*their* angels in heaven." Moreover, it just makes sense that every person has angels assigned to him or her in light of the divine purpose of angels:

"to serve those who will inherit salvation" (Hebrews 1:14). Who is it that's supposed to inherit salvation? People in general—the only physical beings created in the likeness of God. It is true that only genuine believers will inherit salvation, but unbelievers *might* inherit salvation; so angels need to be there for them, particularly when believers pray for them. **And angels cannot readily serve people unless they're readily available.**

We also saw in **Chapter 3** that 'serve' is the Greek word *diakonia (dee-ak-on-EE-ah)*, which literally means serving in the sense of waiting on someone's table. How can angels wait at people's tables—whether they're saved or not saved—if they're not even there to wait on their tables? So, yes, every person has angels assigned to him or her.

Now, say I'm interceding for an unsaved guy and I pray that the LORD would continually bring the gospel to him, one way or another; and, furthermore, provide godly believers to minister to him wherever he goes. Who is it that works behind the scenes to carry out such a prayer? Obviously the angels assigned to this man.

The Power of the Tongue and Your RESPONSIBILITY

The tongue is a powerful gift that the Creator has given us. It has the power of life or death, depending on whether we speak words of life or words of death; words of faith or words of doubt; blessings or curses. This applies to the words we speak over ourselves, as well as the words we speak over others, whether they're present or not. This includes our prayers for people. It is through the words we speak, including our prayers, that angels are released or hindered.

This relates to both heavenly angels and fallen angels. For instance, the girl who was apprehended at the store used her tongue to speak words that *hindered* heavenly angels, yet empowered fallen angels. She didn't repent, but kept it up. And it eventually brought about her doom. This does not negate the responsibility of the sick thug who murdered her, of course, but God had placed a great gift at the girl's disposal and she inadvertently used it to bring about her own destruction! The fact that she was ignorant of the power of the tongue didn't negate the power of this God-given tool. If a boy innocently picks up a gun and kills himself he's dead regardless of whether or not he was aware of its power. The gun is neither good nor evil, but it has the potential for positive and negative results based on the actions of the person using it. The gun can put food on your table or protect you from criminals, but it can also kill you or others if wrongly used. It's the same thing with your tongue working together with belief in your heart.

Speaking of children, who is responsible for the words spoken over them since kids are generally ignorant of the power of words? Obviously their parents, but also any adult figure that has influence over them, like teachers, coaches, relatives and friends' parents.

When I was a kid my dad constantly spoke negative words over me, such as "You're no good," "You're going to turn to $#!&" and worse. These words were implanted in my heart week after week, month after month, year after year, to the point that I started believing them. As soon as I hit 13 my life took a horrible nosedive. I started hanging around the wrong crowd, drinking, doing drugs and committing crimes (like breaking & entering, theft and vandalism). By the time I was 15 I was seriously considering suicide. What brought about this whirlwind of destruction? The negative words constantly spoken over me, which I meditated on, eventually accepted, and repeated with my tongue.

Who's responsible for the destruction that ensued? Surely, I must take responsibility for what I used my mind to dwell on—my thought life—and what I used my tongue to speak. Yet my father was the influential authority figure who planted these negative words in my heart in the first place. So he bore *partial* responsibility for the destruction of my life as a wayward teen.

My point is that we must realize the power of the tongue and take responsibility for the words we speak over ourselves *and others*. Search your heart. If you've been speaking negative words over yourself or others—including gossip, slander and negative-spinning—simply repent and God will forgive you, which means he'll dismiss your offense and wipe the slate clean (1 John 1:8-9).

Repentance tends to have a negative connotation these days, but it's actually a very positive thing; it means to change for the positive by making a 180° turn. We need to regularly "keep with repentance" (Matthew & Luke 3:8). Repentance goes hand-and-hand with the "corrections of instruction," which are the "way to life" (Proverbs 6:23). In other words, we positively change as we receive correct data and adapt accordingly. A wise person changes course upon receiving corrective instruction while a fool stubbornly continues on in his/her foolish way.

Prayer "Releases" Angels to Serve You and Others

I encourage you to regularly pray for yourself and your family & friends, but also for those who are closely connected to you in your neighborhood, at school or work. Pray for them by name and, if you can, do so daily. This "looses" God, the Holy Spirit, and angels to function in their lives.

We're now going to go over some meaty material to discern how this works. If it gets too heavy for you I encourage you to skip ahead to the next chapter; you can always come back when you're ready for it.

If the idea that prayer "looses" God and angels to function in people's lives sounds strange to you, it's in line with the principle of binding & loosing, as taught by the Mighty Christ:

> **"I will give you the keys of the kingdom of heaven; whatever you bind on earth will be bound in heaven, and whatever you loose on earth will be loosed in heaven."**
> **Matthew 16:19**

> **"I tell you the truth, whatever you bind on earth will be bound in heaven, and whatever you loose on earth will be loosed in heaven.**
> [19] **"Again, I tell you that if two of you on earth agree about anything you ask for, it will be done for you by my Father in heaven."**
> **Matthew 18:18-19**

In the first passage Jesus said he was going to give believers the "keys of the kingdom of heaven." "Keys" refer to authority or power. If you have the keys to a vehicle you wield the power to take advantage of it. The "kingdom of heaven" of course refers to God's kingdom, the kingdom of light. Jesus was saying that he was giving his disciples the power to take advantage of God's kingdom. This is driven home with the second part of the verse: "whatever you bind on earth will be bound in heaven, and whatever you loose on earth will be loosed in heaven." You could put it this way, Heaven will back us up in any legitimate effort to manifest God's kingdom on earth via faith and love, which are the terms of the new testament (Galatians 5:6).

What exactly does it mean to "bind" or to "loose"? The Greek word for "bind" is *deo (DAY-oh)*, which means to literally bind up or figuratively in the sense of prohibiting or hindering; "loose" is *luo (LOO-oh)*, which means to unbind or release. So *deo* means to lock up whereas *luo* means to unlock. As such, believers have the authority to **hinder** or **prohibit** the kingdom of darkness on Earth and to **release** God's kingdom. The kingdom of darkness is prohibited in Heaven so we can prohibit it on Earth; the kingdom of light reigns in Heaven so we can loose it on Earth.

In the second passage Christ links the principle of binding & loosing to prayer. We bind the kingdom of darkness and loose the kingdom of light through our prayers.

This is supported by what we know as 'the Lord's prayer,' which is the prayer outline that Jesus gave his disciples:

> " **Our Father in heaven,**
> **hallowed by your name,**
> [10] **your kingdom come,**
> **your will be done**
> **on earth as it is in heaven."**
> **Matthew 6:9-10**

Verse 10 is *not* talking about praying for Jesus' return and the set-up of his eternal kingdom on Earth. It's talking about the principle of binding & loosing in this "present evil age." This means *now*. Do you want God's kingdom to reign in your life and the lives of others? Of course you do, but it has to be released it through prayer. Do you want God's will to be done in your life and the lives of others? You have to loose it via prayer. In other words, God's kingdom will not come and reign on this Earth unless a believer releases it through prayer and action; and God's will is not done on Earth unless the church looses his will via prayer and action. Simply put, believers have the power to bind the kingdom of darkness and loose the kingdom of light.

Someone might understandably respond: "Well if God's so Almighty why doesn't he just automatically do everything? Why does He need believers to 'release' his will through prayer and service?"

It is true that the LORD is Sovereign, which means he "reigns supreme." The Bible describes God as "the King of all the earth" (Psalm 47:7) who owns the Earth and everything in it (Psalm 24:1, 50:12 & 1 Corinthians 10:26). Christ himself called Father God "Lord of heaven and earth" (Matthew 11:25). So there's no disputing that the Almighty reigns supreme and "does whatever pleases him" (Psalm 103:19 & 135:5-6).

However, it's also clear in Scripture that the devil is the "god of this age" and the "prince of this world" who rules the kingdom of darkness or Underworld, which is the dark spiritual dimension that underpins the world (John 12:31 & 14:30). Anyone who's not part of God's kingdom is subject to this dark kingdom because they're "by nature objects of wrath" (Ephesians 2:3); this includes everyone who doesn't have a covenant with the Almighty, meaning all unbelievers. The following verses verify this: 1 John 5:19, Revelation 12:9, 2 Corinthians 4:4 and Ephesians 2:1-2.

These passages show that the "whole world" is presently under the control of the kingdom of darkness, which is why the Bible refers to this current era as "the present **evil** age" (Galatians 1:4).

This doesn't, of course, mean that all unbelievers are frothing at the mouth with evil, but rather that they're subject to the kingdom of darkness, whether they realize it or not. The depth of their subjugation is dependent upon how far they choose to embrace the flesh, which is the satanic nature. It's also dependent on how far their belief system deviates from biblical truth.

We see evidence of Satan's ruler-ship and influence all around us constantly: wars, crime, corruption, broken families, immorality, injustice, poverty, false religion, legalism, harmful ideologies, disunity, disease, addiction, death, etc. Don't be alarmed, however, because the above passages show that the devil's control is limited to those designated as "the world," which doesn't include blood-bought, spiritually regenerated believers, *Hallelujah!* Christians are the "church" of Jesus Christ, which literally means "the called-out ones" in the Greek. This signifies that believers have been rescued from Satan's kingdom:

> **For he has rescued us from the dominion of darkness and brought us into the kingdom of the Son he loves,**
> **Colossians 1:13**

Not only have we been rescued from bondage to the kingdom of darkness, we've been transplanted into God's kingdom as his beloved sons and daughters!

When you pray for yourself and those linked to you—family, neighbors and people at school and work—you're binding up the kingdom of darkness and loosing the kingdom of light, which includes loosing the angels assigned to them. Some of the people you intercede for are lost and some are Christians who are ignorant of these things; as such, the angels assigned to them are limited in helping them, to say the least. But your prayers can release them to work in their lives, one way or another.

This doesn't negate freewill, of course. No matter how much you pray for someone and no matter how much they're exposed to the Word of God, the moving of the Holy Spirit and the service of angels, he or she can still stubbornly resist. And that's *their* choice. You did your part; they have to do theirs. If they refuse then that's their problem and they'll be held accountable for it when they stand before the LORD.

Praying for those whom you regularly come in contact with is to your social relations what oil is to a bike chain. Without your prayers the kingdom of light is hindered in these people's lives, which includes the service of angels. When this occurs the kingdom of darkness takes advantage of the situation: Unclean spirits will naturally have more freedom of movement and therefore more negative influence, which isn't good for the individual in question or for your relationship with him or her. Since godly believers are guaranteed to be persecuted, why open the door to unnecessary problems due to skipping out on your duty to intercede? (See 1 Timothy 2:1-4).

My Example in Praying for People

Christian servant-leaders are called to set **an example** for believers (1 Peter 5:1-3), so allow me to share my example. What I usually do when interceding for several people is voice **a general prayer**, such as the apostle Paul's prayer for the Colossian believers:

> **…we have not stopped praying for you. We continually ask God to fill you with the knowledge of his will through all the wisdom and understanding that the Spirit gives, [10] so that you may live a life worthy of the Lord and please him in every way: bearing fruit in every good work, growing in the knowledge of God, [11] being strengthened with all power according to his glorious might so that you may have great endurance and patience, [12] and giving joyful thanks to the Father, who has qualified you to share in the inheritance of his holy people in the kingdom of light.**
> **Colossians 1:9-12**

Notice how Paul prays this excellent general prayer for all the Colossian believers rather than say a similar prayer for each person by name. This makes sense and saves time because it keeps you from saying the same general prayer over and over for each individual.

After praying a general prayer like this I then lift up various names from my intercession list, praying in the spirit as led of the Spirit (Ephesians 6:18). When I get to a certain individual, a specific need might come up and so I pray about it—both with my understanding and by the spirit (1 Corinthians 14:15)—and then move on to the next person.

I mentioned an "intercession list." This is simply a list of names in my mind; in other words, a *mental* list (I'm good with names and have an excellent memory). But I sometimes pray from an actual list as well, at least a couple times a week.

Praying for Governing Authorities

We talked about praying for people linked to you, whether family, friends, neighbors and people at school or work. With this in mind, be sure to also regularly pray for **governing authorities**, whether spiritual or political (1 Timothy 2:1-4). By *spiritual* authorities, I mean key ministerial leaders in your area, nation and otherwise.

If you need some inspiration on this topic I encourage you to see the excellent 2015 movie *War Room*.

What Goes on Behind the Scenes: The Bottom Line

Our subject is: What goes on behind the scenes in regard to angelic help and demonic assault? If you disregard the power of the tongue and use it to speak death rather than life the angels assigned to you will be hindered and demonic spirits will have more freedom of movement to attack and oppress one way or another. The answer to these types of unnecessary attacks is to make a 180° turn and start using your tongue to speak life. This means taking advantage of the spiritual weapons at your disposal and, specifically, utilizing your tongue as the "sword of the spirit," which is the Word of God spoken in bold faith (Ephesians 6:17-18).

The angels around you naturally obey the voice of the Word of God. It's what they do. When angels are loosed evil spirits are hindered, but when angels are hindered evil spirits are loosed.

The Church must get ahold of this.

Spiritual Attacks for Righteousness' Sake

But some demonic attacks are not the result of using your tongue to speak death or opening the door through unrepentant sin (Ephesians 4:27). In fact, some attacks are the direct result of practical righteousness.[18] The example of Job in the Old Testament is Exhibit A. The first two chapters of his book reveal what went on behind the scenes in regards to Job's extraordinary trials.

> One day <u>the angels came to present themselves before the LORD, and Satan also came with them</u>. [7] The LORD said to Satan, "Where have you come from?"
>
> Satan answered the LORD, "From roaming throughout the earth, going back and forth on it."
>
> Then the LORD said to Satan, "Have you considered my servant Job? There is no one on earth like him; he is blameless and upright, a man who fears God and shuns evil."
>
> [9] "Does Job fear God for nothing?" Satan replied. [10] "<u>Have you not put a hedge around him and his household and everything he has</u>? You have blessed the work of his hands, so that his flocks and herds are spread throughout the land. [11] But now stretch out your hand and strike everything he has, and he will surely curse you to your face."
>
> [12] The LORD said to Satan, "Very well, then, everything he has is in your power, but on the man himself do not lay a finger."
>
> Then Satan went out from the presence of the LORD.
>
> **Job 1:6-12**

---

[18] I say "practical righteousness" as opposed to *positional* righteousness, although the foundation of the former is the latter. To explain: All genuine believers are righteous in a positional sense due to spiritual regeneration wherein they receive the "gift of righteousness" (Romans 5:17 and 2 Corinthians 5:21). Practical righteousness, by contrast, is actually walking in righteousness as a result of living according to one's new nature, which is "created to be **like God** in **true righteousness**" (Ephesians 4:22-24). Practical righteousness naturally increases as one matures spiritually.

Satan appears before the Sovereign LORD in Heaven where God proceeds to boast of Job and his extraordinary character. The devil argues that Job is devout merely because the Lord has blessed him so greatly and, furthermore, that God had "put a hedge around him, his household and everything he has," which provided supernatural protection.

Before getting to the meat of this occasion, what do you suppose this "hedge" involved? Surely, this intangible shield was implemented and maintained by angels whose very purpose is to serve and protect people.

In any case, Satan insists that Job would curse God to his face if this "hedge" was taken down and his many blessings were removed. This naturally provokes God to conduct a test by allowing the devil to assault Job and take "everything he has." Thus, using neighboring tribes and weather phenomena, Satan causes Job to lose all his animal stock and his ten children in a single day (Job 1:12-19).

But Job passes the test, saying, "Naked I came from my mother's womb, and naked I will depart. The LORD gave and the LORD has taken away; may the name of the LORD be praised" (verse 21). Job was, of course, unaware of what went down behind the scenes. He didn't know that the devil—whose very name means "slanderer" or "accuser"—incited God to permit the attack in order to test Job's character. He wasn't aware of Satan's role in the proceedings and therefore wrongly attributed the events to the LORD.[19]

This opens the door to round two, which begins when the devil appears before the Creator a second time:

> **Then the LORD said to Satan, "Have you considered my servant Job? There is no one on earth like him; he is blameless and upright, a man who fears God and shuns evil. And <u>he still maintains his integrity, though you incited me against him to ruin him without any reason</u>."**

---

[19] Although Job *was* right in the sense that Yahweh is the Sovereign God who "reigns supreme" and thus would have to *allow* negative events even in cases where the kingdom of darkness is directly responsible.

> ⁴ "Skin for skin!" Satan replied. "A man will give all he has for his own life. ⁵ But now stretch out your hand and <u>strike his flesh and bones, and he will surely curse you to your face</u>."
>
> ⁶ The LORD said to Satan, "Very well, then, <u>he is in your hands</u>; but you must spare his life."
>
> Job 2:3-6

Satan argues that Job passed the first test because he was personally unscathed, but if his body were attacked he'd surely curse God to his face. Thus the LORD permits the devil to attack Job's body with the condition that he couldn't take his life.

In this second round, Satan afflicts Job with painful sores from head to toe, but Job refuses to turn against God even though his distraught wife encourages him to "curse God and die" (verses 7-9).

What I want to drive home here is that Job wasn't attacked by the kingdom of darkness due to opening the door through sin or using his tongue to speak death, which would've bound up angels and loosed evil spirits to oppress him one way or another. Job was so exceptional that God literally boasted to Satan that there was no one on Earth like him—"he is blameless and upright, a man who fears God and shuns evil" (Job 1:1,8). Being "blameless" would include being blameless with the use of his tongue.

So the account clearly shows that **Job was attacked due to being blameless and upright**.[20] As such, Job's incredible trial can be

---

[20] I've heard some theorize that Job opened the door to the devil through fear, which they argue is backed-up by his statement: "What I feared has come upon me; what I dreaded has happened to me" (Job 3:25). But this can be rejected for a few obvious reasons: **1.** We already know in plain language from the previous two chapters of Job that he was *not* being attacked because he opened the door to the Enemy through fear; rather, God praised him as righteous & thoroughly blameless and *this* is what spurred Satan to unjustly bring into question his character, which compelled the LORD to allow the test. Nowhere is it even hinted that Job opened the door for a horrible attack through fear. On the contrary, note what God says in 2:3. Scripture interprets Scripture. **2.** Speaking of that hermeneutical law, the context of Job 3 is of a man relentlessly venting after two horrible satanic assaults wherein he lost his ten children and all his great wealth; then, after seven [continued on next page]

designated as an MIT—a Maturing-Intended Trial, which takes place through no fault of the person tested. To explain, let's consider the three basic types of tests you'll face in life...

Distinguishing SITs, MITs and DITs

David Servant came up with a great way to categorize human trials—SITs, MITs and DITs:

1. **SITs** refer to **Self-Inflicted Trials**, like when someone bangs up his/her body due to careless snow skiing or gets nausea after eating too much junk food or suffers poverty because s/he is too lazy to work (which isn't the *only* reason for poverty, of course). In each case the pain suffered isn't some diabolical spiritual plot, but simply the result of the person's foolish actions and choices.
2. **MITs** refer to **Maturing-Intended Trials**, like Job's test. The LORD permitted Satan to assault Job for the purpose of testing his motivations. Was Job godly and devout solely for the purpose of having God's blessings? Would he curse the Almighty or deny His existence if his many blessings were temporarily removed? Although the rest of the book of Job shows him severely venting to God after the misery and frustration of the ensuing weeks[21] (e.g. Job 10:1-3) Job didn't turn away from his Creator, but rather went *to* Him, and therefore passed the test. God then restored him and blessed him doubly (Job 42:10).

---

literal days of intense silent suffering with a few hushed friends (2:13), Job finally speaks his mind and his verbiage is hysterical: He curses the very day of his birth and argues for non-existence as opposed to life in this troubled world.
3. As David Kirkwood argued, if we are going to dubiously base our entire interpretation of the book of Job on one verse spoken in venting hysterics then we should also be able to argue that Job opened the door to Satan by expecting good based on his later statement (when he was a little more rational): "when I hoped for good, evil came; when I looked for light, then came darkness" (Job 30:26).
[21] Job's trial lasted several weeks, perhaps even months, as verified by the fact that he was reduced to "skin and bones" during the ordeal (Job 19:20).

When New Covenant believers are attacked we need to recognize it for what it is—an attack of the enemy—and resist in faith. If you do this, the enemy will flee like a pathetic cur with its tail between its legs (James 4:7). As with Job, God will "restore you and make you strong, firm and steadfast" "**after** you have suffered a little while" (1 Peter 5:8-10). You will experience greater maturity and favor with God as a result.

3. **DITs** refer to **Discipline-Intended Trials**, which pertain to God permitting us to be inflicted by one or more of the five general curses as a means of rebuke for disobedience. This is why some of the Corinthians were sick or prematurely died, because they brought judgment on themselves due to disobedience (1 Corinthians 11:27-31). It was the same thing with a woman in the church at Thyatira—a self-proclaimed "prophetess"—as well as those who were foolishly following her bad example. Jesus said He gave them time to repent but they were unwilling so he was going to inflict some of them with sickness ("a bed of suffering") and even strike some of them dead (Revelation 2:20-23)!

Needless to say, when we experience one or more of the five mundane curses—**1.** physical illness, **2.** mental illness, **3.** human attack *and* defeat, **4.** the threat of premature death, and **5.** financial lack—we need to ask ourselves if it's an SIT, an MIT or a DIT. If it's a **Self-Inflicted Trial**, we simply need to acknowledge our folly in the matter and make the necessary changes. If it's a **Maturing-Intended Trial**, we should "fight the good fight of faith" with perseverance and victory will be ours. If it's a **Discipline-Intended Trial**, we need to seek the Lord concerning what it was we did to incur His discipline, humbly acknowledge the error, and repent; that is, change for the positive. This would include repenting of foolishly using the power of the tongue to speak against the Word of God, which automatically hinders angels from performing their services and releases demonic spirits to oppress.

Now, someone might point out that Discipline-Intended Trials complicate the issue because they require the believer to determine if the malady in question is an attack from the kingdom of darkness for righteousness' sake or a disciplinary measure on God's part due to unrepentant disobedience. To do this requires an actual *relationship* with the LORD through "the fellowship of the Holy Spirit" (2 Corinthians 13:14). Bear in mind that relationship is what true Christianity is about and separates it from mere human religion. How is this relevant? If a believer has a genuine relationship with God s/he will be able to discern fairly easily if the curse they're hit with is the result of an MIT or a DIT. On the other hand, believers who fail to cultivate such a relationship will have a harder time distinguishing MITs from DITs. So, in reality, this is a spur to go deeper in God!

For important details on spiritual warfare see **Chapter 17, 18, 19** and **20**.

Chapter 7

Who is "The Angel of the LORD"?

The Bible refers to *"The* Angel of the LORD" several times, but it's clear that this is no ordinary angel and he should be differentiated from references to *an* angel of the LORD (e.g. Luke 1:11). In fact, it's obvious that The Angel of the LORD is *deity*—the **Mighty pre-incarnate Christ**. Let's look at the scriptural evidence for this powerful revelation.

The First Appearance of The Angel of the LORD

"The Angel of the LORD" first appears in Genesis 16 when the slave Hagar ran away from her home with Abram and Sarai (who are renamed Abraham and Sarah in the following chapter). The Angel of the LORD appears to Hagar at a spring and instructs her to go back home and submit to her mistress; he then encourages her about her soon-to-be-birthed son, Ishmael, and their countless descendants (verses 7-12).

But how do we know the Angel of the LORD is deity in this passage? Verse 13 makes it clear:

> **She gave this name to <u>the LORD who spoke to her</u>: "<u>You are the God who sees me</u>," for she said, "I have now <u>seen the One who sees me</u>."**
> **Genesis 16:13**

We are told point blank that this "angel" is the LORD. Secondly, Hagar dubs him "the-God-Who-Sees-Me" and, furthermore, testifies that she had now *seen* the-God-who-sees-her.

Someone might argue that no one has ever seen God based on a few clear passages, such as when Moses requested to see God's Glory and the LORD responded: "you cannot see my face, for no one may see me and live" (Exodus 33:20). Another example is 1 Timothy 6:16 where Paul describes God as "whom no one has seen or can see."

Here's another passage:

> **<u>No one has ever seen God</u>, but the one and only Son, who is himself God and is in closest relationship with the Father, <u>has made him known</u>.**
> **John 1:18**

If no one has ever seen God then how do we explain Hagar seeing the LORD in Genesis 16 above? The answer lies within the second part of this verse: No one has ever seen God, the Father, but the Son—who also is God—has made Him known. How did the Son make God known? Two ways:

1. Christ made the Father known through His incarnation, which is confirmed by Jesus' statements: "Anyone who has seen me has seen the Father" (John 14:9), "whoever sees me sees him who sent me" (John 12:45 ESV) and "If you knew me, you would know my Father also" (John 8:19).
2. Christ also made the Father known in Old Testament times *before* his incarnation, as illustrated above when Hagar saw God via The Angel of the LORD.

There are several other appearances of the pre-incarnate Christ—aka "the Angel of the LORD"—in the Old Testament...

The Angel of the LORD Appears to Moses in the Burning Bush

Notice what the Bible says about The Angel of the LORD in the account of the burning bush:

> **Now Moses was tending the flock of Jethro his father-in-law, the priest of Midian, and he led the flock to the far side of the wilderness and came to Horeb, the mountain of God. ² There <u>the angel of the LORD appeared to him in flames of fire from within a bush</u>. Moses saw that though the bush was on fire it did not burn up. ³ So Moses thought, "I will go over and see this strange sight—why the bush does not burn up."**
>
> **⁴ When the Lord saw that he had gone over to look, <u>God called to him from within the bush, "Moses! Moses!"</u>**
>
> **And Moses said, "Here I am."**
>
> **⁵ "Do not come any closer," <u>God said</u>. "Take off your sandals, for the place where you are standing is holy ground." ⁶ Then he said, "<u>I am the God of your father, the God of Abraham, the God of Isaac and the God of Jacob.</u>" At this, Moses hid his face, because <u>he was afraid to look at God</u>.**
>
> **⁷ <u>The LORD said</u>, "I have indeed seen the misery of my people in Egypt. I have heard them crying out because of their slave drivers, and I am concerned about their suffering. ⁸ So I have come down to rescue them from the hand of the Egyptians and to bring them up out of that land into a good and spacious land, a land flowing with milk and honey"**
>
> **Exodus 3:1-8**

As you can see, The Angel of the LORD appeared to Moses in fiery flames from within the bush. When The Angel of the LORD speaks, he testifies to being God and Moses was understandably "afraid to look **at God**." Then this celestial being is referred to as the "LORD" in verse 7, which is the Tetragrammaton—YHWH—the name for God, which we'll look at shortly.

Clearly The Angel of the LORD is God, albeit not the Father, but rather the Son, who is the One who reveals the Father.

The Angel of the LORD Appears to Gideon

Here's another occasion where the Angel of the LORD appears:

> **The angel of the LORD came and sat down under the oak in Ophrah that belonged to Joash the Abiezrite, where his son Gideon was threshing wheat in a winepress to keep it from the Midianites. ¹² When the angel of the LORD appeared to Gideon, he said, "The Lord is with you, mighty warrior."**
>
> ¹³ **"Pardon me, my lord," Gideon replied, "but if the Lord is with us, why has all this happened to us? Where are all his wonders that our ancestors told us about when they said, 'Did not the Lord bring us up out of Egypt?' But now the Lord has abandoned us and given us into the hand of Midian."**
>
> ¹⁴ **The LORD turned to him and said, "Go in the strength you have and save Israel out of Midian's hand. Am I not sending you?"**
>
> ¹⁵ **"Pardon me, my lord," Gideon replied, "but how can I save Israel? My clan is the weakest in Manasseh, and I am the least in my family."**
>
> ¹⁶ **The LORD answered, "I will be with you, and you will strike down all the Midianites, leaving none alive."**
>
> **Judges 6:11-16**

"The Angel of the LORD" appears to Gideon in verses 11-12 and the following verses confirm him to be the LORD, aka Yahweh (verses 14 & 16).

The Angel of the LORD Appears to the Parents of Samson

In Judges 13 The Angel of the LORD appears to the parents of Samson to announce the prophet's birth wherein 'The Angel' gives them instructions on how the child is to be raised consecrated to the LORD. He is referred to as "the Angel of the LORD" several times in this chapter and "the Angel of God" as well (verse 9).

He's also referred to as a "man" a few times (verses 6, 10 & 11), which simply shows that The Angel of the LORD *appeared* as a man to Manoah and his wife. Of course, they could tell that he was no ordinary person because Manoah's wife described him as a "man of God" who "looked like an angel of God, very awesome" (verse 6).

When Manoah asked The Angel's name he responded: "Why do you ask my name? It is beyond understanding" (verse 18) or, as the New Living Translation puts it, "It is too wonderful for you to understand." Clearly, this was a messenger of God far greater than mighty archangels like Michael and Gabriel, who had understandable names.

Who exactly "the Angel of the LORD" is in Judges 13 is cleared up at the close when he ascends to Heaven in the flames of Manoah's offering (verse 20). To which Manoah cries: "We are all doomed to die! We have **seen God!**" (verse 22).

Yes, they saw God, but not God, the Father, since He "lives in unapproachable light, whom no one has seen or can see" (1 Timothy 6:16). Rather they saw God, the Son; the One who *reveals* the Father.

Jacob Wrestles with God

With everything we now know about The Angel of the LORD—that he is God, the Son, who reveals Father God—let's look at the incredible account of Jacob who wrestled with a "man" all night that turned out to *be* God:

That night Jacob got up and took his two wives, his two female servants and his eleven sons and crossed the ford of the Jabbok. ²³ After he had sent them across the stream, he sent over all his possessions. ²⁴ So Jacob was left alone, and <u>a man wrestled with him till daybreak</u>. ²⁵ When the man saw that he could not overpower him, he touched the socket of Jacob's hip so that his hip was wrenched as he wrestled with the man. ²⁶ Then the man said, "Let me go, for it is daybreak."

But Jacob replied, "I will not let you go unless you bless me."

²⁷ The man asked him, "What is your name?"

"Jacob," he answered.

²⁸ Then the man said, "Your name will no longer be Jacob, but Israel, because you have struggled <u>with God</u> and with humans and have overcome."

²⁹ Jacob said, "Please tell me your name."

But he replied, "<u>Why do you ask my name</u>?" Then he blessed him there.

³⁰ So Jacob called the place Peniel, saying, "<u>It is because I saw God face to face</u>, and yet my life was spared."

³¹ The sun rose above him as he passed Peniel, and he was limping because of his hip.

Genesis 32:22-31

While there are a lot of potent truths you can pull from this amazing account we want to focus on the simple fact that Jacob wrestled with someone all night that appeared to be a "man" and this man turned out to be God. As Jacob exclaims at the end: "I saw God face to face."

We know from the rest of Scripture that Jacob didn't see Father God because no one can see the Father and live. He saw the pre-incarnate Son whose job is to reveal Father God. While this passage doesn't refer to the Son as The Angel of the LORD, that's who it is. Notice that Jacob asks for his name and he responds similarly to the way The Angel of the

LORD did to Manoah, as shown in the previous section (Judges 13:18). Moreover, notice what the prophet Hosea says when he references the account of Jacob wrestling with this "man":

> ³ **In the womb he [Jacob] grasped his brother's heel;**
> **as a man he struggled <u>with God</u>.**
> ⁴ **He struggled with <u>the angel</u> and overcame him;**
> **he wept and begged for his favor.**
>
> **Hosea 12:3-4**

Hosea refers to the "man" Jacob wrestled all night as God *and* "the angel," meaning *The* Angel of the LORD, i.e. the pre-incarnate Christ. Scripture interprets Scripture.

The Commander of the Army of the LORD

The Son makes another pre-incarnate appearance before the sack of Jericho where he's not identified as The Angel of the LORD, but rather as the Commander of the Army of the LORD:

> Now when Joshua was near Jericho, he looked up and saw <u>a man</u> standing in front of him <u>with a drawn sword in his hand</u>. Joshua went up to him and asked, "<u>Are you for us or for our enemies</u>?"
> ¹⁴ "<u>Neither</u>," he replied, "<u>but as commander of the army of the Lord I have now come</u>." Then Joshua <u>fell facedown to the ground in reverence</u>, and asked him, "What message does <u>my</u> Lord have for <u>his servant</u>?"
> ¹⁵ The commander of the Lord's army replied, "Take off your sandals, <u>for the place where you are standing is holy</u>." And Joshua did so.
> ¹ Now the gates of Jericho were securely barred because of the Israelites. No one went out and no one came in.

> **² Then <u>the LORD</u> <u>said to Joshua</u>, "See, I have delivered Jericho into your hands, along with its king and its fighting men."**
>
> **Joshua 5:13-6:2**

It doesn't take long for Joshua to realize that this mysterious man with a drawn sword isn't merely a "man" because Joshua falls facedown to the ground in worship. Keep in mind that both the Hebrew and Greek words for 'worship' literally mean to prostrate oneself in adoration or reverence. This was Abraham's response to the LORD, as observed in Genesis 17:3 and 18:1-2, which document two other appearances of the pre-incarnate Christ.

Joshua then proceeds to call this curious man "Lord" and refers to himself as his "servant" (verse 14).

Further evidence that this Commander of the Army of the LORD is deity can be observed in that he immediately commands Joshua to remove his sandals because he was standing on holy ground. This recalls what The Angel of the LORD instructed Moses at the burning bush (Exodus 3:5).

Lastly, the Commander of the LORD's Army is identified at the end of the passage simply as "the LORD" (verse 2) wherein He supplies Joshua with the strategy he needed to conquer the pagan city. Keep in mind that there were no chapter divisions in the original manuscripts; these were added 2600 years *after* the book of Joshua was written.

So the Commander of the Army of the LORD is the pre-incarnate Christ.

Now, let me ask you: Does this Commander come across as a milksop or does he strike you as a mighty warrior that commands respect and awe? Notice what he says when Joshua asks him if he's on Israel's side or Jericho's side: "Neither, but as commander of the army of the LORD I have come." This response is simple and succinct, but it's potent and speaks volumes: Jesus Christ is so magnificent, so great—so incredibly awesome—he's above the mundane conflicts of this world and the politics thereof. Bringing this home for us today: The Mighty Christ is above the perpetual squabbling of the left-wing and right-wing factions of our governments. Enough said.

Understanding God's Name—YHWH

All these passages reveal that The Angel of the LORD is God, with several identifying him as the "LORD," which is YHWH in the Hebrew. This is the Tetragrammaton *(teh-truh-GRAM-uh-tawn)*, which is the actual name of God in the Bible. YHWH is typically rendered "LORD" in English versions of Holy Scripture (all capitals).

From the 2nd or 3rd century BC The Name was considered too holy to speak in Jewish culture and therefore substitute words for YHWH were used, like *Adonai (ah-doh-NAHY)* and *Elohim (eh-LOH-him* or *EL-oh-HEEM)*. *Adonai* is a title of reverence for God and *Elohim* simply means "God."

Since YHWH became ineffable, the actual pronunciation was lost over time, although *YAH-way* is the likely pronunciation (or *YAH-hoo-way* for devout Hebrews). "Jehovah" is merely the English form of the Tetragrammaton (JHVH) with the vowels of *Adonai* inserted.

Basically, when God told Moses "I AM WHO I AM," he was giving the translation of what Yahweh means (Exodus 3:13-14). "I AM WHO I AM" is *Ehyeh Asher Ehyeh* in Hebrew. He was saying in effect, "My name is the fact that I exist."

Now, isn't that a perfectly fitting name for the **Almighty**?

In response to this fascinating information someone wrote me quoting Romans 10:13, which says "Everyone who calls on the name of the Lord will be saved." She understandably asked:

> So what name exactly? Since the one mentioned is too holy and we don't really know the correct pronunciation (and probably for the best in light of the third commandment).

To answer, let's read Romans 10:13 with the surrounding verses:

> **Moses writes this about the righteousness that is by the law: "The person who does these things will live by them." ⁶ But the righteousness that is by faith says: "Do not say in your heart, 'Who will ascend into heaven?'" (that is, to bring <u>Christ</u> down) ⁷ "or**

'Who will descend into the deep?'" (that is, to bring <u>Christ</u> up from the dead). ⁸But what does it say? "The word is near you; it is in your mouth and in your heart," that is, the message concerning faith that we proclaim: ⁹If you declare with your mouth, "<u>Jesus is Lord</u>," and believe in your heart that God raised <u>him</u> from the dead, you will be saved. ¹⁰For it is with your heart that you believe and are justified, and it is with your mouth that you profess your faith and are saved. ¹¹As Scripture says, "Anyone who believes <u>in him</u> will never be put to shame." ¹²For there is no difference between Jew and Gentile—the same Lord is Lord of all and richly blesses all who call <u>on him</u>, ¹³for, "Everyone who calls <u>on the name of the Lord</u> will be saved."

¹⁴How, then, can they call on the one they have not believed in? And how can they believe in the one of whom they have not heard? And how can they hear without someone preaching to them? ¹⁵And how can anyone preach unless they are sent? As it is written: "How beautiful are the feet of those who bring good news!"

Romans 10:5-15

Paul was quoting the prophet Joel in verse 13 and the Hebrew word translated as "LORD" in that Old Testament passage is YHWH. Hence, we are to call upon the name of YHWH. But the very next verse—Romans 10:14—implies that Paul was talking about calling upon the name of the Lord *Jesus* and believing in Him. "Jesus" is the Greek rendition of the Hebrew Yeshua (or Joshua), which means "Yahweh saves" or "Yahweh is salvation."

Jesus Christ is the topic of this section of Scripture, as verified by verses 6, 7 and 9; and Jesus is even referred to as "Lord" in verse 9. This is the Greek word *kurios (KOO-ree-os)*, which is the very same word used to translate the Hebrew YHWH from Joel 2:32 in verse 13! In other words, **the same Greek word for "Lord"—*kurios*—is used to translate the Hebrew YHWH and is also used as a reference to Jesus**

Christ in the same context. So, whether Yahweh or Yeshua it's all good. Keep in mind what Jesus said: "Anyone who has seen me **has seen the Father**" and "I and the Father **are ONE**" (John 14:9 & John 10:30).

I suggest keeping this data in mind for the next time a Jehovah's False Witness tries to scam you about the Father and the Son who, as you can plainly see, **are both YHWH**. Romans 10:5-15 above is strategic in proving this.

Speaking of the Jehovah's Witnesses, they make this big deal about referring to God by his proper name YaHWeH, which they pronounce as "Jehovah." The problem with this is threefold:

1. YHWH is actually pronounced Yahweh *(YAH-way)*, not Jehovah, as explained above.
2. The Tetragrammaton—YHWH—actually does not appear in the New Testament, at least not in any extant text. As noted above, the Greek word *kurios* is used to translation it (Joel 2:32 & Romans 10:13). *Kurios,* by the way, means "Lord, master, sir."
3. When Jesus Christ instructed us how to pray he said we are to address Yahweh as our "heavenly **Father**" or our "**Father** in heaven" (Matthew 6:9-13). This corresponds to *familial* relation where we're Yahweh's ***children*** through spiritual rebirth (1 John 3:9, 1 Peter 1:23 & Titus 3:5). As such, we are to naturally refer to Yahweh as *"abba* Father" (Romans 8:15). The Aramaic *abba* is a term of *tender endearment* by a beloved child for his/her father; it's an *affectionate, dependent* word akin to "Daddy" or "Papa." Think about your relationship with your earthly father. Do you call him by his proper name or do you use a term of endearment, like "Daddy," "Dad," "Pa," "Pops" or "Father"? This is why Christ said we are to address YHWH as "Father" when we commune, which isn't to say we *can't* refer to him as Yahweh (more on this in a moment).

As to the pronunciation of YHWH, as noted above *YAH–way* (or *YAH-hoo-way* to devout Jews) is the accepted pronunciation, but proper pronunciation has nothing to do with the third Old Testament commandment—"You shall not misuse the name of the LORD your God" (Exodus 20:7)—especially in light of varying dialects. For instance, people of northern and southern Israel pronounced *Adonai* and *Elohim* differently, with the accent on different syllables. The idea that the LORD would reject someone merely because he or she put the accent on a different syllable than someone else is silly. God looks to the heart not to whether or not they pronounce a word perfectly (1 Samuel 16:7).

As far as YHWH becoming ineffable, that didn't happen until the Hellenistic period which coincided with the inter-testamental period (i.e. "between testaments"—approximately 400 BC to the time of Christ). And it's actually unbiblical in light of David—"a man after God's own heart"—**utilizing YHWH frequently in his prayer time, as seen throughout the Psalms, which shows that God** *approves* **of people using YHWH in our communion with Him.** To exclusively use substitute names and titles on the grounds that we might severely offend God by mispronouncing YHWH is unbiblical.

Taking the LORD's name in vain refers to **the wrongful use of The Name**, not mispronunciation based on one's dialect or whatever; unless, of course, someone were to *intentionally* mispronounce it in a mocking sense.

If Christ is "The Angel of the LORD" Is He an Angel?

The answer to this question is an emphatic "No" for several reasons:

1. **The Angel of the LORD is constantly identified as the LORD—Yahweh—albeit the Son, not the Father.** We've seen several examples of this (e.g. Exodus 3:1-12 & Judges 6:11-22).
2. **"The Angel of the LORD" is a *title* of the Son, Yeshua, not a name.** The Hebrew word for "angel" is *malak (mal-AWK)*, which simply means "a messenger, supernatural or human." The word appears 213 times in the Old Testament and typically refers to *supernatural* messengers (Genesis 19:1) but often refers to *human* messengers as well (Genesis 32:3,6). Just as the "envoys" to Egypt in Isaiah 30:4 aren't conventional angels, neither is The Angel of the LORD a conventional angel.

Why did the Father give the Son this title? Two reasons: Yeshua is called The Angel of the LORD—The *Messenger* of the LORD—**because that's what he does**: He reveals God to people because the Father dwells in unapproachable light and no one can see Him (1 Timothy 6:16). Since no one can see Him we can't receive from Him directly. Thus the Son is The Messenger of the LORD. The second reason is...

3. **"The Angel of the LORD" is likely the Father's term of endearment for the Son, such as a man calling his wife or daughter his "angel."** This is akin to *"abba* Father," which is how believers refer to Father God by the Spirit (Romans 8:15). As noted in the previous section, the Aramaic *abba* is a term of *tender endearment* of a child for his/her beloved father; it's an *affectionate* word denoting dependence, similar to "daddy."
4. **God has provided for us an *entire chapter* of the Bible—Hebrews 1—to prove that Jesus is not a conventional angel in the manner of Michael, Gabriel or lesser angels.** If you're not familiar with it, I encourage you to read this chapter; let's look at some of its key statements...

Father God Speaks to People through the Son, who Created all Things!

Observe the opening two verses of the first chapter of Hebrews:

> **In the past God spoke to our ancestors through the prophets at many times and in various ways, ² but <u>in these last days he has spoken to us by his Son</u>, whom he appointed <u>heir of all things</u>, and <u>through whom also he made the universe</u>.**
> **Hebrews 1:1-2**

In Old Testament times God spoke to people through prophets, like Moses and Isaiah, but in these "last days"—which means the time spanning from the Messiah's arrival to His return[22]—the heavenly Father speaks through His Son, Jesus Christ. This doesn't just include the actual words of Christ, as chronicled in the four Gospels, but also to those who "spoke from God as they were carried along by the Holy Spirit" since the Holy Spirit is the "Spirit of Christ" (2 Peter 1:21 & Romans 8:9).

The fact that Father God speaks to people through the incarnated Son is a general truth and does not mean that Father God didn't occasionally speak to people via the pre-incarnate Christ, as shown earlier. Remember the hermeneutical rule: Scripture interprets Scripture.

In any case, verse 2 verifies the main point of this chapter—that Jesus Christ is The *Messenger* of the LORD who speaks for the Father because the Father cannot have direct contact with people, lest they perish. This is why Yeshua has the title The Angel of the LORD—The *Messenger* of the LORD.

Notice in the second part of verse 2 that Jesus is designated as "the heir of all things... through whom he [Father God] made the universe." All things in Heaven and Earth where made through Christ (John 1:3); this includes ***all angels***:

> **For in him <u>all things were created</u>: things in heaven and on earth, <u>visible and invisible</u>, whether thrones or powers or rulers or authorities; <u>all things have been created through him and for him</u>.**
> **Colossians 1:16**

"Powers," "rulers" and "authorities" comprise supernatural hierarchies, including the devil and his ranks of fallen angels (Ephesians 6:12). This isn't to say, of course, that Christ created these disgraced spirits in their fallen state—He created them in a perfect condition and they later foolishly rebelled, which we'll look at further in **Chapter 9** and **11**.

So Christ is superior to angels *because he created them!*

All I can say about this is: *Wow!* Jesus ain't no conventional angel!

---

[22] See Acts 2:17, James 5:3, 1 Peter 1:20, 2 Peter 3:3-4.

Jesus Christ: *Superior* to Angels

Let's look at the next two verses of Hebrews 1:

> **The Son is the radiance of God's glory and the exact representation of his being, sustaining all things by his powerful word. After he had provided purification for sins, <u>he sat down at the right hand of the Majesty in heaven</u>. ⁴So he became as much <u>superior to the angels</u> as <u>the name he has inherited is superior to theirs</u>.**
>
> **Hebrews 1:3-4**

The fact that Christ sat down at the right hand of Father God in Heaven distinguishes Him from angels, like Michael and Gabriel who, at most, merely stand in the presence of God (Luke 1:19). This is further emphasized several verses later:

> **To which of the angels did God ever say,**
>
> > **"Sit at my right hand**
> > **until I make your enemies**
> > **a footstool for your feet"?**
>
> **Hebrews 1:13**

The quote is from the opening verse of this Psalm:

> **The LORD says to my Lord:**
>
> > **"Sit at my right hand**
> > **until I make your enemies**
> > **a footstool for your feet."**
>
> **Psalm 110:1**

Father God is speaking to the Son here. The former is referred to by the Hebrew Tetragrammaton—YHWH—which is rendered "LORD" (all capitals) whereas the latter is a different Hebrew word for "Lord." When Christ quotes this verse in the New Testament both words are the *same* Greek word, *kurios (KOO-ree-os)*, which is the Greek word for YHWH, noted earlier (Matthew 22:44). My Point? Jesus *is* YHWH, albeit the Son, not the Father.

Now let's revisit verse 4:

> **So he became as much <u>superior to the angels</u> as <u>the name he has inherited is superior to theirs</u>.**
> **Hebrews 1:4**

Here it is emphasized in plain language that Yeshua is *superior* to angels. The Greek verb translated as "became" refers to a change of state and not a change of existence because we know that the Son has existed from eternity, just as the Father:

> **In the beginning was the Word, and the Word was with God, and the Word was God. ²He was with God in the beginning. ³<u>Through him all things were made; without him nothing was made that has been made</u>...**
> **¹⁴The Word became flesh and made his dwelling among us. We have seen his glory, the glory of the one and only Son, who came from the Father, full of grace and truth.**
> **John 1:1-3,14**

This explains why *both* Father and Son refer to themselves as "I Am" (Exodus 3:14, John 8:58 & 18:6) and as "the first and the last" (Isaiah 44:6 & Revelation 22:13).

The reason Hebrews 1:4 says that Jesus "became" superior to angels is simply because he "was made lower than the angels for a little while" when he was incarnated (Hebrews 2:9). Notice what the Bible says about this:

...Christ Jesus:

⁶ <u>Who, being in very nature God</u>,
    did not consider equality with God
    something to be used to his own advantage;
⁷ rather, <u>he made himself nothing</u>
    by <u>taking the very nature of a servant</u>,
    being <u>made in human likeness</u>.
⁸ And being found in appearance as <u>a man</u>,
    he humbled himself
    by becoming obedient to death—
        even death on a cross!

⁹ Therefore God exalted him to the highest place
    and gave him the name that is above every name,
¹⁰ that at the name of Jesus every knee should bow,
    in heaven and on earth and under the earth,
¹¹ and every tongue acknowledge that Jesus Christ is Lord,
    to the glory of God the Father.

Philippians 2:6-11

As you can see, before Christ's incarnation he was "in very nature God" but "made himself nothing" by "being made in human likeness." This is when he became lower than the angels for a little while (Hebrews 2:9) and it explains why Hebrews 1:4 says that he "became" superior to the angels when he ascended to the Father and "sat down at the right hand of the Majesty in heaven" (Hebrews 1:3).

What Does it Mean that Jesus is God's "Firstborn"

Let's consider another verse from Hebrews 1:

And again, when God brings his firstborn into the world, he says,

"Let all God's angels worship him."
Hebrews 1:6

As you can see, the Son is referred to as God's "firstborn." This is observed in other passages as well:

The Son is the image of the invisible God, the firstborn over all creation.
Colossians 1:15

Cults like the Jehovah's False Witnesses use these texts to support their belief that Jesus was the first created being of the LORD; and then God used Jesus to create everything else. However, Scripture interprets Scripture and we know from other passages examined in this chapter that Jesus *is* Yahweh (YHWH), albeit the Son, not the Father.

So what do these verses mean by describing Yeshua as the "firstborn." The apostles, like Paul, borrowed this term from their Hebraic upbringing where "firstborn" meant especially honored. For instance, the nation of Israel was referred to as God's "firstborn," but this obviously didn't mean Israel was the first nation that ever existed (Exodus 4:22). Similarly, God referred to David as His "firstborn" when he was hardly the first male God created, not to mention David was the youngest of Jesse's eight sons (Psalm 89:20,27). Furthermore, David was the *second* king of Israel. In light of all this, when Christ is referred to as the "firstborn" it simply means that the Son has a place of honor before the Father, shared by no one else; as well as a place of honor over all creation.

There are several other reasons for rejecting the idea that Christ was God's first created being. Here are two obvious ones:

1. Jesus cannot be both "first created" and "one and only Son" (John 1:14 &18, 3:16 & 18, 1 John 4:9). Think about it.
2. John 1:3 (above) says that "Through him [Christ] **all things were made; without him nothing was made that has been made**." If Yeshua is the Creator of **all things** he cannot also be the first created. It's simple logic.

Angels Worship Jesus

Now let's consider the second part of verse 6:

> **"Let all God's angels worship him."**
> **Hebrews 1:6**

This is further evidence of Christ's superiority to angels—**angels worship Him**. As such, if Jesus *was* an angel he'd have to worship himself!

Why do angels worship Yeshua? Because he's **their Creator**, as shown earlier in Colossians 1:16. Furthermore, all authority in Heaven and on Earth has been given to Him (Matthew 28:18) and notice who's submitted to Him:

> **Jesus Christ, who has gone into heaven and is at God's right hand — with angels, authorities and powers in submission to him.**
> **1 Peter 3:22**

Also, we saw in **Chapter 1** that the Word of God forbids the worship of angels and advocates the worship of God alone (Revelation 19:10 & 22:9); and the Messiah is clearly worshipped by people and angels alike (Matthew 2:11, 14:33, 21:9 & 28:9).

You can study the rest of Hebrews 1 for yourself. I just wanted to show that there's **an entire chapter in God's Word** that proves Jesus Christ is superior to angels.

'Wouldn't Calling Jesus "The Angel of the LORD" Mislead Some People?'

Some folks have been misled into concluding that Christ was merely a mighty angel in the manner of Michael, with some even believing he *is* Michael. All I can say is: They must not know how to read in light of the clear scriptural data that shows Yeshua *is* the LORD—Yahweh—albeit the Son and not the Father. Seriously, how much clearer could God be in his Word that Christ is superior to angels?

The fact that some people fall into error because Jesus is "The Angel of the LORD" (etcetera) reveals why it's important to "rightly divide" the Scriptures, as encouraged in the Bible:

> **Do your best to present yourself to God as one approved, <u>a worker who does not need to be ashamed</u> and who <u>correctly handles the word of truth</u>.**
>
> **2 Timothy 2:15**

Who is God's "worker who does not need to be ashamed"? Answer: The one who correctly handles the written Word. It's only the person who *in*correctly handles God's Word that should be ashamed because he or she *wrongly* interpreted it. This, of course, spreads error, which naturally puts people into bondage since only the truth can set them free, not error (John 8:31-32).

In order to "rightly divide" the Scriptures we must make sure that we're adhering to the four common-sense rules of hermeneutics, that is, Bible interpretation:

1. **Context is king:** Meaning the surrounding text reveals the obvious meaning of each passage.
2. **Scripture interprets Scripture:** Meaning every passage must be interpreted in light of the larger context of the entire Bible and thus the Bible itself is the best interpreter of a passage. In other words, one's interpretation of a passage must gel with what the rest of Scripture teaches on the topic in question; the more overt and detailed passages obviously expand our understanding of the more sketchy and ambiguous ones.
3. **Take the Bible literally unless it's clear that figurative language is being used:** In which case you look for the literal truth that the symbolism intends to convey.
4. **If the plain sense makes sense—and is in harmony with the rest of Scripture—don't look for any other sense lest you end up with nonsense:** This includes the "plain sense" of the whole of Scripture on any given topic. In other words, if an individual or group comes up with an interpretation that is opposed to the plain-sense meaning that all the passages in the Bible obviously point to on a subject then it must be rejected. This fourth rule is essentially the other three combined.

These "rules" are really just common-sense guidelines for discovering truth and being set free from error, whether secular or religious. Although the Bible is simple enough that the simplest of persons can receive from it and be blessed, it's also deep and complex, which means that as believers grow in the Lord they naturally grow in knowledge, understanding and wisdom.

Anyone who unbiasedly adheres to these four hermeneutical rules will be able to discern the truth on any given topic. The 'truth' is simply "the way it really is." But we *have* to be honest with the Scriptures and free from the bias of sectarianism[23] in order to discern it.

---

[23] Sectarianism is **faction-ism**, which is actually cited as a work of the flesh in the Bible (Galatians 5:19-21). In the Greek it's *hairesis (HAH-ee-res-is)*, meaning "a religious or philosophical **sect**" and the resulting division it causes. As such, some translations render the word as "divisions." It's a "self-chosen opinion" rooted in sectarian loyalty—i.e. based on the beliefs of one's favored sect— rather than a viewpoint rooted in the rightly-divided [continued on next page]

Something else to consider is the fact that—believe it or not—the LORD and godly characters in the Bible have been known to set out "stumbling blocks" to *intentionally discombobulate proud fools, whether legalists or libertines*. See, for example, Ezekiel 3:20, Romans 11:9 and Psalm 69:22.

Frankly, people who teach that Yeshua isn't the LORD, but rather a created angel are fools who have fallen prey to this stumbling block due to their sectarianism and superficial "studies." They should be ashamed for spreading such blatant error; and they'll be held accountable for it when they stand before the Lord (2 Corinthians 5:10-11, Romans 14:10,12 & James 3:1).

The Angel of the LORD in the New Testament

The book of Revelation contains over 300 references to Old Testament passages, far more than any other New Testament book. Is it any wonder that The Angel of the LORD appears in it:

> **Then I [John] saw another <u>mighty angel</u> coming down from heaven. <u>He was robed in a cloud</u>, with <u>a rainbow above his head; his face was like the sun</u>, and <u>his legs were like fiery pillars</u>. ² <u>He was holding a little scroll, which lay open in his hand</u>. He planted his right foot on the sea and his left foot on the land, ³ and <u>he gave a loud shout like the roar of a lion</u>. When he <u>shouted, the voices of the seven thunders spoke</u>.**
>
> **Revelation 10:1-3**

Word of God. The Pharisees and Sadducees were strict sectarians and their faction-ism prevented them from seeing obvious truths in Scripture, even though they diligently studied them (John 5:39-40). Sectarian ministers are essentially "yes men" to their sect (party) whereas more independent ministers who focus on God's Word are naturally more reliable. This *does not* mean, by the way, that if you belong to a sect—like Baptists—you're automatically guilty of sectarianism.

Several things point to this being The Angel of the LORD—i.e. the Mighty Christ—and not just another angel:

1. The Greek word for 'another' in "I saw *another* mighty angel" is *allos (AL-os)*, which can mean "different" as well as another of the same kind (Strong 10). And it's clear that this angel—i.e. *messenger* of the LORD—is vastly different than the angels that appeared up to this point in John's vision.
2. This angel's shout is likened to a roar of a lion and Jesus Christ is the Lion of Judah (Revelation 5:5).
3. Speaking of whom, the "scroll" that this angel holds presumably refers to the scroll of Revelation 5, which only the Lion of Judah—that is, Jesus Christ, the "Lamb, who was slain"—could take from Father God and open! After all, what other scroll would it refer to? Scripture interprets Scripture.
4. The context of both Revelation 5 (where **only the Son** could take the scroll from the Father and open it) and Revelation 10 (where the Angel holds the scroll as he descends from Heaven, planting one foot on land, one foot in the ocean and shouting a victory cry) shows that the scroll must be **the title deed to the Earth**. Only Christ can hold it because **A.** He's the Creator of Heaven and Earth (Colossians 1:16), **B.** He's "the King of kings and Lord of lords" (Revelation 17:14 & 19:16) who **C.** possesses "all authority in heaven and earth" (Matthew 28:18).
5. The description John gives of the Angel is akin to other stunning descriptions of Deity in the Bible (Ezekiel 1:26-28 & Revelation 1:13-18):

    - "**a rainbow above his head**" (Ezekiel 1:28).
    - "**his face was like the sun**" (Revelation 1:16 & Ezekiel 1:27).
    - "**his legs were like fiery pillars**" (Revelation 1:15 & Ezekiel 1:27).
    - His legs being like fiery pillars, by the way, is symbolic of judgment and only the Son has authority to judge the Earth (John 5: 22).

- "**When he shouted, the voices of the seven thunders spoke**" (Revelation 1:15).

The evidence leads me to believe that this angel is The Angel of the LORD—i.e. Jesus Christ—and not any ol' strong angel. For anyone who disagrees, that's fine; it's not something worth arguing over.

We'll look at another interesting reference to The Angel of the LORD in the New Testament next chapter.

The Angel of the LORD distinguished from *an* Angel of the LORD

The Angel of the LORD understandably does *not* appear during Christ's incarnation on Earth because this "Angel" *is* Christ. Keep in mind that the Son is the living "Word of God" because He's everything the Father wants to *say* to humanity (John 1:1-3 & Hebrews 1:1-2). The Hebrew & Greek words for 'angel' mean "messenger." Thus Christ—the Word of God—is The Angel of the LORD, The Messenger of the LORD. The Father conveys the "message of reconciliation" through the Son and all those born of his seed (2 Corinthians 5:18-20).

Obviously it's imperative to distinguish *The* Angel of the LORD from *an* angel of the LORD in the Scriptures. The former is Deity whereas the latter is not. For instance, Luke 1:11 shows "an angel of the Lord" appearing to Zechariah, the husband of Elizabeth and father of John the Baptist. Several verses later this angel is identified as Gabriel (19 & 26) and is undoubtedly the same angel who appeared to the shepherds immediately following Christ's birth, as chronicled in the following chapter (Luke 2:7-15). Scripture interprets Scripture.

It should be noted that in the original Hebrew and Greek text there's no article in front of the words for "angel" (*malak* and *angelos* respectively) and so English translators must determine if a text refers to *The* Angel of the LORD or *an* angel of the LORD and render it accordingly. In the passages from Luke 1-2 above translators rightly rendered it "an angel of the Lord" because the context reveals the angel to be Gabriel.

Unfortunately, in the King James Version of Matthew 28:2 the translators wrongly rendered the text as "the angel of the LORD" in reference to an angel who appears to some women at Christ's tomb. However, we know this angel is *not* The Angel of the LORD—God, the Son—because he informs the women that Jesus wasn't there, but that He had risen and, in fact, had gone ahead of them to Galilee where they would find Him (verses 5-7). As they say, "Context is King."

Incidentally, the Luke account of these events reveals that there were actually *two* angels at Christ's tomb whereas the Matthew and Mark accounts only mention one. Why? Obviously because the latter two accounts focus on the angel that spoke to the women. This is further evidence that the angel was not The Angel of the LORD.

Jesus Christ—Mighty LORD, Not Milksop

No doubt this chapter has given you a more balanced view of Jesus Christ. The image that the world and religion offers of Jesus is that of a wimpy milksop, but nothing could be further from the truth.

Sterile religion and worldly culture has fostered this false image to the point that it's the general perception of most people, spoken or unspoken. As such, when the average person thinks of Jesus Christ they think of "gentle Jesus meek and mild" rather than the awesome Lion of Judah or the stunning Angel of the LORD. I'm not saying that Jesus doesn't have a gentle side—He does for those humble folks who warrant it (Matthew 11:28-30)—but how about some **balance**?!

Even when Jesus was on Earth and ministered for 3½ years he was anything but some effeminate weakling. Consider the proof: He was brilliant in argumentation (Matthew 22:15-22); He astonished and silenced his enemies (Luke 20:26) to the point that "no one dared ask him anymore questions" (Mark 12:34). Does this sound like an impotent milksop?

Furthermore, Christ was dynamic during his earthly ministry— full of energy, power, passion and life. He had an aura of pizzazz, not stultifying dullness. Want evidence?

- Jesus said he *was* life and could therefore offer abundant life to any humble soul who chose to follow him (John 14:6 & 10:10).
- Because Christ possessed abundant life he had a vibrant spirit of joy; he was not always ultra-solemn and sorrowful; and he certainly wasn't boring.
- Yeshua had wholehearted conviction about what he knew—he truly believed what he preached and his air of authority was palpable (Matthew 7:28-29).

Jesus was incredibly bold, outspoken and had no qualms about offending pompous fools deserving of correction:

- He was invited to a dinner party with some Pharisees and immediately began insulting the host and honored guests, not because he was abusive but because they *needed* rebuked (Luke 11:37-54). This is **tough love**.
- Christ was forthright and honest—he got straight to the point when necessary and didn't beat around the bush with overly diplomatic discourse (Matthew 15:1-20 & 18:7).

One of the most amazing examples of Jesus' incredible boldness & power can be observed when he cleared the Temple of ungodly fools:

> **On reaching Jerusalem, Jesus entered the temple area and began <u>driving out</u> those who were buying and selling there. He <u>overturned the tables of the money changers and the benches of those selling doves,</u> [16] and <u>would not allow anyone to carry merchandise through the temple courts</u>.** [17] **And as he taught them, he said, "Is it not written: 'My house will be called a house of prayer for all nations, but you have made it a den of robbers.' "**
>
> [18] **The Chief priests and the teachers of the law heard this and <u>began looking for a way to kill him</u>, for <u>they feared him</u>, because the whole crowd <u>was amazed</u> at his teaching.**
>
> **Mark 11:15-18**

Notice that **Christ radically threw over tables and benches and would not allow anyone to carry merchandise through the Temple courts**. Does this sound like "gentle Jesus meek and mild" or the bold Lion of Judah? Can you imagine Jesus *not allowing* anyone to carry goods into the Temple? And no one dared defy him! A soft pushover wouldn't be able to do this. Of course, it wasn't a case of Christ intimidating people with fleshly brawn & bluster, but rather his potent spiritual passion, anointing and boldness.

Believe it or not, Jesus cleared the Temple in this manner *twice* during his earthly ministry. This account took place near the end of his public service, but he also cleared the Temple near the beginning—three years earlier—as detailed in John 2:13-17. On this earlier occasion **he made a whip and utilized it in driving out the animals, yelling and scattering coins!** Why did the Messiah have to clear the Temple a second time? Obviously because the 'snakes' withered back in over the course of the next three years.

Now notice the response of the sterile legalists in Mark 11:18: They *feared* Christ! They feared him so much that they decided to kill him and remove him from the scene altogether. Let me tell you something, impotent milksops don't inspire fear and they certainly don't provoke VIPs to plot murder. Also, note how the people who witnessed his clearing of the Temple responded: They were *amazed!* Dull sissies don't inspire amazement, but people who are dynamic, courageous and authoritative do! (And by "authoritative" I *don't* mean authoritarian, which is abusive. 'Abuse' is the misuse of power).

All over the gospel accounts we see evidence of Christ being courageous, astonishing, amazing, authoritative and even frightening! For verification, just look up these passages: Matthew 7:28-29, 14:26, Mark 1:27, 2:10-12, 4:37-41, 7:37, Luke 5:8-11, 7:14-16, 20:20-26, 20:40 and the aforementioned John 2:13-17. Needless to say, people who insinuate that Jesus was some effeminate weakling obviously don't know how to read!

Is it any wonder that the Bible encourages us to *not* provoke the Son? Speaking of which…

Chapter 8

DON'T Vex Angels

We saw in **Chapter 6** that failing to voice God's Word in faith will tie-up your angels, so to speak, and prevent them from fulfilling their God-given mandate to serve you. In the vacuum, wicked spirits naturally have more liberty of movement to harass and oppress.

This is bad enough, but it would be worse to *vex* the angels assigned to you—that is, annoy and provoke them. How do you vex angels? Through a stubborn spirit of unbelief and the corresponding words & actions. We saw a good example of this in **Chapter 1** when the archangel Gabriel appeared to Zechariah to inform him of his wife's pregnancy and their forthcoming Nazarite son, John the Baptist:

> Then <u>an angel of the Lord appeared to him</u>, standing at the right side of the altar of incense. ¹² When Zechariah saw him, <u>he was startled and was gripped with fear</u>. ¹³ But the angel said to him: "Do

> not be afraid, Zechariah; your prayer has been heard. Your wife Elizabeth will bear you a son, and you are to call him John. ¹⁴ He will be a joy and delight to you, and many will rejoice because of his birth, ¹⁵ for he will be great in the sight of the Lord. He is never to take wine or other fermented drink, and he will be filled with the Holy Spirit even before he is born. ¹⁶ He will bring back many of the people of Israel to the Lord their God. ¹⁷ And he will go on before the Lord, in the spirit and power of Elijah, to turn the hearts of the parents to their children and the disobedient to the wisdom of the righteous—to make ready a people prepared for the Lord."
>
> ¹⁸ Zechariah asked the angel, "<u>How can I be sure of this? I am an old man and my wife is well along in years</u>."
>
> ¹⁹ The angel said to him, "<u>I am Gabriel. I stand in the presence of God, and I have been sent to speak to you and to tell you this good news</u>. ²⁰ And now you will be silent and not able to speak until the day this happens, <u>because you did not believe my words</u>, which will come true at their appointed time."
>
> **Luke 1:11-20**

It's understandable that the sudden appearance of a supernatural being "startled" Zechariah and so he was "gripped with fear." However, after Gabriel conveyed his wonderful message Zechariah responded in unbelief, doubting that he & Elizabeth could have a baby due to their age. This offended Gabriel and so he strikes Zechariah dumb for nine months until the baby was ready to be birthed (verses 57-64). Why was Gabriel so irked? Because he was astounded by Zechariah's unbelief in response to the supernatural appearance of a ruling angel who regularly stood in the very presence of the Almighty.

This is evidence that our negative actions—persistent unbelief or sin—can provoke angels, resulting in some type of penalty or discipline. It goes without saying that we should respond in faith to God's Word, wherever it comes from, and not react with doubt and unbelief!

Why do you think Gabriel struck Zechariah dumb? Because "the tongue has the power of life and death" (Proverbs 18:21). If Zechariah continued to speak his unbelief **it would've prevented the miracle of John's birth from taking place!** Thus Gabriel silenced his tongue until John was born.

Mary, by contrast, did not respond in unbelief to Gabriel's message regarding her miraculous pregnancy and the coming Messiah:

> **The angel went to her and said, "Greetings, you who are highly favored! The Lord is with you."**
> <u>²⁹ **Mary was greatly troubled at his words and wondered what kind of greeting this might be.**</u> ³⁰ But the angel said to her, <u>**"Do not be afraid, Mary; you have found favor with God.** ³¹ **You will conceive and give birth to a son, and you are to call him Jesus.** ³² **He will be great and will be called the Son of the Most High.**</u> **The Lord God will give him the throne of his father David,** ³³ **and he will reign over Jacob's descendants forever;** <u>**his kingdom will never end."**</u>
> ³⁴ **"How will this be," Mary asked the angel, "since I am a virgin?"**
> ³⁵ **The angel answered, "The Holy Spirit will come on you, and the power of the Most High will overshadow you. So the holy one to be born will be called the Son of God.** ³⁶ **Even Elizabeth your relative is going to have a child in her old age, and she who was said to be unable to conceive is in her sixth month.** ³⁷ **For no word from God will ever fail."**
> ³⁸ **"I am the Lord's servant," Mary answered. "May your word to me be fulfilled." Then the angel left her.**
>
> **Luke 1:28-38**

Mary's question was a legitimate one and not unbelief in light of the fact that she was a virgin. After Gabriel explained how the miracle would take place she humbly responds in faith: "I am the Lord's servant. May your word to me be fulfilled."

She wasted no time in visiting Elizabeth where she ecstatically proclaimed: "the Mighty One *has done* great things for me" (verse 49). Mary spoke of her miracle in the past tense even though there was zero physical evidence of her supernatural pregnancy at this point, which shows faith.

So Zachariah vexed an angel through stubborn unbelief and thus suffered humiliating dumbness for nine months whereas Mary responded in faith and was blessed. Take heed.

Don't Provoke *The* Angel of the LORD

We are responsible for the words we speak and what we believe in our hearts—our thought life—including the words we speak & believe over other people. Combined with the force of belief, our words have power, both positive and negative. Why do you think Christ said: "For by your words you will be acquitted, and by your words you will be condemned" (Matthew 12:37)?

Speaking of Jesus Christ, we must be careful to *not* provoke The Angel of the LORD through unrepentant rebellion. Consider the following example where the LORD addresses the Israelites after their deliverance from bondage in Egypt on their way to the Promised Land of Canaan:

> "See, I am sending <u>an angel</u> ahead of you <u>to guard you along the way</u> and <u>to bring you to the place I have prepared.</u> [21] <u>Pay attention to him and listen to what he says. Do not rebel against him; he will not forgive your rebellion, since my Name is in him.</u> [22] If you listen carefully to <u>what he says and do all that I say</u>, I will be an enemy to your enemies and will oppose those who oppose you. [23] <u>My angel will go ahead of you and bring you into the land</u> of the Amorites, Hittites, Perizzites, Canaanites, Hivites and Jebusites, and I will wipe them out."
>
> **Exodus 23:20-23**

As you can see, a mighty "angel" was assigned to the Israelites to:

1. Guard the Israelites along their way (verse 20).
2. Give instructions from the LORD (verses 21-22).
3. Go ahead of them (verse 23).
4. Lead them into the Promised Land (verses 20 & 23).

Who is this angel? We saw last chapter that the Hebrew word for "angel" is *malak (mal-AWK)*, which simply means "a messenger, supernatural or human." The word appears over two hundred times in the Old Testament and most often refers to *supernatural* messengers (Genesis 19:1) while sometimes referring to *human* ones (Genesis 32:3,6 & Isaiah 30:4).

We also saw last chapter that *malak* is used several times in reference to "The Angel of the LORD," the pre-incarnate Christ. A good example is when The Angel of the LORD appeared to meek Gideon (Judges 6:11,14). We observed that this was no ordinary angel, but rather God, the Son, and how a whole chapter of the Bible is devoted to proving that Christ is vastly superior to angels (Hebrews 1).

So what about this "angel" that went ahead of the Israelites and led them into the Promised Land? Was it a conventional angel or The Angel of the LORD, the pre-incarnate Christ? The latter. Here's the evidence:

1. The LORD said that His name—YHWH—was "in him" (verse 21). "In him" is one word in the Hebrew, *qereb (KEH-reb)*, meaning in the "midst" or "within." In other words, God's name is intrinsically linked to this specific messenger and there's only one "angel" (*malak*) in the Bible with this particular honor, The Angel of the LORD.
2. The statement that this "angel" would "not forgive" their rebellion (verse 21) obviously meant not forgiving those who were incorrigibly rebellious. How do we know this? Because the LORD *always* forgives the humbly repentant (1 John 1:9, Psalm 32:5 & Proverbs 28:13). So this Angel had the capacity to forgive or *not* forgive sin, which is a divine quality.

Conventional angels, by contrast, are mandated to serve people in the sense of waiting on their tables, so to speak; they don't have the authority to forgive or not forgive sin.

3. This "angel" is mandated to *lead* the Israelites into their Promised Land (verses 20 & 23) and, in the New Covenant, the Holy Spirit is the one who *leads* believers, not angels. Angels *serve* believers. The Holy Spirit is, of course, the "Spirit of Christ" (Romans 8:9). Just as The Angel of the LORD led the Israelites into their earthly Promised Land so the Spirit of Christ leads New Covenant believers into their earthly "promised land" (I say *earthly* "promised land" to distinguish it from our *eternal* Promised Land, which is the "new heaven and a new earth, the home of righteousness" - 2 Peter 3:13). We'll look at this further at the end of this chapter and, especially, in **Chapter 20** (the last two sections).

4. The key to victory in the forthcoming takeover of Canaan would not be the Hebrews' military might, but rather the presence of The Angel of the LORD, who is Christ, along with the Israelites' obedience. Just the same, believers in the New Testament do not conquer their "promised land" by their own might, but rather through the power of Christ and our compliance (Philippians 4:13). I add "and our compliance" because a covenant is an agreement or contract between two parties where each party has terms to fulfill. In our case, believers are obligated to *believe* (that is, walk in faith) and endure on the foundation of love— love for God and love for people as we love ourselves. This is "Faith working through love." We'll go over these things in **Chapter 20** (in the section *The New Covenant is Superior to the Old Covenant*).

"Do Not Rebel Against Him"

With the understanding that this "angel" is The Angel of the LORD—the pre-incarnate Christ—God instructed the Israelites to listen to what he said and not rebel against him (verse 21). The King James Version phrases this as "provoke him not" whereas the New King James

Version says "do not provoke him." The Hebrew word for "provoke" is *marar (maw-RAR)*, which is used 13 times in the Old Testament and means to make bitter, grieve, provoke, enrage or vex.

What can we get from this? Rebellion against the Angel's divine messages would provoke him—grieve him, vex him, enrage him. He would not forgive obstinate rebellion and hence the guilty Hebrews would have to suffer the corresponding punishment. And what is the wages of unrepentant sin? Death (Romans 6:23 & James 1:14-15).

Unfortunately, the Israelites foolishly provoked The Angel through their incorrigible rebellion and suffered accordingly.

Bear in mind that **it was God's express will for them to escape slavery in Egypt and inherit the Promised Land** (Exodus 3:8,17 & 13:5). In fact, The Angel of the LORD was commissioned to fulfill this, but success *hinged* on the Israelites' faithfulness (Exodus 23:20-23). Sadly, the Hebrews kept rebelling with their persistent spirit of unbelief.

A good example is when twelve spies explored the Promised Land in preparation to conquer it and ten of them came back with a negative report that contradicted God's will. Joshua and Caleb were the only two who were faithful to the LORD's Word (Numbers 13-14). The negative report spread and thus the Israelites said in unison: "**If only we had died in Egypt! Or in this wilderness!** Why is the LORD bringing us to this land only to let us fall by the sword? Our wives and children will be taken as plunder. Wouldn't it be better for us to go back to Egypt?" (Numbers 14:2-3).

Notice God's response:

> "**As surely as I live, declares the LORD, <u>I will do to you the very thing I heard you say</u>:** [29] <u>**In this wilderness your bodies will fall**</u>—**every one of you twenty years old or more who was counted in the census and who has grumbled against me.** [30] **Not one of you will enter the land I swore with uplifted hand to make your home, except Caleb son of Jephunneh and Joshua son of Nun.**"
>
> **Numbers 14:28-30**

The disobedient Israelites were punished **according to their own unbelieving words**. They *said* they would die in the desert and thus it would be so over the course of the next forty years, starting with the immediate deaths of the ten unfaithful spies via plague (verses 36-37). Thankfully, the LORD did not hold those under 20 years of age accountable. The only two older than 19 (at the time) to enter the Promised Land four decades later were Joshua and Caleb because they walked in obedience to God's Word and did not provoke The Angel of the LORD who was leading them to Canaan.

I want to stress: It *was* God's will for all of them to live and inherit the Promised Land. But they stubbornly and stupidly opposed God's will by believing a negative report and used the power of their tongues to voice words of unbelief. So the LORD gave to them accordingly. They said "We're going to die in the desert" and that's exactly what happened. What you *say* and *believe* is what you get.

It's important to drive this home: Our words have the power of life and death (Proverbs 18:21). Make sure you speak life and not death. Make sure you speak *according to* God's will and not *against* it because otherwise you risk hindering heavenly angels from servicing you and consequently opening the door for fallen angels to attack. Even worse, those who walk in exceptional unbelief and incorrigible rebellion risk vexing their angels and even provoking the Mighty Christ.

For anyone who finds this incredulous, please consider that...

What Happened to the Israelites are Examples for Us

Are these Old Testament events applicable to us today? And, if so, how? Assuming you're a New Covenant believer, notice what the New Testament says in this regard:

> Now these things occurred **as examples** to keep us from setting our hearts on evil things as they did. [7] Do not be idolaters, as some of them were; as it is written: "The people sat down to eat and drink and got up to indulge in revelry." [8] We should not commit

sexual immorality, as some of them did—and in one day twenty-three thousand of them died. ⁹ <u>**We should not test Christ**</u>, as some of them did—and were killed by snakes. ¹⁰ <u>**And do not grumble, as some of them did**</u>—<u>**and were killed by the destroying angel**</u>.

¹¹ These things happened to them <u>**as examples**</u> and were written down <u>**as warnings for us**</u>, on whom the culmination of the ages has come.

1 Corinthians 10:6-11

As you can see, what happened to the Israelites in the Old Testament was chronicled as sobering "**examples**" and "**warnings**" for us—New Covenant believers—so that we would not foolishly walk in the same transgressions and suffer accordingly. Four sins and the corresponding occasions are named:

1. **Idolatry:** This means worshiping something *above* the LORD, which doesn't have to be a literal idol; it could be something like mammon (money). Paul got this example from Exodus 32 where the Israelites—barely out of Egypt—fell into gross idol worship.
2. **Sexual immorality:** This includes all forms of sexual sin—fornication, adultery, homosexuality and so forth. This also refers to what took place in Exodus 32. The figure of 23,000 deaths is a combination of the 3000 killed by the Levites at Sinai for instigating the mass orgy (verse 28) and the participators who died from the subsequent plague (verse 35).
3. **Testing Christ:** This refers to questioning the goodness and plan of the Almighty, who created us, leads us, protects us and provides for us. This example comes from Numbers 21:4-9 where the Israelites became impatient and frustrated due to Moses' circuitous route to the Promised Land where they proceeded to speak "*against* God and *against* Moses" (verses 5 & 7). Thus the LORD sent venomous snakes against the rebels and killed them (verse 6). The only way those bitten could live

was to look at a snake on a pole made by Moses at the LORD's instructions, which foreshadowed Jesus' death on the cross.[24]

Two significant things bear noting from this account: First, the attacking snakes were types of the devil & filthy spirits. How's this apply to us? Simple: Unbelief and the corresponding disobedience hinders protective angels and looses evil spirits ("snakes"). Secondly, Paul by the Spirit says that the Israelites tested "Christ" whereas the Old Testament account in Numbers specifically says they spoke against "God" and the "LORD" (verses 4 & 7). You see, Christ *is* the LORD, albeit the Son, not the Father. The Israelites were speaking against The Angel of the LORD whose job was to lead them through the wilderness and into the Promised Land. Thus the Israelites "spoke against the LORD," which "tested Christ." Chew on that.

4. **Grumbling:** This means complaining — murmuring and muttering in smoldering discontent — which includes complaining against God's will, his Word and his leading, not to mention his God-anointed servant-leaders, like Moses & Aaron were to the Israelites. Paul says that those who obstinately grumbled were "killed by the destroying angel." This refers to Numbers 16 where Korah, Dathan & Abiram and their 250 followers grumbled against the LORD and his chosen leaders (verse 11). It also includes the thousands of Israelites who grumbled the day after these rebels were slain by the LORD, which brought about the death of 14,700 more Israelites. These complaining rebels "were killed by the destroying angel"!!

Do you want to be slain by the destroying angel? Of course you don't. So don't grumble against the LORD, his Word, his will or his anointed servant-leaders. For anyone who would argue that this doesn't apply to New Testament believers and our assemblies, the above passage plainly says otherwise.

This doesn't mean, of course, that you should tolerate abuse from ministers (abuse is the misuse of power). In the case

---

[24] Why would Christ be pictured as a *snake* on the cross? Because, although Jesus *didn't* sin, he was *made* "sin on our behalf, so that we might become the righteousness of God in Him" (2 Corinthians 5:21 NASB).

of Numbers 16 Moses & Aaron were *not* guilty of abuse. As a matter of fact, Moses was the humblest, godliest man on the face of the Earth at the time (see Numbers 12:3-8), which is in contrast to some modern arrogant "ministers" ('minister,' by the way, means "servant"). If you have legitimate evidence of abuse by spiritual leaders, pray about it and confront the person as led of the Spirit, as humbly as possible. If the person is unrepentant then get one or two witnesses for support in a follow-up confrontation. Christ Himself instructed us to do this (Matthew 18:15-17). If the "minister" remains obstinate about his/her abuse then do what the Messiah adamantly instructed: "*Leave them*; they are blind guides" (Matthew 15:14).

More on the Application of 1 Corinthians 10:6-11

Needless to say, 1 Corinthians 10:6-11 is a sobering passage and we need to regularly examine ourselves to see if we're honestly in the faith and repent as necessary (2 Corinthians 13:5).

The four transgressions listed—idolatry, sexual immorality, testing God and grumbling—are common sins (1 Corinthians 10:13). All believers miss it now & then and anyone who says they don't is a liar (1 John 1:8). But servant-**leaders** are *supposed* to be spiritually mature and therefore freed-up from the bigger sins (1 Timothy 3:1-7). After all, if *they* aren't free from sin how can they help others walk free?

Regardless, *all* believers must learn to daily "put off the old self"—the flesh—and "put on the new self" (Ephesians 4:22-24). This is a *process* that requires "keeping with repentance," meaning humbly 'fessing up when you miss it, which keeps God's grace and forgiveness flowing in your life (1 John 1:9). Theologians refer to this process as **sanctification**, which means purification. It's a purification of the mind that naturally occurs as believers grow spiritually.

The last two sins listed—testing Christ and grumbling—are applicable to the topic of angels, which is why we're addressing this passage:

Testing Christ. Believers commit this sin when they speak against the LORD, his Word or his genuine servant-leaders. This automatically ties-up angels because angels only obey the voice of God's Word. If believers are speaking *against* God's Word, angels have nothing upon which to act. Instead, evil spirits—"snakes"—will be released to kill, steal and destroy (John 10:10). If you don't want this happening in your life then don't speak against God's Word, his will or his genuine servant-leaders.

Grumbling. Amazingly, Korah and his fellow rebels grumbled against the LORD and Moses for delivering them from the bondage of Egypt (!), which they outrageously referred to as "a land flowing with milk and honey" (Numbers 16:12-13). I say "outrageously" because this was how God described the Promised Land he wanted to give the Israelites (Exodus 3:8). They also complained about being taken from Egypt to be killed in the desert. *After* Korah & his rebels were judged and wiped off the face of the Earth, thousands of Israelites complained about it and thus 14,700 were killed by "the destroying angel" via a plague that came out from the LORD (Numbers 16:46). The Bible applies this Old Testament account to New Testament believers. Needless to say, if you don't want to be "killed by the destroying angel" then don't be a grumbler.

But this leaves us with a question…

Who is "the Destroying Angel"?

Believe it or not, the "destroying angel" refers to the LORD, the Son—*The* Angel of the LORD. If you find this incredulous, allow the Scriptures to prove it to you beyond any shadow of doubt.

Let's start by revisiting the verse in question:

> **And do not grumble, as some of them did—
> and were killed by <u>the destroying angel</u>.**
> **1 Corinthians 10:10**

As detailed above, Paul is referring to the events of Numbers 16. On this occasion three sets of rebels were killed:

1. **Korah, Dathan & Abiram, their families and Korah's men:** They were killed when the Earth opened up beneath them and swallowed them alive (Numbers 16:25-34). Moses specified that it was "**the LORD**" who did this (verse 30).
2. **The 250 community leaders who supported Korah's rebellion and offered incense:** They were killed when "fire came out from **the LORD** and consumed them" (Numbers 16:35).
3. **The 14,700 Israelites who complained against Moses and Aaron because the LORD slew the rebels en masse.** They were killed when wrath came out from "**the LORD**" in the form of a plague (Numbers 16:41-50). Many more would've died if atonement hadn't been made through Moses and Aaron.

According to the account itself, who killed the grumbling rebels? **The LORD Himself** through **1.** the Earth opening up, **2.** fire and **3.** plague. There is no mention of a conventional angel in Numbers 16 carrying out these just executions. Thus when Paul says they were "killed by the destroying angel" in 1 Corinthians 10:10 he was referring to the LORD.

I should point out that the Greek word for 'angel' does not actually appear in 1 Corinthians 10:10, which is why some versions read like so:

Nor grumble, as some of them did, and were destroyed by <u>the destroyer</u>.
1 Corinthians 10:10 (NASB)

The King James Version also translates it this way.

"The destroying angel" (in the NIV) or "the destroyer" (in the NASB and KJV) is just one word in the Greek, *olothreutés (ol-oth-ryoo-TACE)*, which only appears this single time in Scripture. The word stems from the noun *olethros (OL-eth-ros)*, which means "ruin, doom, destruction, death." *Olethros* can refer to physical death, but Paul also used it in reference to human damnation:

> ...**This will happen when <u>the Lord Jesus</u> is revealed from heaven in blazing fire with his powerful angels. ⁸<u>He will punish those who do not know God</u> and do not obey the gospel of our Lord Jesus. ⁹They will be punished with <u>everlasting destruction</u>** *(olethros)* **and shut out from the presence of the Lord and from the glory of his might**
> 2 Thessalonians 1:7-9

This refers to the fate of unredeemed people who refuse Christ as LORD. Since they reject the Redeemer and His gracious gift of eternal life they must justly suffer the wages of sin, which is death (Romans 6:23). This passage describes their fate as "everlasting destruction," meaning destruction that lasts forever with no hope of resurrection. John described it as "the second death," the result of being discarded in the lake of fire, which is God's garbage dump (Revelation 20:11-15).

Notice that the above passage—2 Thessalonians 1:7-9—clearly shows "the Lord Jesus" as the one who issues out this destruction. Father God doesn't do it because he "lives in unapproachable light, whom no one has seen or can see" (1 Timothy 6:16). The heavenly Father speaks to people through the Son. He *creates* through the Son. In fact, as observed last chapter, **everything seen and unseen has been made by the Son** (Hebrews 1:2 & Colossians 1:16). This explains why Christ has the authority to destroy, *if* necessary. Why? Because He's the One who created in the first place. If you legally build a structure on your property the only one who has the authority to destroy it is you. It's the same principle here. We'll talk about this more in a moment.

With all this in mind, let's return to 1 Corinthians 10:10. Paul said that the grumbling rebels put to death in Numbers 16 were killed by "the destroying angel" or "the destroyer." Who is this destroyer? It's the LORD Himself, the Son. We know this because, as noted above, the account **three times** attributes the just executions of the rebels to the LORD. No other being is mentioned as their destroyer, except the

LORD, who performed the executions through **1.** the Earth opening up, **2.** fire and **3.** plague.

Believers are "Saved" from the LORD's Wrath

Christians are said to be "saved," but saved from what? Many believers don't realize this but we are actually saved from God's wrath. In other words, **we are saved from** *God Himself*. This is plainly observed in John's solemn declaration: "Whoever rejects the Son will not see life, for **God's wrath** remains on them" (John 3:36). Here's further evidence:

> **But because of your stubbornness and your unrepentant heart, you are storing up wrath against yourself for** the day of God's wrath, **when his righteous judgment will be revealed.**
> **Romans 2:5**

> **Since we have now been justified by his [Jesus'] blood, how much more shall we be** saved from God's wrath through him?
> **Romans 5:9**

> **Jesus, who rescues us from** the coming wrath.
> **1 Thessalonians 1:10**

> **For God did not appoint us to suffer** [his] wrath **but to receive salvation through our Lord Jesus Christ.**
> **1 Thessalonians 5:9**

As you can see, Christians are saved from God's wrath which, according to Romans 2:5 above, will be executed on the Day of Judgment, referred to as "the day of God's wrath."[25]

Yet, what exactly is God's wrath? In the Old Testament anyone who incurred God's wrath was to suffer destruction at *his* hands (see, for example, Psalm 106:23 and Ezekiel 20:13). In the same way, when God's wrath is poured out on Judgment Day, whoever's name is not found written in the book of life will suffer destruction at his hands.

This explains why Hebrews 10:31 says "It is a dreadful thing to fall into **the hands of the living God**." The context of this text is human damnation, as verified by verses 26-27:

> **If we deliberately keep on sinning after we have received the knowledge of the truth, no sacrifice for sins is left, [27] but only a fearful expectation of judgment and of raging fire that will consume the enemies of God.**
> **Hebrews 10:26-27**

This is reminiscent of the way the 250 followers of Korah were justly executed by the LORD, i.e. the Son:

> **And fire came out from the LORD and consumed the 250 men who were offering the incense.**
> **Numbers 16:35**

So, when Hebrews 10:31 says "It is a dreadful thing to fall into **the hands** of the living God," who's "hands" is it talking about? Not the Father, but the Son.

Now let's revisit three of the verses cited above:

---

[25] Many people will experience God's wrath poured out on this Earth during the coming Tribulation, but the vast majority of unsaved humanity will not experience his wrath until their Judgment Day (Revelation 20:11-15).

> **Since we have now been justified by his [Jesus'] blood, how much more shall we be <u>saved from God's wrath</u> <u>through him</u>?**
>
> **Romans 5:9**

> **<u>Jesus</u>, who rescues us from <u>the coming wrath</u>.**
>
> **1 Thessalonians 1:10**

> **For God did not appoint us to suffer** [his] **<u>wrath</u> but to receive salvation <u>through our Lord Jesus Christ</u>.**
>
> **1 Thessalonians 5:9**

Observe how these verses *specify* that it's the Lord Jesus Christ who **saves us** from Father God's wrath. With this in mind, consider this passage:

> **There is only one Lawgiver and Judge, the one who is able to <u>save</u> and <u>destroy</u>.**
>
> **James 4:12**

You see, the LORD is either going to **save people** or **destroy them** based on how they respond to his gracious offer of forgiveness and eternal life (Acts 20:21). In light of this, ponder something Jesus said:

> **"Do not be afraid of those who kill the body but cannot kill the soul. Rather, be afraid of <u>the One</u> who can <u>destroy</u> both soul and body in hell."**
>
> **Matthew 10:28**

The Greek word for 'hell' here is *Gehenna (GHEH-en-nah)*, which literally referred to the Valley of Hinnom *(HIN-om)*, a constantly smoking trash dump outside the SW walls of Jerusalem where garbage was eradicated. Jesus was simply using Gehenna as a figure for the lake of fire. Note what he says will happen to unrepentant rebels cast into the lake of fire: "the One" will destroy both soul and body. Who is "the One" who will destroy them? The LORD, of course, but more specifically the Son. In other words, Jesus was warning his listeners of what *he himself* would do to the willingly irredeemable on Judgment Day.

"Kiss the Son, Lest... You Perish in the Way"

What we're talking about is clearly observed in this Old Testament passage:

> ¹⁰ Therefore, <u>you kings</u>, be wise;
> be warned, <u>you rulers of the earth</u>.
> ¹¹ Serve <u>the LORD</u> with fear,
> And rejoice with trembling.
> ¹² Kiss <u>the Son</u>, lest He be angry,
> And you perish *in* the way,
> When His wrath is kindled but a little.
> Blessed *are* all those
> who <u>put their trust in Him</u>.
> **Psalm 2:10-12** (NIV/NASB[26])

The passage is speaking to "kings" or "rulers of the earth"—encouraging them to "serve the LORD with fear." This is referring to Yahweh but, more specifically, the Son.

World leaders—and all people by extension—are instructed to "kiss the Son," which simply means to honor him, i.e. worship him. This includes putting your trust in Him. The first part of verse 12 says that those who refuse to do so risk angering the Son and thus they will "perish in the way."

You see, Christ is our Creator—the "Lawgiver and Judge, the One who is able to **save** and to **destroy**" (James 4:12)—and he will save or destroy based on our response to His graciousness. In our case, this means his gracious offer of eternal life that is received through repentance and faith (Acts 20:21). Only the stupidest of fools would reject such an awesome free gift and continue on the path of certain death.

---

[26] Verse 10 is from the NIV whereas verses 11-12 are from the NASB.

There's nothing morally or judicially wrong with the fact that the Lord is going to irreversibly destroy sinful people who reject his gift of eternal life. How so? Because the Bible repeatedly makes it clear that the wages of sin is death and, furthermore, our Creator—Christ—has made sure that every human heart instinctively realizes this (Romans 1:32). Thus, people who reject redemption through Christ in favor of living a sinful lifestyle are indeed choosing the wages of their actions, death (whether choosing it consciously or subconsciously). And Yeshua will unenthusiastically accommodate them because he respects their freewill. The LORD alone is the ultimate authority and giver of life and therefore he has the authority and right to take life away—*if* he must.

Justice, after all, demands the execution of the penalty of the law. In this case the penalty of the law is death—eternal death—death with no hope of resurrection. As noted earlier, Paul referred to this sentence as "everlasting destruction" in 2 Thessalonians 1:9. Its execution is necessary in order that God may be just. A government that never calls offenders of the law to account is contemptible and wicked. The biblical doctrine of eternal punishment is our assurance that God is essentially and unchangingly holy and just. (Please note that I said "eternal punishment" and not "eternal punish*ing*").

See my book *HELL KNOW* for scriptural details on human damnation.

Examples of The Angel of the LORD Destroying

With the understanding that **1.** Christ is The Angel of the LORD and **2.** that he has the authority to justly destroy anything he creates, *if* necessary, let's examine a couple examples of this from the Old Testament.

This first example concerns the LORD destroying the firstborn males of Egypt in order to provoke Pharaoh to let the Israelites go free; Moses is speaking to the elders of Israel:

> "When **the LORD goes through the land to strike down the Egyptians, he will see** the blood on the top and sides of the doorframe and will pass over that doorway, and he will not permit **the destroyer** to enter your houses and strike you down."
>
> ²⁴ "Obey these instructions as a lasting ordinance for you and your descendants. ²⁵ When you enter the land that the LORD will give you as he promised, observe this ceremony. ²⁶ And when your children ask you, 'What does this ceremony mean to you?' ²⁷ then tell them, 'It is the Passover sacrifice to **the LORD, who passed over the houses of the Israelites in Egypt and spared our homes when he struck down the Egyptians.**' "
>
> Exodus 12:23-27

Observe that it's the LORD Himself who was going to pass through Egypt; and the final verse specifies that it is **the LORD who would strike down the Egyptians, i.e. slay all the firstborn males**. But verse 23 specifies further that it is "the destroyer" who would actually smite them. While I suppose this "destroyer" *could* be an archangel, like Michael (the chief angel who enforces law and judgment, as covered in **Chapter 1**), it's more likely the pre-incarnate Christ—The Angel of the LORD—in light of the specificity of verse 27.

A passage in the Psalms sheds additional light:

> ⁴² **They** [the Israelites] **did not remember his**
> [God's] **power**—
>   the day **he** redeemed them from the oppressor,
> ⁴³ the day **he** displayed his signs in Egypt,
>   **his wonders** in the region of Zoan.
> ⁴⁴ **He** turned their river into blood;
>   they could not drink from their streams.
> ⁴⁵ **He** sent swarms of flies that devoured them,
>   and frogs that devastated them.
> ⁴⁶ He gave their crops to the grasshopper,
>   their produce to the locust.

> ⁴⁷ <u>He</u> destroyed their vines with hail
>   and their sycamore-figs with sleet.
> ⁴⁸ <u>He</u> gave over their cattle to the hail,
>   their livestock to bolts of lightning.
> ⁴⁹ <u>He</u> unleashed against them his hot anger,
>   his wrath, indignation and hostility—
>   <u>a band of destroying angels</u>.
> ⁵⁰ <u>He</u> prepared a path for his anger;
>   <u>he</u> did not spare them from death
>   but gave them over to the plague.
> ⁵¹ <u>He struck down all the firstborn of Egypt</u>,
>   the firstfruits of manhood in the tents of Ham.
> ⁵² But <u>he brought his people out like a flock</u>;
>   he led them like sheep through the wilderness.
>
> **Psalm 78:42-52**

This is a brief, poetic account of the ten plagues of Egypt, which occurred after the pharaoh refused to let the Israelites go. As you can see, it was the LORD Himself—the pre-incarnate Christ—who executed the ten plagues, but verse 49 shows that he had the assistance of "a band of destroying angels" to carry out at least some of these judgments; the text doesn't specify which ones.

As far as the execution of the firstborn is concerned, however, Exodus 12:23 above doesn't say that the LORD used *angels* (plural) to accomplish this, just that he would release "the destroyer" (singular) to do so. Since Exodus 12:27 cites the LORD as the One who struck down the firstborn we may conclude that the pre-incarnate Christ—The Angel of the LORD—is this "destroyer."

Offering support is this passage, which concerns God's judgment on Israel after David arrogantly took a census of his fighting men:

> **Before David got up the next morning, the word of the LORD had come to Gad the prophet, David's seer:** ¹² **"Go and tell David, 'This is what the LORD says: I am giving you three options. Choose one of them for me to carry out against you.' "**

> ¹³ So Gad went to David and said to him, "Shall there come on you three years of famine in your land? Or three months of fleeing from your enemies while they pursue you? Or three days of plague in your land? Now then, think it over and decide how I should answer the one who sent me."
>
> ¹⁴ David said to Gad, "I am in deep distress. <u>Let us fall into the hands of the LORD</u>, for his mercy is great; but do not let me fall into human hands."
>
> ¹⁵ So <u>the LORD sent a plague on Israel from that morning until the end of the time designated, and seventy thousand of the people from Dan to Beersheba died.</u> ¹⁶ When <u>the angel</u> stretched out his hand to destroy Jerusalem, <u>the LORD</u> relented concerning the disaster and said to <u>the angel</u> who was afflicting the people, "Enough! Withdraw your hand." <u>The angel of the Lord</u> was then at the threshing floor of Araunah the Jebusite.
>
> **2 Samuel 24:11-16**

God offered King David three options as punishment for his sin: **1.** three years of famine in Israel, **2.** three months of Israel being defeated by their enemies or **3.** three days of plague. David chose the last one, likely because it involved the shortest length of judgment, but also because suffering plague would be a case of falling "into the hands of the LORD" and David was familiar with God's great mercy, which was preferable to falling "into human hands" (verse 14). Note that David attributes the ensuing plague to the LORD Himself.

The next verse specifies that it is "the LORD"—Yahweh—who sends the plague on Israel, which kills 70,000 Hebrews. Verse 16 then shows the LORD preventing **The Angel of the LORD** from destroying Jerusalem by commanding him: "Enough! Withdraw your hand." We saw last chapter that The Angel of the LORD is the pre-incarnate Christ.

If this is so, how do we explain that the LORD talks to The Angel of the LORD as a separate person? Simple, it's evidence of what theologians call "the Trinity": Father God instructed the Son to withhold his hand from destroying the capital city and the Son complied. This is in harmony with what Jesus testified—He only does what the Father commands (John 8:29 & 15:10).

This isn't something peculiar to 2 Samuel 24:16 as we observe the same thing in other passages, like this one:

> That night <u>the angel of the Lord</u> went out and put to death a hundred and eighty-five thousand in the Assyrian camp. When the people got up the next morning—there were all the dead bodies!
>
> **2 Kings 19:35**

And this one:

> Then <u>the angel of the LORD</u> said, "<u>LORD Almighty</u>, how long will you withhold mercy from Jerusalem and from the towns of Judah, which you have been angry with these seventy years?" [13] So <u>the LORD spoke kind and comforting words to the angel</u> who talked with me.
>
> **Zechariah 1:12-13**

This passage shows that both "the angel of the LORD" and Father God were present at the same time. Since we know Christ is The Angel of the LORD this text is simply depicting two persons of the Trinity talking to each other. This explains, by the way, why God refers to Himself in the plural in the creation account:

> Then God said, "<u>Let us</u> make mankind in <u>our image</u>, in <u>our likeness</u>..."
>
> **Genesis 1:26**

> And the Lord God said, "The man has now become <u>like one of us</u>, knowing good and evil. He must not be allowed to reach out his hand and take also from the tree of life and eat, and live forever."
>
> **Genesis 3:22**

This plurality doesn't indicate the false notion of polytheism, however, because the Bible emphasizes that God is one (Deuteronomy 6:4 & Isaiah 45:5,6,18). Rather, it's an indication of one God in three persons: Father, Son and Holy Spirit (Matthew 28:19 & 2 Corinthians 13:14).

In any case, The Angel of the LORD who was about to "destroy Jerusalem," as detailed in 2 Samuel 24:16, is the same Angel the Israelites were warned *not* to provoke in Exodus 23:21—the mighty pre-incarnate Christ.

Is it possible, or even likely, that Christ utilized the services of "destroying angels" to carry out the just destruction in question? Yes. But this does not make him any less "the destroyer" as the angels who assisted him wouldn't destroy anything without his authorization. Speaking of which…

The LORD Utilized the Help of Destroying Angels

Let's go back to Psalm 78:

He [God] unleashed against them his hot anger,
   his wrath, indignation and hostility—
   <u>a band of destroying angels</u>.
                                                    Psalm 78:49

What we see here is the LORD utilizing the services of angels to carry out his wrath on those judged; in this case, the destruction of Egypt through the various plagues. Examples of this can be observed in both the Old and New Testaments. Let's look at an example from each…

Just before the obliteration of Sodom & Gomorrah three "men" appeared to Abraham with one turning out to be the LORD, the pre-incarnate Christ (Genesis 18:1-3,10). The LORD informed Abraham of his intentions of destroying these wicked cities because "the outcry against Sodom and Gomorrah is so great and their sin so grievous" (verse 20).

The two "men" who accompanied the LORD then left for Sodom while Abraham spoke to the LORD on behalf of the two cities (verses 22-33). Christ agreed to not destroy Sodom & Gomorrah if ten righteous people could be found there; unfortunately, this wasn't the case and the cities were doomed.

The two men who went to Sodom were angels masquerading as men (Hebrews 13:2). They went to the city to get Lot and his family out of the city before its destruction. We observe the wickedness of Sodom when men from every part of the city surrounded Lot's house in order to have perverted "sex" with Lot's two guests (Genesis 19:4-5). These angelic visitors were likely exceptional looking and word spread around town, stirring up degenerate lust in the male populace.

This was certain proof for God's angelic spies that the cities were wicked enough to incur judgment so they instructed Lot to get his family members and flee the city. They said:

> "...<u>**we are going to destroy this place**</u>**. The outcry to the Lord against its people is so great that** <u>**he has sent us to destroy it**</u>**."**
> **Genesis 19:13**

While verse 29 says that "God destroyed the cities on the plain" he obviously enlisted two destroying angels to carry out the judgment.

Interestingly, when Lot hesitated escaping the area, the angels "grasped his hand and the hands of his wife and of his two daughters and led them safely out of the city, for the Lord was merciful to them" (verse 16). I point this out to show that these angels carried out their God-given mandate—**to serve those who are to inherit salvation** (Hebrews 1:14).

In the New Testament there's the example of Herod Agrippa, who unjustly arrested many Christians and even had James the son of Zebedee executed (Acts 12:1-5). God is merciful and therefore showed Herod much patience even though he was severely persecuting His church. But when Herod imprisoned Peter and put James to death his days were numbered and he was dangerously nearing the limit of God's tolerance (1 Thessalonians 2:15-16).

Unfortunately, Herod chose to repeatedly spurn God's awesome grace and so the Lord withdrew his mercy and decisively executed stern judgment at a political speech where Herod accepted praise due only to the Almighty and thus "an angel of the Lord struck him down" (Acts 12:21-23). What happened? Herod's pomp and unjust acts reached the limit of God's tolerance and thus judgment fell. The LORD utilized the services of an angel to carry out his judgment, which was death, the wages of sin.

This occurred in the New Testament era and this is our LORD whom Jesus and Paul said we should emulate (Matthew 5:48 & Ephesians 5:1). Chew on that.

Christ the Destroyer?

I realize that some reading this might be having a hard time wrapping their heads around the idea that Christ is both savior and destroyer. This is the result of years of religious indoctrination where Jesus has been made out to be little more than a harmless smiley guy who walks around in a white dress. It's the "Gentle Jesus, Meek and Mild" syndrome,[27] which is a thoroughly unbalanced perception. Sure, Jesus has a gentle, merciful and loving side and we're astronomically blessed because of it. But God's Word offers us a three-dimensional perspective.

We saw at the end of the previous chapter how Christ was brilliant in argumentation during his earthly ministry (Matthew 22:15-22) and astonished his enemies (Luke 20:26) to the point that "no one dared ask him anymore questions" (Mark 12:34). He was utterly dynamic, exuding life to the full (John 14:6 & 10:10). He was authoritative (not authoritarian), bold, outspoken and had no qualms about offending pompous people who were deserving of correction (Matthew 7:28-29, Luke 11:37-54 & Matthew 15:1-20 & 18:7). He radically cleansed the Temple of carnal fools twice, yelling, throwing over tables, scattering money and whirling a whip, which amazed the onlookers and struck fear in the hearts of religionists (Mark 11:15-18 & John 2:13-17). Christ was courageous, astonishing, amazing, authoritative and even frightening

---

[27] *Gentle Jesus, Meek and Mild* was a sacred poem/hymn written by Charles Wesley and published in 1742

(Matthew 7:28-29 & 14:26; Mark 1:27, 2:10-12, 4:37-41 & 7:37; Luke 5:8-11, 7:14-16, 20:20-26 & 20:40).

And, yes, Christ is also **the destroyer** for those who reject him as savior:

> **There is *only* one Lawgiver and Judge, the One who is able <u>to save</u> and to <u>destroy</u>;**
> **James 4:12** (NASB)

Now someone might object on the grounds that Christ's purpose in the New Covenant is to give life to the full, not kill and destroy, which is the Enemy's modus operandi (John 10:10). While this is true, it doesn't negate the above passage, which shows that **the Mighty Christ is both Savior of the humble repentant and Destroyer of the incorrigibly rebellious**. We must be *balanced* in our studies. "Scripture interprets Scripture" is a hermeneutical rule for a reason. People who disregard it become unbalanced and thus fall into error or, at least, limit their perception of reality.

Besides, there's a vast difference between the Mighty LORD justly destroying the worthless wicked (who will simply reap the wages of their unrepentant sin) and the devil & filthy spirits who destroy people indiscriminately, including unjustly attacking the righteous, like Satan did with Job (Job 1-2).

Angels are Assigned to You to Help You Enter *Your* "Promised Land"

I've heard Christians speak of the Promised Land as a type of eternal life in the new Heavens and new Earth (typically referred to as "Heaven"). This is true, as far as our *eternal* "Promised Land" is concerned. Even the Old Covenant saints had an eternal Promised Land for which they longed (Hebrews 11:10,16). Yet, just as the Hebrews had an earthly Promised Land, so believers have an earthly "Promised Land," but it's not some literal piece of real estate, as the land of Canaan was for the Hebrews. For the believer, the Israelite's Promised Land is a type of walking in our promised blessings in general and, more specifically, fulfilling whatever mission or dream the Lord gives you. In short, the Promised Land is a type of your inheritance during your temporal life on this Earth. Let's consider a few examples of **1.** promised blessings in general and **2.** fulfilling the mission God gives you.

The New Testament promises healing for believers (1 Peter 2:24 & James 5:14-15). In 2013 my left knee swelled up and became stiff. It was difficult to merely get up and walk across the room. The problem required surgery, but I decided to stand on the healing promises of my covenant. It took faith & persistence but, after a few months, the healing fully manifested and I've been lovin' it ever since—jogging five times a week, enjoying long daily walks and even skiing in the winter.

That same year, our semi-flat roof over our upstairs bedroom was heavily leaking and needed serious repairs. Standing on the promise of God's provision (Philippians 4:19), Carol & I spoke in faith over the roof on a daily basis. After several weeks of faith & persistence (Hebrews 6:12) the means came to not only fix the roof, but replace it entirely, *plus* receive a new ceiling for the entire upstairs! God does "immeasurably more than all we can ask or imagine" (Ephesians 3:20)!

As far as the Promised Land of fulfilling one's God-given dream is concerned, I had taught at numerous local churches for several years and eventually graduated Bible college. Carol & I sought the Lord and were led to start a non-sectarian ministry that focused on teaching God's Word through books, websites, videos, social media, newsletters, sermons and other mediums. We knew it was the Lord's will so we stuck to our guns in faith & perseverance—*despite* gossipy opposition from so-called "Christians." And here we are with several books out and two websites, reaching the world with the life-changing truths of God's awesome Word.

These are real-life examples of New Covenant believers walking in *their* earthly Promised Land. Every believer is called to do this, but you must put off the flesh, seek the LORD and learn to walk in faith & patience, not to mention *DON'T* provoke angels or The Angel of the LORD through a grumbling spirit that opposes God and his will (not to mention the other sins listed earlier this chapter). Rather loose angels to assist you in your service by giving voice to God's Word.

We'll look at the blessings of our covenant and how to walk in them in more detail in **Chapter 20**.

Chapter 9

Understanding Fallen Angels (Evil Spirits)

Fallen angels refer to the angels that fell from Heaven after their failed coup. These disgraced angels are one-and-the-same as evil spirits, which are demons, as witnessed here:

> ...**Jesus traveled about from one town and village to another, proclaiming the good news of the kingdom of God. The Twelve were with him, ² and also <u>some women who had been cured of evil spirits</u> and diseases: Mary (called Magdalene) <u>from whom seven demons had come out</u>; ³ Joanna the wife of Chuza, the manager of Herod's household; Susanna; and many others.**
>
> **Luke 8:1-3**

As you can see, fallen angels are described as **evil spirits**. The Greek word for "evil" is *ponéros (pon-ay-ROSS)*, meaning "bad, wicked, malicious." This shows that evil spirits are the opposite of heavenly angels, which are good spirits. The latter function in submission to the LORD and therefore serve people (Hebrews 1:14) whereas evil spirits are "bad" and so do the precise opposite—they seek to hurt people one way or another. This is in line with their leader's mandate "to kill, steal and destroy" (John 10:10).

Speaking of their leader, Satan is the "father of lies" (John 8:44) and so his wicked minions constantly try to *deceive* people. Take 'ghosts,' for example, which are supposedly the disembodied souls of the dead stuck on this plane and haunting a particular environment. Isn't it possible or even likely that this type of paranormal phenomena is the deceptive activity of demons?

Unclean (Filthy) Spirits

Evil spirits are also referred to as *unclean* or *impure* spirits:

> **Jesus called his twelve disciples to him and gave them authority to drive out impure spirits and to heal every disease and sickness.**
> **Matthew 10:1**

The Greek word for "impure" here is *akathartos (ak-ATH-ar-tos)*, which simply means unclean or impure. It reveals that evil spirits are filthy. This makes sense in light of the fact that 'holy' refers to absolute purity, the natural result of being separated unto God. The LORD is absolutely pure—holy—and so anyone consecrated unto Him must be pure. Thus anyone who rejects the Almighty and is cast from his presence becomes the opposite—*un*holy, *im*pure. Since you can't get further from God than the irredeemable fallen angels, they're utterly unholy—unclean, impure, filthy.

Being filthy, there's a stench to unclean spirits in the spirit realm. This explains why one spiritually-sensitive minister said he could always recognize someone who was walking in sexual perversion, like homosexuality, when they came up for prayer at his meetings. He said there was a foul odor in the spirit.

One of my relatives married a wicked witch (seriously) and she wasted no time in getting her new husband to totally separate from his family. My nephew met her when he was a child and he kept curiously asking "What's that smell? Something stinks!" He was just a little kid at the time and said the odor smelled like vomit. No one present knew what he was talking about, so he was obviously picking something up in the spirit. Children are more sensitive to the spiritual realm and are therefore apt to pick up things that hardened adults can no longer perceive. Consider the typical scenario where kids think there's a "monster" under the bed or in the closet. Is it simply their imagination or are they picking up an evil spirit in the vicinity?

All this explains why the Bible instructs us:

> **Therefore, <u>get rid of all moral filth</u> and the <u>evil that is so prevalent</u> and humbly accept the word planted in you, which can save you.**
> **James 1:21**

While believers are *born* holy in their spirits when they receive spiritual regeneration (Titus 3:5), **practical** holiness only occurs as you learn to put off your flesh—the "old self"—and live according to your new righteous nature—the "new self"—with the help of the Holy Spirit (Ephesians 4:22-24). This is what theologians refer to as the process of sanctification—*purification*—and part of this process includes doing what James instructed: "get rid of all moral filth and the evil that is so prevalent."

How does this tie-in to our topic? Simple: Impure spirits are naturally attracted to that which is morally impure. Just as flies are attracted to dog doo-doo and rats are drawn to garbage, so filthy spirits are attracted to that which is morally filthy. So get rid of all moral filth and you'll stop attracting filthy spirits! It's just common sense.

We'll look at this further in **Chapter 18** (in the section *Purify Your Heart*).

Getting back to Luke 8:1-3, notice what verse 2 says:

> **...some women who had been cured of evil spirits and diseases: Mary (called Magdalene) from whom seven demons had come out;**
>
> **Luke 8:2**

Some women were cured of **evils spirits** through Christ's ministry and one of these was Mary Magdalene, who was exorcized of seven **demons**. This shows that...

Evil Spirits are Demons

Evil spirits are one-and-the-same as demons. We see this above and also in Jesus' encounter with the demon-possessed man in the region of Gerasenes *(JAIR-ah-seens)*. The man is described in Scripture as being possessed by multiple evil spirits that spoke to Jesus through him:

> **The demons begged Jesus, "Send us among the pigs; allow us to go into them." ¹³ He gave them permission, and the impure spirits came out and went into the pigs.**
>
> **Mark 5:12-13**

This is further evidence that demons are synonymous with filthy spirits.

I said earlier that evil spirits are fallen angels. While I think this is obvious, some people have brought this into question with highly creative (to be nice) alternative views. In order to prove that evils spirits are fallen angels let's first establish that...

Satan was a "Cherub" who Fell from Heaven

Jesus said he "saw Satan fall like lightning from heaven" (Luke 10:18). This monumental event is chronicled in the Old Testament using the kings of Babylon and Tyre as types (Isaiah 14:12 & Ezekiel 28:12-

17). The passage in Ezekiel shows that Satan was once a "**cherub**," an **angel** (28:14,16).

The New Testament offers a fascinating flashback to Satan's fall from Heaven:

> **Then another sign appeared in heaven: an enormous <u>red dragon</u> with seven heads and ten horns and seven crowns on its heads. ⁴ Its tail swept <u>a third of the stars out of the sky and flung them to the earth</u>...**
>
> **⁷ Then war broke out in heaven. Michael and his angels fought against <u>the dragon</u>, and <u>the dragon and his angels</u> fought back. ⁸ But he was not strong enough, and <u>they lost their place in heaven</u>. ⁹ <u>The great dragon was hurled down</u>—that ancient serpent called <u>the devil</u>, or <u>Satan</u>, who leads the whole world astray. He was hurled to the earth, <u>and his angels with him</u>.**
>
> **Revelation 12:3-4,7-9**

This prophecy is actually a double reference and therefore has two applications: It refers to the devil's last gasp attempt to conquer Heaven during the mid-point of the future seven-year Tribulation (Revelation 6-19), but it's also a flashback to his original fall. Verse 4 figuratively indicates that **a third of the angels** fell with the devil—the "red dragon"—to the Earth. Keep in mind that "stars" are a metaphorical reference to angels (Job 38:7).

The notion that this passage is a "double reference" is in line with **the law of double reference**, which is the tendency of biblical prophecies to have two applications—one relevant to the general time of the prophecy and another far-flung, whether the distant future or past. We'll look at his "law" in more detail in **Chapter 11**.

By the way, the fact that the devil & his filthy spirits *again* attempt to conquer Heaven shows that they're hopelessly incorrigible. They never learn from their mistakes. It's reminiscent of the saying: "Insanity is doing the same thing over & over again expecting different results." If this is accurate, Satan & his minions are decidedly insane.

The Devil & His Angels Dwell in the Underworld

So Satan is described as a cherub—an angel—who was kicked out of Heaven, along with a third of the subordinate angels who rebelled with him.

Jesus said that the lake of fire was "prepared for the devil **and his angels**" (Matthew 25:41) as their eternal tormenting prison, but they currently roam the Earth, not in the physical realm, but the spiritual:

> **For our struggle is not against flesh and blood, but against the rulers, against the authorities, against the powers of this dark world and against <u>the spiritual forces of evil in the heavenly realms</u>.**
> **Ephesians 6:12**

The "spiritual forces of evil" dwell in "the heavenly realms." This refers to the **Underworld**, which is the dark spiritual dimension that underpins the Earth & Universe (Philippians 2:9-11 & Revelation 5:2-3). This is where the devil & his fallen angels operate. They don't dwell in hell because the lake of fire is hell and no one has been cast there yet. They inhabit the dark realm of the Underworld and operate from this plane—"roaming the earth, going back and forth in it," as Satan put it (Job 1:7 & 2:2). This explains something Peter said:

> **Be alert and of sober mind. Your enemy the devil prowls around like a roaring lion looking for someone to devour.**
> **1 Peter 5:8**

All this biblical data helps us conclude with confidence that demons or evil spirits *are* fallen angels.

Addressing Two Alternative Views

Some people have challenged this, suggesting that evil spirits are either **1.** the spirits of the giant Nephilim *(NEF-ah-lim)*, which were wiped out in the worldwide flood of Noah's day, or **2.** the spirits of a mysterious "pre-Adamic" race who perished in a worldwide flood that occurred sometime between Genesis 1:1 and 1:2.

The reason these people argue that demons *aren't* fallen angels is because of two verses in the New Testament which show that fallen angels are imprisoned in *tartaroó (tar-tar-OH)*, awaiting God's judgment (2 Peter 2:4 & Jude 1:6). However, these passages aren't referring to *all* fallen angels because the chief fallen angel, Satan, is still roaming about (1 Peter 5:8). We'll look at why these evil spirits were imprisoned in *tartaroó* momentarily.

In regard to demons being the spirits of the Nephilim who died in the flood: While the Nephilim were powerful and legendary because their bloodline was mixed with demonic DNA, the Bible nevertheless describes them as "men" (Genesis 6:4). As such, when they died their lifeless souls went to Sheol (Hades) to be held for Judgment Day, just like the souls of all unregenerate **people** (Revelation 20:11-15). Nowhere does the Bible suggest that the spirits of the slain Nephilim are wandering the Earth.

Even more creative is the idea that demons are the spirits of some ambiguous "pre-Adamic race." The small number of people who embrace this peculiar theory are staunch gap theorists who suggest that Satan ruled nations of a pre-Adamic race—a race that they won't call human because the Bible clearly refers to Adam as the "first man" (1 Corinthians 15:45,47). If they weren't really human, then what exactly were they? Sasquatches maybe? Cha-Ka's cousins perhaps? (☺).[28]

---

[28] For an honest biblical evaluation of the dubious pre-Adamic race doctrine see the article *How Old is the Earth?* at the Fountain of Life website.

Hierarchies and Territories of Evil Spirits

Returning to Ephesians 6:12, notice what the text says about fallen angels:

> For our struggle is not against flesh and blood, but against <u>the rulers</u>, against <u>the authorities</u>, against <u>the powers</u> of this dark world and against the spiritual forces of evil in the heavenly realms.
> **Ephesians 6:12**

The "spiritual forces of evil" are comprised of three different categories—"the rulers," "the authorities" and "the powers." This reveals a hierarchy in the spiritual realm with the devil as the wicked despot of his dark kingdom with "rulers," "authorities" and "powers" under his command.

These demonic authorities are assigned regions on Earth in which they negatively influence political powers and the corresponding populace. For instance, in Daniel we observe "the prince of Persia" and "the prince of Greece," both demonic authorities consigned to these areas (Daniel 10:13,20). Additional evidence can be observed when a conglomerate of demons named "Legion" begged the Mighty Christ not to send them out of the region (Mark 5:10). Why? Obviously because it was their assigned territory, their 'home.' Also, the glorified Lord said Pergamum was where Satan's throne was located (Revelation 2:13).

This data corresponds to the fact that the devil is "the god of this world" and thus "the whole world is under the control" of the kingdom of darkness to one degree or another (2 Corinthians 4:4 & 1 John 5:19). Some places, like Pergamum in the 1st century, are subject to greater satanic control than others. San Francisco, Hollywood and New York City are prime examples in modern America.

Why Do Demons Desire to Possess People (and Sometimes Even Animals)?

Evil spirits seek to possess men & women in order to operate more concretely in the physical realm. Being spiritual in nature, they're limited to the spiritual plane and only operate in the physical realm in an indirect manner, unless they can totally take possession of a person, which they can only do with the person's consent, conscious or subconscious (we'll address this shortly). This explains why they seek to possess people.

The afore-cited Mark 5:12-13 shows that demons sometimes even seek to possess animals, but they can only do this with authorization from the Sovereign LORD. Why do they need Christ's permission? Obviously because animals lack the ability to grant or reject consent.

That said, the afore-noted Genesis 6:1-4 shows that demons have the power to operate in the physical realm in a more direct manner. On this occasion fallen angels—the "sons of God"—copulated with women, which gave birth to the Nephilim. God considered this a great transgression and so imprisoned these evil spirits in *tartaroó* to be held for judgment (2 Peter 2:4 & Jude 1:6). As such, the rest of the fallen angels have never again sinned in this manner and, therefore, the height of their manifestation in the physical realm is through possession of a person or animal.

We'll examine the nature of the Nephilim and look more closely at why some fallen angels were imprisoned in *tartaroó* next chapter.

Keep in mind that evil spirits naturally hate human beings because:

1. People are created in the image of God.
2. Angels lack the privilege and position granted redeemed people; that is, being co-heirs with Christ and thus seated with Him at the right hand of the Father in a positional sense (Romans 8:17, Hebrews 1:13 & Ephesians 2:6).

3. Unlike them, people are redeemable.[29]
4. Angels are commissioned to serve people, and since arrogant angels didn't want to do this they rebelled, which resulted in their ouster from Heaven.

The Prime Directive of Evil Spirits

As noted earlier, Christ encountered a man in the area of the Gerasenes:

> They went across the lake to the region of the Gerasenes. ²When Jesus got out of the boat, <u>a man with an impure spirit</u> came from the tombs to meet him. ³This man lived in the tombs, and no one could bind him anymore, not even with a chain. ⁴For <u>he had often been chained hand and foot, but he tore the chains apart and broke the irons on his feet. No one was strong enough to subdue him.</u> ⁵<u>Night and day among the tombs and in the hills he would cry out and cut himself with stones.</u>
>
> ⁶When he saw Jesus from a distance, he ran and fell on his knees in front of him. ⁷He shouted at the top of his voice, "What do you want with me, Jesus, Son of the Most High God? In God's name don't torture me!" ⁸For Jesus had said to him, "Come out of this man, you impure spirit!"
>
> ⁹Then Jesus asked him, "What is your name?"
>
> "<u>My name is Legion</u>," he replied, "<u>for we are many</u>." ¹⁰And he begged Jesus again and again not to send them out of the area.
>
> **Mark 5:1-10**

---

[29] Fallen angels are *ir*redeemable because they had full knowledge of the consequences of their rebellion whereas Adam & Eve did not. We'll look at this in **Chapter 11** and **12**.

This demon-possessed man[30] had great strength, to the point that no one could subdue him. People in the area were understandably scared of him. Yet notice that the spirits who possessed him were terrified of the Mighty Christ (more on this in **Chapter 15**).

The man's great strength can be attributed to the numerous wicked spirits that possessed him. They interestingly referred to themselves in a composite sense as "Legion," which is a Latin word for a division of the Roman army, 5120 infantry with additional cavalry at the time of Christ. In general terms, the word refers to a very large number and so we can assume that there were hundreds or even thousands of demons in this man. Think of it in terms of a snake pit where hundreds of snakes writhe together. The name of this group of demons—"Legion"— is akin to the names delinquent gangs adopt, like The Bloods, The Warriors or The Mecca Knights.

Notice what these evil spirits compelled the man to do—he wandered amongst the tombs and hills crying out in torment day & night, regularly cutting himself with stones. Today we call this type of behavior self-harm or self-injury. People who do this are being harassed by demonic spirits. They may not necessarily be possessed (yet), but they're definitely being oppressed to the point of harming themselves. Anytime you come across people bent on self-destruction you can be sure that evil spirits are involved.

A good example of this is this Swedish band that promotes suicide and self-harm in all its forms. The vocalist nonchalantly informed that there have been several cases of fans committing suicide or, at least, *trying* to commit suicide upon digesting the group's music. He testified in an interview to his own struggles with depression & torment, including frequent stays at mental health facilities. Needless to say, evil spirits are attracted to this band like snakes to a snake pit; and they use this man & his music to spread mental illness and self-destruction to anyone attracted to the group.

---

[30] Luke's account of these events also records only *one* demon-possessed man (Luke 8:26-39) whereas Matthew's rendition cites *two* possessed men (Matthew 8:28-34). How do we explain this seeming discrepancy? Obviously one of the demoniacs was much more prominent, likely due to the myriad demons possessing him, and so Mark & Luke simply disregarded the secondary man in their accounts.

The mass-murderer Richard Speck, who slew eight nursing students at a Chicago dorm in July, 1966, tried to commit suicide in his hotel room two days later. His senseless murder spree was obviously inspired by the kingdom of darkness. You see, wicked spirits *use* people to carry out their prime directive—destroy life—and then *lose* them, inspiring them to destroy their very selves.

Demons revel in the destruction of people because they hate us for the four reasons cited above. They're gravely envious and mad as hell, literally, because fallen people are redeemable whereas they're *ir*redeemable. Thus demons do the very opposite of heavenly angels. Angels *serve* people (Hebrews 1:14) whereas evil spirits harass and destroy.

In fact, wicked spirits are hell-bent on destroying life period. This explains why the three Hebrew letters of Satan's very name—shin/tet/nun—define his prime directive: the destruction of anything that contains life and any continuation of it.

The fact that filthy spirits are obsessed with destroying life can be observed by this conglomerate of demons—"Legion"—who begged Christ to allow them to possess a herd of pigs nearby, which he allowed. Thus the spirits left the man and went into the roughly 2000 swine wherein the herd promptly rushed down the steep bank and into the lake where they drowned (Mark 5:11-13). Why on Earth would they drive the pigs to do this? Because demons are hell-bent on the destruction of life in any form. They *thrive* on it.

How Do You Prevent Demonic Oppression or Possession?

How did this man get possessed by so many demons? (I'm not talking about cases where people are afflicted by "spirits of infirmities," which we'll look at momentarily). Was he just innocently walking along one day and an evil spirit suddenly possessed him and proceeded to invite his buddies to join in? No. As noted earlier, demons are *impure* or *filthy* spirits and so they're naturally attracted to that which is morally filthy. If a person yields to fleshly thoughts and starts to dwell on them to the point of obsession and the corresponding evil behavior it'll attract demonic spirits, which leads to oppression and, ultimately, possession. Once a person is possessed, additional demons are attracted to the wicked "party."

This is one of the reasons why the aforementioned James 1:21 instructs us to "get rid of all moral filth and the evil that is so prevalent" and, instead, feed on the Word of God (Matthew 4:4). It's why Paul encouraged believers to get in the habit of meditating on what is true, noble, right, pure, admirable, excellent and praiseworthy; he even stressed that this attracts the peace of God (Philippians 4:8-9). Do you want the peace of God in your life or the torment of wicked spirits? Obviously the former. Then **"be careful what you think, because your thoughts run your life"** (Proverbs 4:23 NCV).

This is what the Bible calls **renewing the mind** (Romans 12:2 & Ephesians 4:22-24). It's simply changing your thought life from the bad and destructive to the good and productive. If we truly knew the power and life that is available to us through using our imagination for the positive we'd be so full of dynamic power we'd jump up & down with enthusiasm!

All this is linked to what theologians call **the process of sanctification**. 'Sanctification' is one of those big words of which few know the meaning. It simply refers to **purification**, which starts with spiritual rebirth (Titus 3:5) and continues throughout the believer's life as you're "transformed by the renewing of your mind." This not only saves believers from flawed ideologies and poisonous mindsets, it protects us from demonic oppression or, worse, possession. Poisonous mindsets, by the way, are *noémas (noh-AY-mahs)*, which are mental strongholds that develop over time and by-and-large determine a person's actions. There are whole ideologies that are demonic in nature, like communism.

As important as it is to "get rid of all moral filth and the evil that is so prevalent" and feed on God's Word (James 1:21), it's just as vital to **cultivate a relationship with the LORD** by drawing near to Him:

> **Submit yourselves, then, to God. <u>Resist the devil, and <u>he will flee from you.</u></u> ⁸<u>Come near to God and <u>he will come near to you.</u></u> Wash your hands, you sinners, and purify your hearts, you double-minded. ⁹ Grieve, mourn and wail. Change your laughter to**

> mourning and your joy to gloom. ⁱ⁰**Humble yourselves before the Lord, and he will lift you up.**
>
> **James 4:7-10**

Verse 7 says to "resist **the devil** and **he** will flee from you." This is not solely referring to Satan himself, but rather to the kingdom of darkness in general and specifically the evils spirits that are attacking the believer. How do I know? Because James was addressing multitudes of believers scattered amongst many nations, which includes us today (James 1:1), and the devil's *not* omnipresent, like the Almighty (i.e. everywhere at the same time). As such, Satan can only attack one believer or a group of believers at a point in time, like he did with his temptation of Christ in the desert (Matthew 4:1-11). To attack numerous believers across the globe he *has* to use the network of demonic powers under him (Ephesians 6:12). Think about it in terms of one nation attacking another. We say, for instance, that "Bush invaded Iraq" when, in fact, Bush was half a planet away. It's the same thing in the kingdom of darkness. The devil may be assaulting you, but it's not Satan himself, but rather wicked spirits working under his perverse command.

With this understanding, notice what this passage says about deflecting the kingdom of darkness: The key to accomplishing this is to simply **draw near to God**, which automatically results in God drawing near to you. Coming near to the LORD includes repenting of immorality and feeding on His Word, but it's also a matter of fostering a close *relationship*. This sends evil spirits fleeing!

That said, spirits of infirmities are a different issue. These types of evil spirits induce a mental or physical malady in those they assault, such as muteness/deafness (Mark 9:17-29) or a crippling condition (Luke 13:10-16). The victims of these spirits are not necessarily involved in moral filth, but rather are people who are spiritually feeble and ignorant, particularly in regards to spiritual warfare. In other words, **spirits of infirmities take advantage of *ignorance***. Thankfully, knowledge and wisdom empower people and will protect you from such spirits (Proverbs 24:5), which is why this book exists. We'll look at spirits of infirmities in **Chapter 16** & **17** and spiritual warfare in **Chapter 19** & **20**.

Evil Spirits are Attracted to "Dry Places"

Christ taught that impure spirits naturally seek "arid places," which means dry, waterless areas (Matthew 12:43). This isn't referring to places that are *physically* dry, like deserts, but rather spaces that are *spiritually* dry; that is, **places where God is absent**. You see, the LORD is likened to Living Water in the Bible—He's ***The* Fountain of Life** who gushes forth life (Psalm 36:9). This corresponds to what Christ said about Himself and the Holy Spirit:

> ...Jesus stood and said in a loud voice, "<u>Let anyone who is thirsty come to me and drink</u>. ³⁸ Whoever believes in me, as Scripture has said, <u>rivers of living water will flow from within them</u>." ³⁹ By this he meant <u>the Spirit</u>, whom those who believed in him were later to receive.
>
> **John 7:37-39**

The Lord encourages those who are spiritually thirsty—spiritually dry—to come to Him and drink. He then points out that those who receive the Holy Spirit will have "rivers of living water" flowing within them.

The key to repelling demonic spirits is to stay well-watered by cultivating a relationship with the LORD. Saturate yourself with the things of God: prayer, simple communion, Scripture reading & meditation, praise & worship, fellowship with genuine believers, mutual submission (Ephesians 5:21), etc. As you do this, you automatically stave off wicked spirits. How so? Because **demons seek dry places—waterless spaces absent of God's presence**.

This reveals the danger in becoming spiritually dry. When a pastor & his assembly become spiritually arid it attracts evil spirits, who'll start "whispering in their ears." Spiritually-dry people are naturally susceptible to "doctrines of demons," which gets them off track if embraced (1 Timothy 4:1). "Doctrines" refers to teachings or instructions; so "doctrines of demons" simply means *teachings* or *instructions* of demons. Take, for example, white or black fellowships that embrace racist ideology: Members of the KKK typically profess to be Christians, with some members even being church leaders. Then you have Jeremiah Wright's hateful, crackpot false gospel. How can people of God—even fulltime ministers—go so far astray? Because they allowed themselves to become spiritually dry, which attracted evil spirits; and out of desperation they gave ear to doctrines of demons.

The "Put Off" / "Put On" Principle

Let's read the full passage where Jesus said demonic spirits seek dry places:

> **"When an impure spirit comes out of a person, it goes through arid places seeking rest and does not find it. ⁴⁴ Then it says, 'I will return to the house I left.' When it arrives, it finds the house unoccupied, swept clean and put in order. ⁴⁵ Then it goes and takes with it seven other spirits <u>more wicked than itself</u>, and <u>they go in and live there</u>. And the final condition of that person is worse than the first.**
>
> **Matthew 12:43-45**

When a filthy spirit leaves a person it naturally seeks rest in arid places—spaces absent of God and the living waters thereof. The presence of God torments wicked spirits and so they seek succor where He's absent. If the demon can't find such a place it will simply go back to the "house" it left—*if* it can, that is.

But why wouldn't a demon be able to find a waterless place—a space lacking God and the things of God? We can only conjecture based on the scriptural evidence. We know that evil spirits are territorial; that is, they're assigned specific areas (Daniel 10:13,20). We also know that they're lazy. In Jesus' hypothetical example the demon couldn't find anywhere in its immediate territory for rest so it lazily goes back to the person it left and finds him "swept clean and put in order" yet "unoccupied." This reveals that the person had enough discipline to get his life in order and "cleaned up his act," but he wasn't occupied with God and the corresponding things of God. It was an outward change lacking inward reality. So the demon acquires seven other spirits more malevolent than itself and returns to the unoccupied "house." Needless to say, the end state of the man is worse than before.

This is a spur to seek more than mere superficial change based on self-discipline. You can't just "quit a habit" or "break a habit" without filling the vacuum with something positive. And God—who is *The Fountain of Life* (Psalm 36:9)—is the most positive 'thing' to fill yourself. That's why the Bible teaches the principle of "putting off" *and* "putting on" (Ephesians 4:22-24). Right patterns must replace wrong ones. Good behaviors must replace sinful activities. Productive thoughts must displace destructive ones.

On a side note, this passage shows that some demons are more malevolent than others.

Evil Spirits getting attached to Kids or Youths

Demons can get attached to people when they're kids or youths if they're regularly in an unhealthy environment where there's significant demonic activity. For instance, if a child grows up in a household where there's substantial immoral activity (including pharisaical religiosity) or one of the parents is demon-possessed or if they get involved with libertine gangs or groups.

The reason demons are able to attach themselves to children or youths in such situations is because—being young and influence-able—they're vulnerable. Parents and guardians have a responsibility to protect kids under their authority, not just physically, but spiritually. Why do you think Jesus took the time to bless the children (Matthew 19:13)? Yet, even in these cases, evil spirits *have* to have the permission of the individual—conscious or subconscious—to increasingly oppress them and ultimately possess them.

We'll address this topic in more detail in **Chapter 17**.

Chapter 10

The Nephilim and the "Sons of God"

Genesis 6 speaks of the Nephilim *(NEF-ah-lim)* and the "sons of God" who fathered them. Let's look at the key verses in this chapter with the understanding that these events take place just before the Noahic flood:

> When human beings began to increase in number on the earth and daughters were born to them, ²<u>the sons of God</u> saw that the daughters of humans were beautiful, and they married any of them they chose. ³Then the Lord said, "My Spirit will not contend with humans forever, <u>for they are mortal</u>; their days will be a hundred and twenty years."

> **⁴The Nephilim were on the earth in those days—and also afterward—when the sons of God went to the daughters of humans and had children by them. They were the heroes of old, men of renown.**
>
> **Genesis 6:1-4**

The "Nephilim" were literal giants, apparently the product of "the sons of God" procreating with women. Who were these "sons of God"? The phrase is *ben Elohim*[31] in the Hebrew and refers to angels, as shown here:

> **while the morning stars sang together**
> **and all the angels** *(ben Elohim)* **shouted for joy?**
>
> **Job 38:7**

This poetic verse is an example of synonymous parallelism where the second line repeats the first line in different words. As such, the "morning stars" in the first line and the *ben Elohim* in the second are both references to angels. While the NIV translates *ben Elohim* as "angels," most English translations render the words literally as "the sons of God."

In any case, the context of this verse is when God created the Earth, which was before Satan's rebellion and subsequent fall. As you can see, *all* the angels—the "sons of God" (*ben Elohim*)—were rejoicing at the LORD's awesome creation of the physical Universe.

Yet even after Satan & his angels fell from Heaven they were still the "sons of God," the *ben Elohim*. We observe this in Genesis 6:1-4 above.

These two passages also show that the *ben Elohim* refer to angels:

> **One day the angels** *(ben Elohim)* **came to present themselves before the LORD, and Satan also came with them.**
>
> **Job 1:6**

---

[31] *Elohim* is pronounced *eh-LOH-him* or *eh-LOH-heem*, but I also hear *EL-oh-HEEM* a lot.

> On another day <u>the angels</u> *(ben Elohim)* **came to present themselves before the LORD, and <u>Satan also came with them</u> to present himself before him.**
>
> Job 2:1

Which angels came to present themselves before the LORD? Neither verse says but, as pointed out in **Chapter 1**, it was likely the archangels—the ruling angels—reporting to God, like Michael and Gabriel. Both verses add "and Satan also came with them," as if to say that it wasn't just the heavenly archangels who reported to God on this occasion, but the disgraced archangel as well. This shows us that, fallen or not, Satan still has to regularly report to the Sovereign LORD and give account.[32]

I should add that the Apocrypha and Pseudepigrapha[33] also interpret "the sons of God" in Genesis 6:1-4 as angels.

A variant position is that the "sons of God" of Genesis 6 were not the angels who fell with Lucifer, but rather heavenly angels who came down and had relations with women as humanity was multiplying. Those who support this view argue that these angels fell due to lust rather than already having fallen due to partnering with the devil's rebellion. While I don't embrace this view and wonder if those who support it watched *City of Angels* one too many times, I'm sharing it as an alternative possibility for you to consider in your studies.

Either way, the mixing of angelic DNA with human DNA produced the Nephilim, giants described in verse 4 as "heroes of old, **men** of renown" or, as the Holman Bible renders it, "powerful **men** of old, the famous **men**" who understandably became legendary before the flood.

---

[32] See 2 Chronicles 18:18-21 for another fascinating example where the angels appear before the LORD's throne in Heaven, both good and bad spirits. The angels on this occasion, however, are not limited to archangels. (It's also chronicled in 1 Kings 22:19-22).

[33] The Apocrypha *(ah-POK-rah-fah)* and Pseudepigrapha *(soo-doh-PIG-rah-fah)* are collections of uninspired books written during the intertestamental period after the cessation of Old Testament prophecy. Not one of them was written in the Hebrew language.

Some oppose this interpretation on the grounds that Christ indirectly said that angels "neither marry nor are given in marriage" (Luke 20:34-36), but this is different than saying that angelic beings *can't* marry or *can't* have sex. Furthermore, Jesus was talking about heavenly angels, not fallen angels; the latter would obviously rebel against any such moral constraints by the very nature of their fallen-ness.

By the way, angels *can* appear in the natural in human form, as verified by the two angels who appeared to Lot as *men*; moreover, the perverted men of Sodom wanted to have "sex" with them (Genesis 19:1-5). The fact that these angels appeared as *men* shows that they weren't necessarily genderless, which is corroborated by Mark 16:5. We'll explore this topic further in **Appendix A**.

Why Did the Nephilim Copulate with Women?

Assuming the "sons of God" refer to the fallen angels who rebelled with Satan, why did they procreate with women? We can only speculate from the biblical data and it leads to the sound conclusion that they wanted to taint the human bloodline in order to block the "seed" that the LORD prophesied would come through the female and "crush" Satan's head (Genesis 3:15). The "seed" is a reference to Christ, the Anointed One, who came "to destroy the devil's work" (1 John 3:8).

This satanic plot resulted in God's judgment and the corresponding flood:

> **The Lord saw how great the wickedness of the human race had become on the earth, and that every inclination of the thoughts of the human heart was only evil all the time. ⁶ The Lord regretted that he had made human beings on the earth, and his heart was deeply troubled. ⁷ So the Lord said, "I will wipe from the face of the earth the human race I have created—and with them the animals, the birds and the creatures that move along the ground—for I**

> regret that I have made them." ⁸But Noah found favor in the eyes of the Lord.
>
> **Genesis 6:5-8**

It stands to reason that these verses (and the rest of Genesis 6, as well as Genesis 7) are somewhat related to what took place in verses 1-4. The LORD thus flooded the Earth with only eight human survivors, through whom the anointed seed would eventually come and destroy the devil's work, providing redemption for humanity.

In order for this to never happen again, God condemned the "sons of God" who committed this act:

> **For if God did not spare <u>the angels</u> when <u>they sinned</u>, but cast them into hell** [*tartaroó* in the Greek, not *Hades*, aka *Sheol*], **delivering them in chains to be held in gloomy darkness until their judgment;**
>
> **2 Peter 2:4**

> **And the angels who did not keep their positions of authority but <u>abandoned their proper dwelling</u> — these he has kept in darkness, bound with everlasting chains for judgment on the great Day.**
>
> **Jude 1:6**

We know that this particular judgment only came upon the fallen angels who "sinned" and not to *all* fallen angels because there are evil spirits active on Earth to this day (Ephesians 6:12). This is supported by the fact that Jude 1:6 (above) is solely referring to the fallen angels who "abandoned their proper dwelling." What does this mean? It's likely a reference to them leaving the spiritual realm—their natural habitation—to manifest in the physical realm in physical form for the purpose of polluting the human bloodline and thereby preventing the birth of the Anointed One. Remember, evil spirits are "the spiritual forces of evil **in the heavenly realms**." The dark heavenlies are their proper dwelling and so to appear on Earth and have sex with women they'd *have* to abandon both their spiritual dwelling and spiritual nature in order to accomplish it.

So that this would never happen again to pollute the human bloodline God imprisoned these wicked angels in *tartaroó (tar-tar-OH)* to await their judgment and banishment to the lake of fire, which the LORD "**prepared for** the devil and his angels" (Matthew 25:41).

Were the Nephilim in the Promised Land?

The so-called Nephilim mentioned in Numbers 13:33 by the ten doubting Hebrew spies were not actually Nephilim because the LORD had imprisoned the "sons of God" of Genesis 6:2,4 in *tartaroó* and the Nephilim that existed before the flood perished in it. This put an end to the Nephilim altogether.

Keep in mind that the doubting spies are the ones speaking in Numbers 13:33. They are the words of disobedient men struck with fear and trying to discourage the Hebrews from invading the Promised Land. No doubt there were *some* giant people in the land and surrounding regions—Goliath, for instance, was 9½' tall—but they weren't actual Nephilim, i.e. powerful humans whose bloodline was mixed with demonic DNA.

The tallest human on record in modern times, incidentally, was Robert Pershing Wadlow, who stood one inch shy of 9', which means he was only **half a foot *shorter* than Goliath**. He passed away in 1940. I bring up Wadlow to show that a person can be a giant, but this doesn't mean he's a Nephilim.

Chapter 11

The Chief "Enemy" Angel

    Satan is the leader of the fallen angels. His name is a Hebrew word[34] that simply means "adversary" or "enemy." As such, when you hear believers talk about "the enemy" it's a reference to Satan and, by extension, his kingdom. This is the perfect name for the ultimate loser seeing as how he's the willful **enemy** of the Creator and all that is good or life-giving.

    Scripture shows that he is a created being who's in opposition to the LORD, but he's not equal to the Almighty and is actually no threat to God's supreme reign (Isaiah 45:5-7). Note, for instance, how easily God defeats Satan's final rebellion in Revelation 20:7-10.

    Interestingly, the word 'satan' in the Hebrew is made up of the three letters of the Hebraic alphabet—shin/tet/nun:

---

[34] Originally pronounced *saw-TAWN*.

- **Shin** is a picture of two front teeth meaning "sharp or destructive."
- **Tet** is a picture of a basket meaning "surrounding, enclosing or containing."
- **Nun** is a picture of a seed meaning "life or the continuation of life."

What's the point? The letters of Satan's very name define his prime directive—the destruction of anything that contains life and any continuation of it. Is it any wonder that Christ described the Enemy as a "thief" who "comes to steal and kill and destroy"? This is the express opposite of the LORD's purpose, which is to **give life and give it to the full** (John 10:10). You see, God *is* **the Fountain of Life** (Psalm 36:9): Just as a mighty geyser gushes forth water, so the LORD gushes life into the lives of all who come near to Him (James 4:8). The Enemy, by contrast, works to steal or destroy life. Yahweh is the Creator while Satan is the de-creator. God only justly destroys as a last resort based on the incorrigible will of the individual (Ezekiel 18:30-32). Satan destroys indiscriminately because that's his mission; he *thrives* on it.

Slanderer, Liar, Murderer

Satan is also known as the devil, which is translated from the Greek *diabolos (dee-AB-ol-os)*, meaning "**slanderer**." The term comes from the verb *diabálló (dee-ab-AL-loh)*, meaning "to slander, accuse, defame, complain." Moreover, Christ called the devil a "**murderer** from the beginning" and "the father of **lies**" (John 8:44).

These are the bad fruits of the devil and the satanic nature, which is the flesh — slandering, defaming, complaining, lying and murdering. Needless to say, if you know people, groups or organizations that regularly operate in such tactics it tells you everything you need to know—they're "of the devil." The libertine party of choice in the USA, the Demoncraps, is Exhibit A.[35]

---

[35] Speaking as someone who's politically independent. No doubt more conservative parties are also guilty of such transgressions on occasion, but the Demoncraps—and hedonism in general—are out of hand in the US today.

How did Satan—the Enemy—come to be this way? Let's look at…

Lucifer: Before he became "the Enemy"

Many details about the Enemy are relayed in prophecies that have two applications. Theologians refer to this as **the law of double reference**, which is the tendency of biblical prophets to prophesy two things simultaneously—one relevant to the general time of the prophecy and the other relating to the distant past or far-flung future. A good example can be observed in the first two chapters of Isaiah where the prophet jumps from the restoration of Jerusalem to the future Millennium and the new Earth. From a warning to the people of Jerusalem of looming judgment to a notice of God's Day of Judgment of all unredeemed souls throughout history (see 2:12-22). What was about to take place in Jerusalem was just a prefiguring of what will happen to the entire Earth. Just as Jerusalem was restored, so the Earth will be restored after God's reckoning.[36]

With the law of double reference in mind, let's consider a prophecy from Ezekiel 28 that concerns the king of Tyre, Ithobaal II. Tyre was (and still is) a city just north of Israel along the coast of the Mediterranean. The great wealth that Ithobaal II had amassed resulted in pride to the point that he perceived himself as god (verse 2). Such pomposity drew righteous judgment as the LORD said he would send foreign nations to humble the king by drawing "their swords against his beauty and wisdom," bringing him "down to the pit" through a "violent death" (verses 7-8). God's judgment ends with this humbling pronouncement:

---

[36] Why did the LORD hide prophecies concerning the distant future or past in ones that had a more immediate application? In other words, why is there a "Law of Double Reference" at all? Perhaps because the prophecies of Old Testament prophets had to be 100% accurate. If their words were proven to be false, they were to no longer be regarded as prophets and, in fact, were to be put to death (Deuteronomy 18:20-22). As such, their prophecies *had* to have a more immediate application.

> ⁹ Will you then say, "I am a god,"
>   in the presence of those who kill you?
> You will be but a mortal, not a god,
>   in the hands of those who slay you.
> ¹⁰ You will die the death of the uncircumcised
>   at the hands of foreigners.
>
> Ezekiel 28:9-10

The LORD's judgment on Ithobaal II was to die prematurely, which is in line with the biblical axiom "the wages of sin is death" (Romans 6:23).

The next nine verses are *another* prophecy against the same king, but this time it is paralleled with the fall of Satan and his banishment from Heaven to the Underworld:

> **This is what the Sovereign Lord says:**
>
> " 'You were <u>the seal of perfection</u>,
>   full of wisdom and <u>perfect in beauty</u>.
> ¹³ <u>You were in Eden,</u>
>   <u>the garden of God</u>;
>   <u>every precious stone adorned you</u>:
>   carnelian, chrysolite and emerald,
>   topaz, onyx and jasper,
>   lapis lazuli, turquoise and beryl.
>   <u>Your settings and mountings were made of gold</u>;
>   <u>on the day you were created they were</u>
>   <u>prepared</u>.
> ¹⁴ <u>You were anointed as a guardian cherub,</u>
>   <u>for so I ordained you</u>.
>   You were on the holy mount of God;
>   you walked among the fiery stones.
> ¹⁵ <u>You were blameless in your ways</u>
>   <u>from the day you were created</u>
>   <u>till wickedness was found in you</u>.
> ¹⁶ Through your widespread trade
>   you were filled with violence,

> and you sinned.
> So I drove you in disgrace from the mount of God,
> and <u>I expelled you, guardian cherub,</u>
> from among the fiery stones.
> ¹⁷ <u>Your heart became proud
> on account of your beauty,</u>
> and <u>you corrupted your wisdom
> because of your splendor.</u>
> <u>So I threw you to the earth</u>;
> I made a spectacle of you before kings.
> ¹⁸ By your many sins and dishonest trade
> you have desecrated your sanctuaries.
> So I made a fire come out from you,
> and it consumed you,
> and I reduced you to ashes on the ground
> in the sight of all who were watching.
> ¹⁹ All the nations who knew you
> are appalled at you;
> you have come to a horrible end
> and will be no more.' "
>
> Ezekiel 28:12-19

Why would God parallel Lucifer's fall with the king of Tyre's doom. Because the devil was the evil spiritual authority who pulled the strings of this pagan king. With this understanding, Ezekiel 28:12-19 is speaking of either Satan or the king of Tyre, and sometimes both, depending on the verse. It's our responsibility to "rightly divide" God's Word to discern which.

Verses 12-17 refer to Lucifer and could only be applied to the king of Tyre in a figurative sense. After all, the person addressed is described as "the seal of perfection... and perfect in beauty" (verse 12) who dwelled in "Eden, the garden of God" (verse 13). On top of this he's called a "guardian **cherub**"—an angel (verses 14 & 16). Needless to say, none of these descriptions are literally applicable to a flawed human monarch.

Take another look at the final part of verse 13:

> **Your settings and mountings were made of gold;
> <u>on the day you were created they were
> prepared</u>.**
> **Ezekiel 28:13**

Notice that it says "on the day you were created" and not "on the day you were born." This indicates that it's talking about Lucifer and not the king of Tyre. Secondly, it says that Lucifer's gold "settings" and "mountings" were prepared *on the day he was created*. What's this talking about? A couple of other translations shed insight:

> **the workmanship of <u>thy tabrets</u> and of <u>thy pipes</u> was prepared <u>in thee</u> <u>in the day that thou wast created</u>.**
> **Ezekiel 28:13** (KJV)

> **Gold work of <u>tambourines</u> and of <u>pipes</u> was <u>in you</u>.
> In the day that you were created they were prepared.**
> **Ezekiel 28:13** (WEB)

Not only was Lucifer created "full of wisdom and perfect in beauty" and a "guardian cherub," it also appears that he was created with built-in instrumentation—tambourines and musical pipes—the very day he was created. This is where theologians get the idea that Lucifer was in charge of worship in Heaven.

If you compare various translations you'll see that there is some speculation concerning the Hebrew word translated as "pipes," which is used in Scripture this sole time. The NIV translates it as "mountings" and another version as "engravings." However, the word translated as "tabret" or "tambourine" literally refers to a timbrel or tambourine. It appears 16 other times in the Hebrew Scriptures where the King James Version and the New American Standard Bible unanimously cite it as a musical instrument, whether "tambourine," "timbrel" or "tabret" (i.e. a tabor). Seeing as how the first word definitely refers to a musical instrument—a tambourine or tabor—it stands to reason that the second word refers to an instrument as well. And, since a tabor is a small drum used to accompany a pipe or drum, it's reasonable that the word refers to pipes or fifes of some sort.

This intrinsic musical anointing that Lucifer had explains how the devil uses music to mislead people, particularly the youth. Like the Pied Piper, Satan will utilize music to lead astray whole generations. And I'm not talking about a specific *style* of music, but rather the *content* of it, regardless of style. Consider, for example, the Beatles hit song from late 1963 "I Want to Hold Your Hand," which debuted at the beginning of so-called Beatlemania. It's a catchy ditty about innocent youthful romance and had no ill effect on the teen and tween-ager masses. Yet less than 14 years later the band Queen released the sexually explicit "Get Down, Make Love" aimed at the same audience. It was a bait-and-switch tactic using the power of music to mislead a generation and its descendants into sexual hedonism.

In any case, Lucifer was more likely to have such wealth, beauty, wisdom, perfection and musical instruments at his creation than some ancient earthly king at his birth.

"Anointed Guardian Cherub"

As noted, verses 14 and 16 show that Lucifer was "anointed" a "guardian cherub."

'Anoint' means "to dedicate to the service of God" and indicates the LORD's favor. This explains why Jesus is called Christ (from the Greek *christos*) or Messiah (from the Hebrew *mashach*), both of which mean "anointed one." So Lucifer was handpicked by God for the privilege of guarding—i.e. covering—the LORD's throne, similar to the cherubim who were assigned to guard the Garden of Eden after Adam & Eve were banished (Genesis 3:24).

This is evidence that Lucifer had regular access to the glorious presence of the Almighty.

"You were Perfect in Your Ways"

Let's read verse 15 from a different translation:

> **You were perfect in your ways from the day that you were created, until unrighteousness was found in you.**
> **Ezekiel 28:15** (WEB)

Lucifer was perfect in angelic beauty before his fall and thus was praised as "the seal of perfection… and perfect in beauty" (verse 12). This obviously wasn't wholly true of Ithobaal II, but it was true of Satan when he was Lucifer, before iniquity was found in him.

The first part of the passage shows how proud God was of Lucifer: This magnificent cherub was God's pattern of perfection and beauty. Yet the second half resonates with disappointment, even mourning.

Lucifer's Fall

What was it that led to Lucifer's rebellion and fall from Heaven? Verse 17 shows that Lucifer's root transgression was pride:

> **<u>Your heart</u> became proud**
>   **on account of your beauty,**
> **and you corrupted your wisdom**
>   **<u>because of your splendor</u>.**
> **So I threw you to the earth;**
>   **I made a spectacle of you before kings.**
> **Ezekiel 28:17**

This is a great warning against allowing our blessings to go to our heads. Lucifer became arrogant *because* of his great beauty, wisdom and splendor. His inherent blessings puffed up his ego to the point that he thought he was all that and a bag of chips, so to speak. The New Testament corroborates this (1 Timothy 3:6). The root of sin is always traced to what's going on **in one's heart**.

Understandably, the LORD throws this archangel out of Heaven to the Earth in disgrace. We know this isn't referring to Ithobaal II because he never left the Earth in the first place.

Verses 18-19, however, more clearly apply to the earthly king of Tyre because they show his body being "reduced to ashes" in the sight of spectators as he comes to "a horrible end" and is "no more." Since we know from other passages that Lucifer wasn't reduced to ashes when he fell to the Earth and didn't become "no more," these statements obviously refer to Ithobaal II and not Satan. The latter's alive and not-well on planet Earth to this day.

The main point about Lucifer rings loud and clear: This blessed archangel was corrupted by pride due to his incredible beauty and other endowments, which resulted in his foolish rebellion and ousting from glory.

Thus the LORD threw Lucifer to the Earth or, more specifically, the Underworld, which is the spiritual dimension that underpins the Earth and Universe. Isaiah paralleled Satan's fall with the king of Babylon's doom:

> [12] **How you have fallen from heaven,**
>   **morning star** [Lucifer]**, son of the dawn!**
>   **You have been cast down to the earth,**
>   **you who once laid low the nations!**
> [13] **You said in your heart,**
>   **"I will ascend to the heavens;**
>   **I will raise my throne**
>   **above the stars of God;**
>   **I will sit enthroned** **on the mount of assembly,**
>   **on the utmost heights of Mount Zaphon.**
> [14] **I will ascend above the tops of the clouds;**
>   **I will make myself like the Most High."**
> [15] **But you are brought down to the realm of the dead** [Sheol]**,**
>   **to the depths of the pit.**
> [16] **Those who see you stare at you,**
>   **they ponder your fate:**
>   **"Is this the man who shook the earth**
>   **and made kingdoms tremble,**
> [17] **the man who made the world a wilderness,**
>   **who overthrew its cities**
>   **and would not let his captives go home?"**
>
>   Isaiah 14:12-17

This is another example of **the law of double reference** where two things are simultaneously prophesied—one relevant to the general time of the prophecy and the other relating to the distant past or far-off future. In this case, Isaiah prophesies Sennacherib's doom[37] and parallels it with the much earlier fall of Lucifer, who became Satan. Verse 12, for instance, is an obvious reference to Lucifer and could only be applied to the king of Babylon in a figurative sense. After all, did Sennacherib literally fall from Heaven down to the Earth, like the devil? Was he nicknamed "morning star," aka "Lucifer" (which is how the King James and New King James translate the Hebrew word for "morning star")? Furthermore, Jesus partially cites verse 12 as a reference to the devil:

> **"I saw Satan fall like lightning from heaven."**
> **Luke 10:18**

This is reinforced by Revelation 12:7-10 (covered in **Chapter 9**).

Why would the LORD draw a parallel between the king of Babylon and Satan? The same reason Jesus rebuked Peter as "Satan" in Matthew 16:23 for being a mouthpiece for the devil's ungodly agenda. Just as Satan was the spiritual force *behind* Peter's rash words, so he was the diabolic authority *behind* Sennacherib's oppressive reign.

Whereas verses 12-14 obviously refer to the devil and only figuratively to Sennacherib, verses 15-17 solely relate to the earthly king (although verses 16-17 *may* refer to the devil by extension). Verse 15 shows Sennacherib's soul being housed in "the pit" after his death, which is Sheol, the "realm of the dead" located in the heart of the Earth.[38] The point is that death awaits those who arrogantly presume to be God.

---

[37] FYI: Assyrian king Sennacherib *(suh-NAK-uh-rib)* conquered Babylon and hence dubbed himself *the King of Babylon*.
[38] See my book *SHEOL KNOW* for details.

Lucifer's Pride wouldn't allow Him to Serve God or People

We observed last chapter that angels already existed when the Earth and Universe were created, as shown in God's humbling response to the venting Job:

> "Where were you <u>when I laid the earth's foundation</u>?
> Tell me, if you understand.
> ⁵ Who marked off its dimensions? Surely you know!
> Who stretched a measuring line across it?
> ⁶ On what were its footings set,
> or who laid its cornerstone—
> ⁷ <u>while the morning stars sang together
> and all the angels shouted for joy</u>?"
>
> **Job 38:4-7**

The angels "sang together" and "shouted for joy" when the Almighty created the Earth. Satan's rebellion occurred sometime after this because there had to be an Earth and the corresponding Underworld for him to fall to and inhabit. As explained in **Chapter 9**, the "underworld" is simply the spiritual dimension that undergirds the Earth. Not being physical beings, the devil and his fallen angels operate from this spiritual realm to negatively influence the physical world.

Notice that verse 7 says "**all** the angels shouted for joy" when the Earth was created. The word 'all' is *kol (kohl)* in the Hebrew, meaning "the whole." As noted last chapter, the Hebrew for 'angels' in this verse literally means "the sons of God," the same words used to describe angels elsewhere in Scripture, including the devil & his filthy angels (e.g. Genesis 6:2,4 & Job 1:6, 2:1). My point is that *all* the angels rejoiced when God created the Heavens and the Earth (Genesis 1:1), which would include Lucifer and his subordinates *before* their rebellion and ouster from Heaven.

Yet in Genesis 3:1-15 we observe Satan, after his fall, possessing a serpent-with-legs in order to tempt the first woman. This shows that Lucifer and his cohorts rebelled and were cast from Heaven sometime *after* the creation of the Earth & Universe, but *before* the devil's duping of Eve, which means sometime between Genesis 1:31 and Genesis 3:1.[39] We don't know the exact expanse of time between the two, but it could've been years. In any case, this shows that Satan's rebellion occurred shortly after the creation of human beings.

We know from the previous section that Lucifer's insurgency was due to pride:

> [13] You said **in your heart**,
>   "**I will** ascend to the heavens;
> **I will** raise my throne
>   above the stars of God;
> **I will** sit enthroned on the mount of assembly,
>   on the utmost heights of Mount Zaphon.
> [14] **I will** ascend above the tops of the clouds;
>   **I will** make myself like the Most High."
>
> **Isaiah 14:13-14**

These five "I will" statements reveal Satan's arrogance—he wanted to *be* God rather than be God's servant. This was the first sin ever committed. And notice, again, that sin is traced to what's going on **in one's heart**, which is corroborated by Christ in the New Testament (Mark 7:20-23). No wonder Jesus emphasized this in the Sermon on the Mount (Matthew 5:21-22, 27-28).

We saw earlier in Ezekiel 28 that Lucifer was an exceptionally beautiful angel, God's guardian cherub with an intrinsic musical anointing who dwelt in the presence of the Almighty. But he was not satisfied with his extraordinary blessings and privileges. Instead, Lucifer wanted to *be* God and so, after his defeat, he naturally tempted Adam & Eve with the same basic sin that led to his downfall (Genesis 3:1-5).

---

[39] As footnoted in **Chapter 1**, this is the young Earth perspective, which I believe is the most biblically faithful position on the age of the Earth/Universe. Gap theorists, who embrace the old Earth model, place the fall of Lucifer & his fallen spirits sometime between Genesis 1:1 and 1:2. For details, see the teaching *How Old is the Earth? (The Gap Theory vs. Young Earth Creationism)* at the Fountain of Life website.

Now here's an important point: Lucifer was no doubt having problems with the concept of serving *before* God created Adam & Eve, but once they were created and he caught wind of the fact that angels were commissioned to *serve* people (Hebrews 1:14) his pride couldn't handle it, particularly when he found out human beings were created in the likeness of God. And, worse, that they were expressly created to be *co-heirs* with Christ, seated *with Him* at the right hand of the Father, a privilege and position *not* granted to angels (Romans 8:17, Hebrews 1:13 & Ephesians 2:6). Lucifer's envy went into overdrive and thus he orchestrated his doomed revolt.

Humankind's Slavery to Satan

Incredibly, the Bible teaches that unredeemed humanity is in slavery to Satan. The rest of this chapter we're going to look at what this means, how it happened, and what are its ramifications. In the next two chapters we'll focus on the good news—the *awesome* news—that God has ingeniously provided a way of escape for anyone who wants it.

What is the evidence that humanity is in slavery to Satan? Let's start with John 8 where we observe Christ having a discussion with the Pharisees and likeminded Jews. The Pharisees were the staunchly legalistic religious leaders of Israel at the time. While they were respected conservatives, Jesus frankly told them that they were slaves to sin, which they adamantly denied on the grounds of their Hebrew stock (Abraham being their forefather). The Messiah responded that, if they were truly Abraham's offspring, they would walk righteously as Abraham did. And if they were God's children they would love him—Jesus—since he *came* from God. Instead, they were trying to murder him. Christ went on to candidly tell them that the reason they wanted to kill him was because they were acting in accordance with *their* father's desire. He was talking about the devil, who was a murderer from the beginning (verses 33-44). So Jesus was saying that the devil was their spiritual father.

Of course, no one likes to be called a child of Satan—especially respected religious folk—and so they proceeded to call Jesus names and even attempted to stone him to death. But the Mighty Christ miraculously slipped from their clutches, no doubt assisted by angels (verses 48-59).

The reason I bring this particular occasion up is because **Christ was talking to conservative religious people** whom he said were slaves to sin and children of the devil. These were people who knew the Scriptures like the backs of their hands. This shows that conservativism and religion cannot set us free from sin and make us children of God.

Notice what the Bible point blank says about humanity's slavery to the devil:

> **We know that we** [believers] **are children of God, and that <u>the whole world is under the control of the evil one</u>.**
>
> **1 John 5:19**
>
> …**the devil, or Satan, who <u>leads the whole world astray</u>.**
>
> **Revelation 12:9**

The devil is able to mislead humanity because he's the legal ruler of this world; the Bible even calls him the "god of this world" (2 Corinthians 4:4). Some translations render this as "the god of *this age*," which shows that Satan's dictatorship is limited to "this present evil age" and is not forever (Galatians 1:4).

Christ testified to humanity's slavery to Satan when he commissioned Paul "to open [people's] eyes so that they may turn from darkness to light and **from the dominion of Satan to God**" (Acts 26:18).

But when and how did Satan become humanity's slave master? Let's look at…

The Fall of Humanity

As noted earlier, after Satan's plunge from Heaven he possessed a serpent-with-legs for the purpose of tempting Eve in the Garden of Eden and, through Eve, seduced Adam into outright rebellion against the Almighty. Here's the account:

> **Now <u>the serpent</u> was more crafty than any of the wild animals the Lord God had made. He said to the woman, "Did God really say, 'You must not eat from any tree in the garden'?"**
>
> **² The woman said to the serpent, "We may eat fruit from the trees in the garden, ³ but God did say, 'You must not eat fruit from the tree that is in the middle of the garden, <u>and you must not touch it</u>, or you will die.'"**
>
> **⁴ "You will not certainly die," the serpent said to the woman. ⁵ "For God knows that when you eat from it your eyes will be opened, and you will be like God, knowing good and evil."**
>
> **⁶ When the woman saw that the fruit of the tree was good for food and pleasing to the eye, and also desirable for gaining wisdom, she took some and ate it. She also gave some to her husband, who was with her, and he ate it. ⁷ Then the eyes of both of them were opened, and they realized they were naked; so they sewed fig leaves together and made coverings for themselves.**
>
> **⁸ Then the man and his wife heard the sound of the Lord God as he was walking in the garden in the cool of the day, and they hid from the Lord God among the trees of the garden.**
>
> **Genesis 3:1-8**

Let's start our analysis of this pivotal passage by grasping these four points:

1. While Satan *could* have manifested himself in the physical realm like the "sons of God" later did (Genesis 6:1-4),[40] he obviously wanted to present his temptation to Eve as a harmless creature in order to be successful. This corresponds to something the New Testament says about him—"Satan himself masquerades as an **angel of light**" (2 Corinthians 11:14). So he possessed a serpent, but this reptile was hardly the slithering serpentine creatures with which we're familiar. This reptile had legs and it did not have the negative connotation that snakes have had ever since (Genesis 3:14). Remember, after God created the Universe and all living things the entire creation was called "very good" and this would include the serpent (Genesis 1:31). So this was a striking, shining animal. It was as threatening to Eve as the GEICO gecko would be to us.
2. Someone mocked this event to me on the grounds that Eve was tempted by "a talking snake." But **A.** it wasn't a snake as we know it, as explained above; and **B.** Adam & Eve were clearly *used* to communicating with animals in the Garden of Eden before their fall because Eve wasn't shocked when the serpent spoke to her. She reacted as if conversing with such an animal was a normal thing. If this sounds strange to you, keep in mind that most of us communicate with animals every day. For instance, my cats let me know when they want something to eat, when they want affection, when they want outdoors and when they want in the house; they even give thanks! They may not speak English, but they certainly talk verbally and bodily; and I understand them. Now imagine how heightened such communion would be *before* the fall of creation when the world was perfect. Then add the fact that the serpent was said to be the smartest of the animals God made (Genesis 3:1[41]).
3. Eve appears to have been alone with the serpent when she was tempted, but this seems to be contradicted by Genesis 3:6 where

---

[40] See the previous chapter for details.
[41] This is where the serpent is called "crafty" or "clever," which is translated from the Hebrew word *arum (aw-ROOM)*, which means prudent, shrewd or sensible.

it says she gave some of the forbidden fruit to Adam "who was with her," which he ate. This explains the traditional Judaic position that Adam was present with Eve the whole time and he heard the entire conversation of the temptation. However, saying Adam "was with her" could simply mean that he was with her when she offered him the fruit. According to this scenario, Eve had the discussion with the serpent, believed his lies, partook of the fruit, and *then* went to Adam—who was likely nearby—and offered him some of it once he "was with her." This interpretation helps make sense of the New Testament's point that Eve was deceived by the devil while Adam was not; and death came to humankind through Adam's sin rather than Eve's (1 Timothy 2:13-14 & Romans 5:14-21). Satan obviously knew that Adam would be more open to embracing his deception if it came via the fairer sex. In other words, he knew that women were men's weakness.

4. Eve's actions could perhaps be excused on the grounds that she was deceived by the serpent. Not to mention she was clearly confused in light of her embellishing of God's prohibition against eating from the tree of the knowledge of good and evil wherein she *added* "and you must not touch it" (verse 3). God never said this and it reveals Eve's muddled mental state. For Adam, however, there was no such excuse: He willfully opted to go with Eve, his "hot babe," rather than continue with God. It was a clear-minded decision. Simply put, **he rejected the LORD and chose the way of the "ancient serpent"** (Revelation 12:9 & 20:2).

Now let's consider the bigger picture from Satan's perspective: After his humiliating expulsion from Heaven he & his minions were utterly defeated and devastated, living meaningless lives separate from God in the "dark heavenlies." So the purpose of the devil's diabolic enticement of Adam & Eve was threefold:

1. To get back at God somehow.
2. To ruin the only beings created in God's image and destined to be co-heirs with Christ, of whom he was furiously envious. This ruin would, of course, extend to their descendants and therefore all humanity.
3. To usurp the authority and power that Adam & Eve had over the Earth and Universe. As such, Satan would attain lawful control of God's physical creation.

We'll entertain a fourth possible reason next chapter.

What power did Adam & Eve possess that Satan craved? God originally blessed the primordial couple — and, by extension, all humankind — to "be fruitful and multiply," to "subdue" and "have dominion" over all the Earth:

> **Then God <u>blessed</u> them, and God said to them, "Be fruitful and multiply; fill <u>the earth</u> and <u>subdue it</u>; <u>have dominion</u> over the fish of the sea, over the birds of the air, and over every living thing that moves on <u>the earth</u>."**
>
> **Genesis 1:28** (NKJV)

This blessing was equally a directive, showing that the LORD put humanity in charge of the Earth and its animal inhabitants. No stipulations were given on how to govern except that they were *not* to eat of the tree of the knowledge of good and evil (Genesis 2:15-17). In short, Adam & Eve had power-of-attorney to manage physical creation in God's place. The Creator obviously trusted them because they were created in His likeness and they didn't have a sin nature (Genesis 1:27).

Power mad, Satan craved this authority and so masqueraded as a harmless creature in order to, first, deceive Eve and, second, convince Adam *through her* to make a ruinous decision for them and all humanity, which was in their loins.

Satan's "Power of Suggestion"

Did you notice, by the way, that Satan's strategy in duping Eve was simply the "power of suggestion"? He didn't approach her with a blatant denial of God's Word, which would've shocked her and sent her running. Instead, he worked with her natural curiosity. He knew Eve was *already* curious about the forbidden fruit and so he waited until she "just happened" to be in the area of the tree before conveying his suggestion: "Did God *really* say, 'You must not eat from any tree in the garden'?" The question was designed to get her focused on the sole thing restricted to her & Adam and thus to doubt God's goodness. The Enemy insinuated doubt concerning God's will — His Word — to mislead her to the supposed true interpretation, which was a lie. And she believed it because of the innocuous way Satan approached her, masquerading as a harmless, beautiful creature, which she received as a credible messenger due to the devil's cunning.

Beware: The kingdom of darkness will use these same tactics today to mislead *you* away from God and His will. In order for the Enemy to not outwit you, you must be aware of his schemes (2 Corinthians 2:11).

We'll look at this topic more in **Chapter 17** and **18**.

The Consequences of Sin

The consequence of eating the forbidden fruit was death. God warned Adam "when you eat of it you will surely **die**" (Genesis 2:17). The original text contains the Hebrew word for 'death' twice and so it should be rendered "in dying you will die." [42] In other words, Adam & Eve would die spiritually when they transgressed, which would eventually lead to physically death and, ultimately, eternal death, unless they were redeemed at some point. As such, **they lost their eternal life**.

The condition of spiritual death, by the way, does not mean that the human spirit is dead, but rather that it's dead to God because it lacks the eternal life necessary to function properly. In short, spiritual death

---

[42] See Young's Literal Translation.

kills the human capacity to know the Creator. This can be observed in the fact that Adam & Eve hid from the LORD immediately *after* suffering spiritual death. It robbed humanity of guilt-free access into the presence of God and the precious communion thereof.

Something else devastating happened: Since Adam & Eve willingly believed and obeyed the word of Satan over the Word of God they became slaves to a new master through the acquisition of a sinful nature, which is the satanic nature.

Moreover, they gave their God-given power-of-attorney over to their new spiritual master. In essence, **Satan acquired the legal right to govern the Earth & Universe, including the legal control of all people born from Adam's seed, meaning humanity was now in bondage to the Enemy**.

Somehow a lawful transfer of power from Adam to Satan occurred. But why wouldn't the Sovereign LORD simply take this control back from the devil? Because God is perfectly just and it would be unjust to take away authority that Satan legally obtained. A lawful means of reversing this legal transference would have to be implemented and this is what the gospel of Christ is all about, which is why it's the "good news."

All of this explains why the Bible says "the whole world is under the control of the evil one" who "leads the whole world astray" (1 John 5:19 & Revelation 12:9). It's because Satan possesses legal authority over physical creation. How else would he be able to tempt Christ with the offer of "all the kingdoms of the world" if they weren't legally his to give? See Matthew 4:8-9.

The English Standard Version translates 1 John 5:19 as "the whole world lies **in the power of** the evil one." The word 'world' in the Greek refers to the Earth and Universe but, more literally, "an *ordered* system, like the universe and creation." In short, the devil is legally in control of physical creation and therefore calls the shots, which is why God's Word refers to him as "the god of this world" who is able to blind the minds of those who don't believe (2 Corinthians 4:4). See **Chapter 17** and **18** for enlightening details on how exactly the kingdom of darkness blinds people's minds.

The Ramifications of Satan's Rule

The fact that Satan is the god of this world can be observed every day all over the planet—war, crime, disease, suffering, immorality, corruption, injustice, abuse, perversion, slander, lies, etc.

One of the favorite arguments of atheists against the idea of an Almighty Creator is that, if there *was* an all-righteous God, why does He allow all these horrible things to happen? Why doesn't He stop it? God's Word tells us precisely why: An evil spiritual being usurped authority from our primeval parents and he's been running the show ever since, with the assistance of his filthy underlings.

Thankfully, the LORD in his ingeniousness devised a legal way to take control back from Satan. This transfer of power is already in motion and will culminate with "a new heaven and a new earth, the home of righteousness" (2 Peter 3:13). When this takes place, God's dwelling will be *with* the redeemed "and he will dwell with them. They will be his people, and God himself will be with them and be their God. 'He will wipe every tear from their eyes. There will be no more death' or mourning or crying or pain, for the old order of things has passed away" (Revelation 21:3-4).

So, for anyone who's upset about the world being so messed up, **the LORD's on top of it**. His awesome plan of redemption for humanity, and all creation, is in motion. In fact, he *foreknew* we were going to fall and already had a plan of action (Ephesians 1:4-5).

What is this plan and how can people make sure they're on board?

Chapter 12

The Liberation of Humanity & Creation

The Bible is all about **1.** the LORD creating the Heavens & Earth and all living things, **2.** the rebellion and expulsion from Heaven of Satan & his foul underlings, **3.** humanity's fall, **4.** Satan's usurpation of authority over creation and, most of all, **5.** God's brilliant, loving plan of **redemption**. In this chapter we're going to focus on this fifth element—the LORD's awesome plan of redemption.

Someone might argue that this is off topic in a book about angels, but it's not. Think about it: Satan is the chief Enemy angel who duped humanity into slavery. Our salvation from satanic bondage comes through the Anointed One, who is *The* Angel of the LORD, as explained in **Chapter 7**. Furthermore, if you want to "reign in life"[43] over the devil & evil spirits with the assistance of angels, as Christ did, you're going to **have to** thoroughly *know* your redemption. So, far from being off topic, this chapter is paramount.

---

[43] Romans 5:17

"All the World's a Stage"

The fascinating events of Genesis 3 are drama of the highest order and bring to mind Shakespeare's famous verse:

All the world's a stage,
And all the men and women merely players;

- **The stage** in Genesis 3 is a beautiful garden roughly the size of California or Iraq[44] on a planet called Earth in a solar system in one galaxy of an estimated 200 billion galaxies in the Universe (!).
- **The players** are: **1.** The Almighty Creator, **2.** His nemesis who was kicked out of Heaven and dwells in the dark spiritual dimension that parallels the Earth and Universe, **3.** Adam & Eve (and the human race in their loins), the only beings created in the likeness of God and called to be co-heirs with Christ, and **4.** a harmless, beautiful animal that Satan uses to dupe Adam & Eve and usurp their authority over the Earth and Universe.
- **The prop** is a tree with the forbidden fruit thereof.
- **The suspense** concerns whose word Adam & Eve will believe—God's or Satan's—which will determine their destiny and the destiny of the human race.
- **The tragedy** is their fall, the cursing of creation and the ensuing pathos of life in a fallen world.
- **The challenge** is how the Creator can possibly set things aright without compromising His perfect justice.
- **The story** contains elements of all great dramas—a noble hero, a wicked villain (or foil), protagonists, deceit, the testing of character, tragedy and potential redemption. Speaking of redemption, let's look at…

---

[44] These dimensions are taken from Genesis.

God's Plan of Redemption for Humanity

To 'redeem' means "to liberate through payment of ransom" or "to clear of debt through proper payment." In the 1st century nearly half the people on Earth were slaves in one form or another. The Greek word for 'redeem' was used back then in reference to purchasing freedom for a slave.

While slavery still exists today, it's much less widespread. However, spiritual slavery is rampant because everyone born from Adam is a slave to sin and captive to the kingdom of darkness. The awesome news is that God has purchased our freedom from this spiritual slavery through the precious blood of Christ.

> **For you know that it was not with perishable things such as silver or gold that you were <u>redeemed</u> from <u>the empty way of life handed down to you from your ancestors</u>, [19] but with the precious blood of Christ, a lamb without blemish or defect.**
> **1 Peter 1:18-19**

We've been liberated through the death and resurrection of Christ, which is the gospel (1 Corinthians 15:1-4). Peter summarizes what we've been freed from as **"the empty way of life"** handed down to us from our ancestors. This refers to people's empty existence separate from God as slaves to sin with Satan as slave master. Such bondage was handed down to us by our ancestors, Adam & Eve, as detailed last chapter.

Some will understandably reason that it's unfair for sin and spiritual slavery to be passed from our primordial parents to the rest of us. Answer: This is what theologians refer to as **federal headship**, which simply means that Adam was the human race's spiritual, moral and physical fountainhead, our lone representative. The entire race was in his loins when he deliberately sinned and thus sin was passed on to all descendants (Romans 5:12). Think about it in terms of genetics: We naturally inherit characteristics of our fore-parents, such as facial features and skin color; the same principle is at play in a spiritual sense.

To be set free from this generational curse of sin we'd have to be born of a *new* Adam—a second Adam—one who doesn't transfer sin and death, but rather life, because he was *not* born of the seed of Adam, but of the seed of God. Believe it or not, this is the core message of the gospel. Christ—*The* Angel of the LORD—is the second Adam (1 Corinthians 15:45-49). Let me explain…

Our freedom was purchased through the precious blood of Yeshua:

> **For He has <u>rescued us from the dominion of darkness</u> and brought us into the kingdom of the Son he loves, ¹⁴ in whom we have <u>redemption</u>, the forgiveness of sins.**
>
> **Colossians 1:13-14**

God has rescued us—*liberated us*—from bondage to the kingdom of darkness through Christ. We're no longer slaves to Satan, as long as you've accepted the awesome gospel.

This great salvation corresponds to the LORD's prophecy after the fall of Adam & Eve:

> **"And I [God] will put enmity**
> **between you [Satan] and the woman,**
> **and between your offspring and hers [Christ];**
> **he [Christ] will crush your head,**
> **and you will strike his heel."**
>
> **Genesis 3:15**

The offspring of the woman—Christ—would eventually deal Satan a fatal blow. The best the devil could do to circumvent this was to try to thwart the birth of the Messiah—which he repeatedly tried to do, but failed. The satanic attempt to pollute the bloodline through the "sons of God" copulating with women was one such attempt (Genesis 6:1-4), as covered in **Chapter 10**. Once Yeshua was born, the devil naturally manipulated his puppets in the Roman/Hebrew governments to have Jesus unjustly captured, tortured and executed, which amounted to "striking his heal." Of course this played into God's genius plan as the death and resurrection of Christ were key to our redemption.

The First Adam and the Great Wall

Adam's sin and the passing of a sin nature to his descendants built an impenetrable wall between God and the human race. Yet, *Hallelujah*, the ministry of the second Adam—Jesus Christ, *The* Angel of the LORD—tore that wall down so that we can reconcile with our Creator.

This "great wall" is a barrier consisting of four figurative blocks:

1. **The holy character of God.**
2. **The debt of sin.**
3. **Slavery to Satan.**
4. **Spiritual death.**

Let's look at all four:

The holy character of God. Have you ever known people who were so 'good' that you felt uncomfortable being around them, perhaps inferior? This is magnified when you know they're aware of some of your more hideous "skeletons in the closet." The reason you felt uncomfortable is because their moral standards were so high that you assumed they'd be judgmental of you, which created a sense of alienation.

Now relate this to the human race and God. All humanity is born of Adam's seed and therefore has an inherent sin nature, which stands in stark contrast to the LORD's flawlessness—His absolute purity, righteousness, justice, love, immutableness (unchangeableness), and veracity. Thus God's holy character became a barrier after the fall. Is it any wonder that the Bible says "all our righteous acts are like filthy rags" (Isaiah 64:6)? Notice it doesn't say that our *bad* deeds are like filthy rags, but rather our *righteous* acts! God is so holy—so absolutely perfect—that even what we would consider good works by human standards are offensive by comparison. In short, there's an infinite gap between fallen humanity and the LORD due to God's holy character.

The debt of sin. Back in the 1st century Roman Empire when criminals were judged they were given a Certificate of Debt, which was placed on the door of their cells. This document cited how they failed to live according to the law of Caesar and denoted the corresponding sentence. When the penalty was fulfilled their Certificate of Debt was stamped "Paid in Full" so that they would not be punished again for their crimes. Of course, if the penalty was death this was irrelevant, but if the consequence was *time* it was valuable: If someone tried to accuse them of a past offense all they had to do was show their canceled Certificate of Debt. Until that debt was paid, however, it stood between them and freedom.

Now let's relate this to the human race and the perfect moral Law of God, summed up in the Ten Commandments and the Sermon on the Mount. All of us have sinned against God's Law because the infection of sin passed from our Federal Headship to us. We're all infected with a sinful nature and have missed it one way or another; actually we've transgressed *innumerable* ways, not just "one," particularly when you consider the so-called "little sins," like arrogance, envy, jealousy, rivalry, greed, carnal lust and the like. Since the "wages of sin is death" (Romans 6:23) we've all been assigned a Certificate of Debt, which cites the penalty of our offenses as death (Colossians 2:14). This is why the Bible says "whoever does not believe stands *condemned already*" (John 3:18).

Humanity's debt of sin means that we're in a state of criminality apart from Christ, the second Adam. We're thus "objects of [God's] wrath" (Ephesians 2:3). It's an impassable barrier between us and God and can only be removed if a qualified individual paid the penalty of death in our place.

Slavery to Satan. This third block in the great wall that separates God and humanity was detailed last chapter: When Satan apprehended power-of-attorney over physical creation he became the "god of this age" (2 Corinthians 4:4) or, as Christ called him, "the prince of this world" (John 12:31, John 14:30 & John 16:11). 'Prince' in the Greek is *archon (AR-kohn)*, which means "ruler, governor, leader." The devil is the spiritual ruler of this planet and thus the world is one big slave market where everyone born of the seed of Adam is legally a slave to Satan, whether they know it or not. This explains why the Messiah said the conservative religious leaders of Israel where children of the devil, to their astonishment (John 8:33-44). It's why the New Testament proclaims in no uncertain terms that "the whole world is under the control of the evil one" "who leads the whole world astray" (1 John 5:19 & Revelation 12:9). It explains Christ's commission to Paul to turn people "from the dominion of Satan to God" (Acts 26:18). It explains why Satan is referred to as "the ruler of the kingdom of the air, the spirit who is now at work in those who are disobedient" (Ephesians 2:2).

Unredeemed humanity may be God's creation, but they're *not* God's children. They lawfully belong to their cruel slave master, the devil. The only person born into this world that was not born in subjugation to Satan is our Mighty Savior, Jesus Christ, because he was *not* born of the seed (sperm) of a human father and therefore was not tainted with Adam's sin infection (Luke 1:34-35). To be set free of slavery to Satan a person has to be born of God's seed and thus become a child of God (1 John 3:2,9 & 5:1).

Spiritual death. At the end of the previous chapter we saw that God warned Adam & Eve not to eat of the tree of the knowledge of good and evil because "in the day" that they did so they would "surely die" (Genesis 2:17). It was pointed out that the Hebrew word for 'death'—*muwth (mooth)*—is actually used *twice* in this statement and therefore could be rendered "in dying you will die." In short, something died in Adam & Eve the moment they sinned, which led to their eventual physical decease. Theologians refer to this as spiritual death, which doesn't mean that their spirit ceased to exist, but rather that their spirit became dead to God because Adam & Eve lost their spiritual life or eternal life. Their relationship with their Creator was thus short-circuited; it died. This condition was unfortunately passed on to everyone born into this world ever since.

Of course, God does not hold children accountable until they reach the "age of accountability," which refers to the age that youths are held responsible for their sins. Theologians typically place this age at 13 based on the Jewish custom that a child becomes an adult at 13, but the Bible doesn't actually say this. Interestingly, God only held Israelites 20 years-old and older accountable for serious sins of unbelief committed during the Hebrews' desert journey to the Promised Land (Numbers 14:29-30). No doubt the age of accountability varies according to the maturity level of the individual and the severity of the sin in question. In any case, before the age of accountability children are spiritually alive; after the age of accountability they're spiritually dead (Paul implied this in Romans 7:9). Yet all people inevitably sin—assuming they mature—and therefore they spiritually die due to the sin infection passed from Adam.

Because of this condition of spiritual death there's a great wall between God and humanity. It's impossible for unredeemed people to do anything to change this condition and reconcile to the LORD *by their own efforts*. As such, no human-made religion can reconcile people to their Creator and grant forgiveness of sins or eternal life. This explains a statement Jesus made to his disciples when they asked him who could be saved. He responded:

> "**With people it is impossible**, but not with God; for all things are possible with God."
> **Mark 10:27**

Eternal salvation and everything that goes with it—reconciliation with the LORD, the forgiveness of sins and acquisition of eternal life—are only available through God and not human-made religion, including religious "Christianity," which isn't actual Christianity. These wonderful things are available exclusively from God through the gospel, which explains why 'gospel' literally means "good news."

Paul said that God gives "**all men** life" (Acts 17:25). The word 'life' here is the Greek word *zoe (ZOH-ay)*, which in this context refers to the temporal life *(zoe)* that God grants all people and is acquired simply by being born of the perishable seed of Adam. Consequently, everyone born into this world has temporal life *(zoe)*. To receive eternal life *(zoe)* people must be born-again of the imperishable seed of Christ, the second Adam (see 1 John 3:9, 1 Peter 1:23, Romans 5:16-17 and 1 Corinthians 15:45). This is what the gospel of Christ is all about and it's all summed up nicely in the Bible's most famous passage:

> "**For God so loved the world that He gave His one and only Son that whoever believes in him <u>shall not perish</u> but have <u>eternal life</u>.**"
>
> **John 3:16**

This is the gospel in a nutshell. Speaking of which...

The Second Adam Demolishes the Great Wall

Summing up, the "great wall" that separates God and fallen humanity consists of four impenetrable blocks—**1. God's holy character, 2. our debt of sin, 3. slavery to Satan** and **4. spiritual death**—and no amount of human effort, religion or philosophy can bring it down. We can't even get over the wall with God's aid; the barrier *must* be destroyed.

This is precisely what Jesus Christ—the second Adam—did. To explain, consider this little parable: An entomologist lived by some woods where he studied the various insects. There was a huge ant hill of which he was particularly fond. When news came that the nearby road was going to be extended through the woods and it was on a collision course with the ant hill the entomologist longed to save his beloved ants, but it was impossible to communicate the dangers to them. The only way he could do so would be to become an ant!

I'm sure you see the parallel to God's concern for the human race. Yet there's one huge difference: God didn't just become a human being to warn us to repent or perish (Luke 13:1-9), the Creator sacrificed himself for us by dying in our place.

Let's look at the four works the Mighty Christ did that demolished the great wall between God and humanity:

Propitiation. This somewhat intimidating theological term simply means that Yeshua's sacrifice turned away God's wrath by satisfying violated justice. In other words, propitiation appeased the offense to God's holy character and rendered us favorable to the LORD—reconciling the wrongdoer with the affronted. Thus the

Messiah's act of propitiation—his atoning sacrifice—demolished the block of God's offended character. We observe this here:

> **He is the atoning sacrifice** [aka propitiation] **for our sins, and not only for ours but also for the sins of the whole world.**
>
> **1 John 2:2**

Christ is the "atoning sacrifice" for our transgressions. These two words are one word in the Greek: *hilasmos (hil-as-MOSS)*, which means "a propitiation" or "atoning sacrifice." You'll usually see *hilasmos* translated as one or the other in English Bibles. To atone means to make amends or reparations for an offense or a crime. That's what the Messiah did for us. Praise God!

Redemption. This is the work of Christ that **1.** canceled our debt of sin and **2.** freed us from slavery to Satan. In other words, redemption demolished the next two blocks of the great wall that separates God and humanity.

Concerning canceling our debt of sin, when Yeshua was nailed to the huge cross darkness fell upon the land for three hours whereupon Christ bore the sins of the world. It was at this time that the Son was utterly forsaken by the Father (Matthew 27:45-46). The Father perhaps allowed the pitch blackness so that no one could see the horror of what happened to the Son as he was engulfed by divine wrath when the sins of humanity were put on him.

For the first time Christ experienced the aloneness of being wholly separated from the Father & Holy Spirit with the corresponding sense of emptiness and meaninglessness.

Right before he died Jesus cried out a single, potent word, *teleó (tel-AY-o)*, which means "It is finished" or "Paid in full" (Matthew 27:50 & John 19:30). This was the same Greek word stamped on a Roman prisoner's Certificate of Debt when his or her sentence was completed. In other words, the price was paid for our sins and thus *our* Certificate of Debt was essentially stamped "Paid in Full."

Concerning freeing us from satanic slavery, this passage best details our redemption through Christ's sacrifice:

> **For there is one God and one mediator between God and mankind, the man Christ Jesus, ⁶who gave himself as a ransom for all people.**
>
> **1 Timothy 2:5-6**

As noted earlier, to 'redeem' means "to liberate through payment of ransom; to clear of debt through proper payment." We've been liberated from slavery to the kingdom of darkness through the sacrifice of the Creator. Jesus was qualified to do this because **1.** He wasn't himself a slave to Satan since he wasn't born of Adam's seed, but rather God's seed (Luke 1:35); and **2.** He was a *willing* redeemer. You see, a slave doesn't have the clout to order someone to pay for his or her ransom. The liberator had to do so *voluntarily*, which explains why Christ emphasized this (John 10:17-18).

Yet what was his motivation? Love. Love sent the Lord to the cross to cancel our debt of sin and liberate us from slavery to the devil (John 3:16).

Substitutionary death. Whereas propitiation concerns God and appeasing his offended character; and redemption concerns sin and paying our debt of sin, as well as liberating us from Satan's slave market; substitutionary death concerns the penalty of death, which is "the wages of sin" (Romans 6:23). All "substitutionary death" means is that Christ died in our place, the innocent for the guilty, which we observe in this potent verse:

> **But we do see Jesus, who was made lower than the angels for a little while, now crowned with glory and honor because <u>he suffered death</u>, so that by the grace of God <u>he might taste death for everyone</u>.**
>
> **Hebrews 2:9**

By dying in our place, Christ removed the barrier of spiritual death and all that goes with it—being dead to God, the loss of eternal life, physical death and, ultimately, the dreaded second death (Revelation 20:11-15).

Because death is the wages of sin, substitutionary animal sacrifice was implemented immediately by God to reestablish fellowship after Adam & Eve's fall. Thus an innocent animal had to die when the LORD killed a mammal to cover their nakedness (Genesis 3:21). This established the principle that a guiltless substitute had to perish in order for sin to be forgiven or, at least, temporarily covered.

This blood sacrifice at the beginning of human history was prototypical and therefore cultures in ensuing generations utilized the concept, some staying close to the pattern and others devolving into perverse variations.

It's interesting to observe in Scripture how substitutionary sacrifice applied to **1.** one lamb for one person (Genesis 4:4 & Leviticus 4:32), **2.** one lamb for one family (Exodus 12:3-14), **3.** one lamb (or bull) for a nation (Leviticus 16) and **4.** one "lamb" for the world, which refers to Christ and explains why John the Baptist exclaimed: "Look, the Lamb of God, who takes away the sin of the world!" (John 1:29). The Lord's great sacrifice fulfilled the need for one lamb for one person, one lamb for one family and one lamb for one nation.

It was no coincidence, by the way, that Christ's crucifixion took place on the Day of Passover because he was the world's Passover lamb. Just as the blood of a lamb placed on the doorframes of the homes of the Hebrews would allow the death angel to "pass over" their abodes (Exodus 12:7,12-13), so the blood of Christ sprinkled on the doorposts of our hearts prompts God to "pass over" us, as far as the damning judgment of eternal death goes.

I want to stress again the Lord's motivation for dying for us. Jesus said, "Greater love has no one than this: to lay down one's life for one's friends" (John 15:13). Christ died in our place because **He loved us**!

While the Messiah's propitiation, redemption and substitutionary death demolished the four blocks of the great wall which alienated God from humanity, a final work was necessary to unite us by reestablishing *relationship*:

Reconciliation. To 'reconcile' means to change from a state of enmity to friendship. Reconciliation therefore neutralized hostility between God and humanity and this explains something Paul said:

> **Once you were alienated from God and were enemies in your minds because of your evil behavior. ²² But now he has <u>reconciled you by Christ's physical body through death</u> to present you holy in his sight, without blemish and free from accusation— ²³ <u>if</u> you continue in your faith, established and firm, and do not move from the hope held out in the gospel.**
>
>

Colossians 1:21-23

At its core the gospel is about reconciling to our Creator, which is why the "good news" is also referred to as "the message of reconciliation":

> **All this is from God, who reconciled us to himself through Christ and gave us the ministry of reconciliation: ¹⁹ that God was reconciling the world to himself in Christ, not counting people's sins against them. And he has committed to us <u>the message of reconciliation</u>. ²⁰ We are therefore Christ's ambassadors, as though God were making his appeal through us. We implore you on Christ's behalf: Be reconciled to God.**
>
>

2 Corinthians 5:18-20

As pointed out in **Chapter 3**, the conditions for reconciling with God are repentance and faith (Acts 20:21). Repentance seems to have a negative connotation today, but it simply means to change your mind for the positive, which therefore changes your direction. It means turning from rebellion to compliance, from dark to light, from destructivity to productivity. While it's possible to repent and not believe, it's not possible to *truly* believe and not repent.

A person's embracing of the message of reconciliation is the first stage of what Christ called the "**restoration of all things**," which refers to the liberation of the Earth and all creation from Satan's dominion and the bondage to decay (i.e. entropy). Let's look at that…

Chapter 13

The Restoration of All Things

Peter spoke of "the period of **restoration of all things**" when preaching to a crowd after the miraculous healing of a lame beggar (Acts 3:21 NASB). God's great restoration of creation takes place in four stages:

1. **Spiritual rebirth of people** who accept the gospel.
2. **The redemption of our bodies**, which is when we'll receive glorified bodies and (primarily) takes place at the Rapture.
3. **Christ's millennial reign on Earth** after the seven-year Tribulation.
4. **The establishment of the new Heavens and new Earth**, the eternal home of righteousness.

Let's go over each stage and the scriptural support for each.

STAGE ONE: Spiritual Regeneration through the Gospel

The Messiah noted the restoration of all things here:

> **Jesus said to them, "Truly I tell you, at <u>the renewal of all things</u>, when the Son of Man sits on his glorious throne, you who have followed me will also sit on twelve thrones, judging the twelve tribes of Israel."**
>
> **Matthew 19:28**

The Greek word for 'renewal' in this verse is *paliggenesia (pal-ing-hen-es-EE-ah)*, which means "new birth, regeneration or renewal." It's only used twice in Scripture. The other occasion is Titus 3:5, where it refers to the ***regeneration of the human spirit***. This occurs, of course, when a believer accepts the gospel through repentance and faith (John 3:3,6 & Acts 20:21).

Spiritual regeneration is **the first stage** of God's "renewal of all things." You see, the restoration of all things is jump-started in our current age through the spiritual rebirth of believers. When a person experiences spiritual regeneration they are transferred from the dominion of Satan to the kingdom of God (Acts 26:18). In terms of physical appearance it doesn't look like anything has changed, although their new attitude about life undoubtedly changes their demeanor. This is because, spiritually, they've swapped kingdoms and are **no longer slaves to Satan**, which naturally has an impact on one's disposition.

Think about it in terms of those sci-fi flicks based on Jack Finney's book *The Body Snatchers*; the first two were called *Invasion of the Body Snatchers*. The same basic principle is at play except that the extraterrestrials are wholly good because they're God—Father, Son & Holy Spirit—who want to snatch people from Satan's dominion. The way they do this is through inward regeneration.

STAGE TWO: The Rapture

Spiritual rebirth culminates with Christ's return for His Church, which is **the second stage** of the restoration of all things. All believers are promised this blessing providing they persevere in faith.[45] This stage concerns Jesus' return for his Church where **believers' bodies are finally redeemed**:

> We know that <u>the whole creation has been groaning as in the pains of childbirth right up to the present time</u>. ²³ Not only so, but we ourselves, who have the firstfruits of the Spirit, groan inwardly as we wait eagerly for our adoption to sonship, <u>the redemption of our bodies</u>.
> **Romans 8:22-23**

The "redemption of our bodies" occurs when Christ snatches up His Church, as detailed in 1 Thessalonians 4:13-18. When this Rapture takes place, living believers will be translated to Heaven with new, glorified bodies while believers who physically died previously will be bodily resurrected with the same kinds of awesome bodies. How awesome will these bodies be? The Bible describes them as **imperishable**, **glorified**, **powerful** and **spiritual** in nature (1 Corinthians 15:42-44). Chew on that.

While some claim that the word 'Rapture' isn't biblical, it is. It refers to a phrase used in the main passage that details this event:

> After that, we who are still alive and are left will be <u>caught up</u> together with them in the clouds to meet the Lord in the air. And so we will be with the Lord forever.
> **1 Thessalonians 4:17**

---

[45] See Colossians 1:22-23 for verification. This is just common sense. After all, if it takes faith to be saved, a person can no longer be saved if they give-up at some point and no longer *believe*. We'll look at this issue in more detail in **Chapter 20** (in the section *The Enemy WILL Attack these God-Given Blessings*).

'Caught up' in the Greek is *harpazó (har-PAD-zoh)*, which means to "snatch up" or "obtain by robbery." It's translated in Latin as "rapio" in the Vulgate, which is where we get the English "Rapture." With this understanding, when the Bridegroom, Jesus, comes for His bride, the Church, He's going to obtain us by **robbing us off the Earth**!

STAGE THREE: Christ's Millennial Reign on Earth

The restoration of all things continues after the seven-year Tribulation when Christ returns to Earth and establishes his millennial kingdom, which is what Jesus was specifically referring to in Matthew 19:28 (quoted above). This is **the third stage** of the restoration of all things at which time Old Testament saints will be resurrected while Tribulation martyrs will be bodily resurrected. Both will receive their immortal bodies at this juncture. As for the mortal humans Christ allows to enter the Millennium after The Judgement of Living Nations (aka The Sheep and Goat Judgment—Matthew 25:31-46), their lifespans will return to the lengthy lifespans of people before the flood of Genesis 6.

Glorified believers will be priests of God and will reign with Christ during the Millennium. Such believers will not be able to propagate because, as Jesus taught, "they will neither marry nor be given in marriage… for they are like the angels" (Luke 20:34-36). This doesn't mean, by the way, that we'll *be* angels; simply that we'll be *like* angels in the sense of not marrying and that we'll attain intrinsic immortality, which we don't currently possess (Romans 2:7 & 2 Timothy 1:10).

Isaiah 11:6-9 shows what life will be like during the Millennium: Carnivorous animals will become herbivorous and therefore wolves will live with lambs and leopards will lie together with goats; calves and lions will 'hang out' and be led by little children. Cows and bears will feed together and formerly carnivorous beasts, like the lion, will eat straw like an ox. Furthermore, children will play by the cobra's den and the viper's nest without fear because poisonous creatures will no longer be poisonous.

At the end of the Millennium Satan is released and immediately deceives the nations, inciting a mass attack on the righteous government of Christ in Jerusalem. This rebellion is easily defeated and the devil is cast into the lake of fire forever. Revelation 20:1-10 details these events.

God's Purpose for the Millennium

The Millennium is basically a transitional phase between this present evil age (Galatians 1:4) and the eternal righteous age-to-come (Luke 18:29-30). But what exactly is God's purpose for the Millennium? It's simple when you think about it:

The Millennium is the LORD's irrefutable proof to humanity that the religion of secular humanism is a lie. As you may or may not know, secular humanism is atheistic in nature and therefore anti-God. To those who embrace this godless religion there's no sin problem because there's no God for whom to sin against. To them, the problem of evil isn't humanity's sin nature and the corresponding alienation from our Creator, but rather a negative environment. As such, they believe evil, crime, poverty, war and other ailments will largely be eradicated when the right government is in place and every person is provided an education, a decent job, a nice living environment, protection from crime, and so on. While these things are good, they don't actually remedy the sin problem or reconcile people to their Creator. They cannot set us free from Satan's dominion and the slavery thereof. After all, a white collar man living in a rich suburb is still perfectly able to commit fraud due to a greedy heart, not to mention be a drunkard, drug addict, wife-beater, slanderer, hypocrite, adulterer, murderer, blowhard, oppressor, porn addict or practicing homosexual.

In the Millennium the LORD is going to provide the perfect government and environment for nations of mortals. It will be a veritable worldwide utopia. Since Jesus will be the King over all the Earth and his assistants will be glorified believers who don't have a sin nature there will be zero corruption in the government (imagine that!). Yet, as the population increases over the course of the thousand years, many of the offspring of the original "sheep"—the mortals whom Christ allows to enter into the Millennium (Matthew 25:31-46)—will just go through the motions of being faithful to the Lord while their hearts aren't in it. This is legalism—putting on the airs of godliness without the heart of godliness. Because legalism is an "outward job" it's decidedly inauthentic. As such, when the devil is unleashed at the end of the thousand years these covert rebels will naturally embrace the lies of the kingdom of darkness and unite for war in a harebrained attempt to take over the completely righteous government of Christ! (This shows that Satan is thoroughly incorrigible; he never learns from his mistakes).

Of course the rebellion is quickly quelled and, after the Great White Throne Judgment, the eternal age of the new Heavens and new Earth will manifest (Revelation 20:9-15 & Revelation 21-22).

So the Millennium is the Most High's eternal showcase in disproving the religion of secular humanism.

STAGE FOUR: The Eternal New Heavens and New Earth

As wonderful as the thousand-year reign of Christ will be, it's just another stage in the "restoration of all things." **The fourth and final stage** takes place when God wholly renovates the Earth & Universe and the heavenly city, the new Jerusalem, comes "down out of heaven from God" to rest on the new Earth (Revelation 21:1-4). Thus the renewal of all things climaxes with the renewing of the Earth & Universe. This is the new Heavens and new Earth, the eternal "home of righteousness" (2 Peter 3:13).

The Greek word for 'restoration' in the phrase "the final restoration of all things" is *apokatastasis (ah-pok-ah-TAS-tah-sis)*, which appears only once in the Bible:

> **For he** [Jesus] **must remain in heaven until the time for <u>the final restoration</u>** *(apokatastasis)* **<u>of all things</u>, as God promised long ago through his holy prophets.**
>
> **Acts 3:21**

The root word for *apokatastasis* is *apokathistémi (ah-pok-ath-IS-tay-mee)*, which means "to set up again" and "restore to its original position or condition." That's what the "restoration of all things" is about—**restoring the Earth and Universe to its original condition before the fall, which is the way God originally intended it to be**.

Creation Itself "Waits in Eager Expectation"

The Bible stresses that creation itself *yearns* for the redemption provided in the restoration of all things:

> **For <u>the creation</u> waits <u>in eager expectation</u> for the children of God to be revealed.**
> **Romans 8:19**

What does creation "wait in eager expectation" for? Answer: The children of God to be revealed, which is part of the restoration of all things, as detailed earlier.

What exactly is "the creation" in this verse? It refers to the Earth and Universe and all living things thereof, including the animal kingdom and even the plant kingdom. They will all be partakers in this redemption of the physical Universe. Why else would all creation "wait in eager expectation" for this great restoration if they were not included in it? Of course, animals and trees aren't literally yearning for this renewal, but they yearn for it in a figurative sense because *they're included in it*.

Consider something interesting, noted by David Reagan: When the high priest sprinkled animal blood on the cover of the Ark of the Covenant once a year to atone for the sins of the Hebrews, this blood covered God's Law, which was represented in the Ark via the tablets of the Ten Commandments. This ritual resulted in God's mercy year to year, covering the Israelites' sins. But the blood of animals could only temporarily cover sin, not cleanse it away forever (Hebrews 10:1-4).

The good news is that Jesus Christ, who is the believer's High Priest, offered his *own* blood when he went to the Most Holy Place in Heaven, not merely the blood of animals (Hebrews 9:23-28). Reagan points out that Leviticus 16:15 shows the high priest sprinkling blood *on the ground in front of the Ark* after sprinkling it on the cover. At the time, the Ark was housed in the tent Tabernacle and so the blood was literally poured **on the ground**. Why is this significant? Because the entire ceremony pointed to Christ's blood atonement in Heaven and the high priest didn't just sprinkle blood on the lid of the Ark for the redemption of humanity, but also on the ground for the restoration of all physical creation.

So **"the final restoration of all things"** (Acts 3:21) refers to **the LORD** *restoring everything in creation to the condition it was originally intended*. The Greek word for 'all things' is *pas (pass)*, which means "all, the whole, every kind of." So God is going to restore *all* creation to its initial condition, as He originally intended it to be before Satan duped Adam & Eve and usurped power-of-attorney over physical creation. Revelation 21:5 adds an interesting insight in that God will be "making everything new" and not making new things. There's a difference.

Of course, the LORD *won't* restore those condemned to the lake of fire. This includes damned human beings, the devil & his filthy angels or anything else cast into the lake of fire, such as death and Hades (Revelation 20:10-15 & Matthew 25:41). The lake of fire is basically God's garbage dump. The good news of the gospel of Christ is all about escaping this eternal condemnation and partaking of "the restoration of all things."

Needless to say, make sure YOU are a partaker and do everything in your power to get those linked to you to be partakers as well. As "Christ's ambassador," YOU are a "minister of reconciliation" called to share the "message of reconciliation" (2 Corinthians 5:18-20).

Here's a diagram of the restoration of all things to help you visualize the four stages:

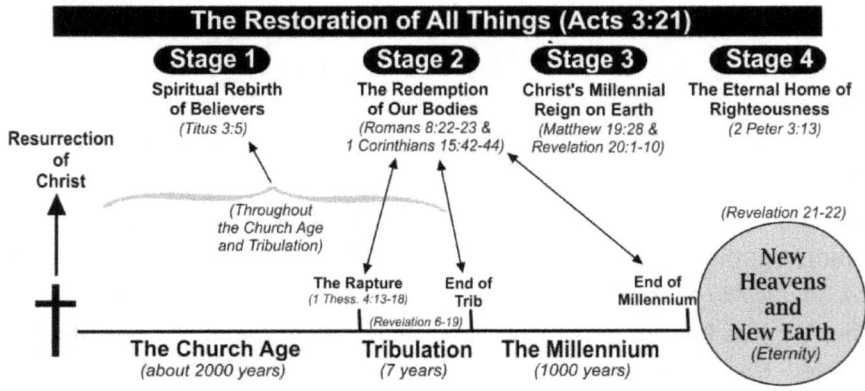

Chapter 14

The DEFEAT of Satan & his Losers

The most important thing you need to understand about the Enemy and his demonic minions is that **they're a defeated foe**. They're *stripped* of their authority and power as far as regenerated believers are concerned:

> **And <u>having disarmed the powers and authorities</u>, he** [Christ] **made a public spectacle of them, <u>triumphing over them</u> by the cross.**
> **Colossians 2:15**

The "powers and authorities" refer to Satan and his sheeple demons. The Bible calls the devil "the god of this world," but **1.** his reign is a temporary one and **2.** he's been "disarmed" for all those *in* Christ. To 'disarm' means to strip or divest. As such, the devil & his filthy angels have been *stripped*—deprived of their property, rights and power for all those who come to Christ. In other words, the enemy has been dispossessed!

The very reason Jesus came to this lost and dying world was to destroy the devil's reign:

> **The reason the Son of God appeared was to destroy the devil's work.**
> **1 John 3:8**

This great mission started with the Messiah's birth, earthly ministry, substitutionary death & resurrection and will culminate with the devil & his filthy angels being cast into the lake of fire (Revelation 20:10 & Matthew 25:41).

How exactly did the Mighty Yeshua "disarm" the devil & his minions and "triumph over them" by his crucifixion and resurrection? By suffering God's wrath in our place, which is what 'substitutionary death' means—the innocent dying for the guilty in order to set them free from their debt of sin and their corresponding bondage to the kingdom of darkness. But—and this is an important "but"—people have to willingly be born-again of the seed of Christ, which is spiritual rebirth (John 3:3,6, Titus 3:5, 1 John 3:9 & 1 Peter 1:23). This regeneration comes through the keys of **repentance** and **faith** (Acts 20:21).

What if You *Don't* Believe?

If you don't have faith—belief—then continue to seek it out. Those who seek shall find (Jeremiah 29:13 & Matthew 7:7). "Come near to God and he'll come near to you" (James 4:8). It's an axiom!

Let me illustrate from my own life: During my adolescence I heard the gospel from a few people and I also collected several tracts that presented the good news of Christ. I don't know how, but I instinctively knew I needed some kind of rebirth—a fresh start in life—and so I prayed the salvation prayer at the end of those tracts on a few separate occasions during those dark years. Nothing happened, however, because I simply didn't have the faith at the time. Simply put, I didn't **believe**... *yet*.

So I carried on in my lost state, but I still genuinely sought the truth—the way it really is—even though some paths ended up being dead ends (like psychology, astrology, etc.). But, years later when I was 20, I was working at a fitness center cleaning the women's shower room well after midnight when something 'clicked' in my mind and I saw the light. All I knew was: "I was blind but now I see!" (John 9:25). I was instantaneously saved and drove home that late night with an amazing sense of peace. The next morning I confessed Christ to my mother and sister with a spirit of newfound joy. The rest is His-story. I've continued to grow in faith as I sought the LORD and the truth, i.e. reality—the way it really is.

Satan & his Loser Angels are Disarmed and Defeated!

For the spiritually reborn believer, the devil & his filthy spirits are disarmed because we're born of the seed[46] of Christ by the Holy Spirit. More than that, God lives in us through the indwelling Spirit and so we are **temples of God** (1 Corinthians 6:19).

This is the mind-blowing "mystery" of the gospel—"Christ **in you**, the hope of glory" (Colossians 1:27). How is Christ in us? Through spiritual rebirth wherein we're "created to be *like* God in true righteousness" (Ephesians 4:22-24) and also through the indwelling Spirit of Christ (Romans 8:9). The kingdom of darkness is disarmed in the lives of all those in Christ; they're *stripped* of all their authority and power. Even more, those born of the Mighty Conqueror have authority and power over all wicked spirits. **Authority means the right to rule whereas power means the ability to rule.** And we have both over the devil & his filthy minions.

We have to get away from this idea that the devil & his loser underlings are these uber-scary creatures. This is only so for the unbeliever who's subject to them. For *believers* born of the seed of the Mighty Christ by the power of the Holy Spirit all filthy spirits have been stripped of their authority and power! Remember: They're spiritual

---

[46] 'Seed' in 1 John 3:9 is the Greek word for sperm; in 1 Peter 1:23 it's *spora (spor-AH)*.

doofuses who foolishly rebelled against the Almighty and lost their glorious place in Heaven and all the blessings thereof. How smart can they possibly be? Not very. Don't be scared of 'em! The truth is, **they're scared of believers who know and walk in their authority and power**. So it's of the utmost importance that you understand who you are in Christ—your position, authority and power. Know who you are and walk like it, talk like it! You'll send the Enemy and his smelly cronies fleeing from you in terror; it's true (James 4:7). We'll look at this more as we progress.

It's of paramount importance that you grasp these truths if you want to walk free of the harassment of evil spirits. This doesn't mean that they won't attack you but, when they do, you are guaranteed the victory as you "fight the good fight faith" (1 Timothy 6:12). If there's a fight to faith there are enemies to faith. You'll never outgrow spiritual warfare; you must simply learn to fight!

'Spiritual warfare,' by the way, simply means to defeat satanic attacks through the spiritual weapons God has provided us. For details see **Chapter 19** and **20**.

Chapter 15

Demons vs. Christ — No Contest!

As with last chapter, I want to drive home a simple but powerful point in this brief chapter. We saw in **Chapter 9** that demons are evil spirits—malevolent spirits—who are also described as unclean or impure spirits. In other words, they're *filthy* spirits, the express opposite of the Holy (absolutely pure) Spirit.

Whether people believe in evil spirits or not, they're viewed as uber-scary beings in our culture and are fittingly the adversaries in many horror novels and flicks. This includes the devil, since he's the principle evil spirit. The *Exorcist* franchise is a good example (not that I'm a fan of those films, although I watched the first one decades ago). With this understanding, did you know that **demons are actually afraid of Jesus Christ**? Observe in this passage how evil spirits respond to the Messiah:

> **They** [Jesus & the disciples] **sailed to the region of the Gerasenes** *(JAIR-ah-seens)*, **which is across the lake from Galilee.** ²⁷ **When Jesus stepped ashore, he was met by a demon-possessed man from the town. For a long time this man had not worn clothes or lived in a house, but had lived in the tombs.** ²⁸ <u>**When he saw Jesus, he cried out and fell at his feet, shouting at the top of his voice,**</u> **"What do you want with me, Jesus, Son of the Most High God?** <u>**I beg you, don't torture me!**</u>**"...**
> ³⁰ **Jesus asked him, "What is your name?"**
> **"Legion," he replied, because many demons had gone into him.** ³¹ **And** <u>**they begged Jesus repeatedly not to order them to go into the Abyss.**</u>
> **Luke 8:26-28,30-31**

As you can see, these demons literally **cry out and beg Christ not to torture them, pleading with Him repeatedly not to order them to go into the Abyss**. "The Abyss" is the furnace-like pit where the most defiant evil spirits are imprisoned (Revelation 9:1-3 & 20:1-3) and **Yeshua had the authority to send these demons there**. (See **Chapter 10** for *why* some rebellious spirits were imprisoned there).

What's so great about the fact that demons are afraid of Jesus Christ? Simple: Our culture holds demonic spirts as the epitome of what is scary and dreadful and yet we observe them in the Bible **shrieking in horror at the mere sight of the Mighty Christ**. More than that, **they literally *beg Him* not to torture them and throw their filthy hind ends into the Abyss**!

As stressed in **Chapter 7** and **8**, we've got to get away from this idea that Jesus Christ was some effeminate milksop walking around in a white dress during his earthly ministry, as if he was some impotent smiley guy. Sure, he walked in love and was gentle and humble (Matthew 11:28-30), but this doesn't negate that **He was also**

courageous, astonishing, amazing, authoritative and frightening. The four Gospels offer thorough evidence of this.[47]

Christ's love walk was a balance between **gentle love** and **tough love**, yet the only side of Jesus that's stressed in our culture is the mild and gentle. What about the fortitude it took to boldly confront the corrupt religious leaders of Israel, which infuriated them to the point of wanting to murder him (Luke 11:37-54)? What about the passion and fierceness it took to clear the Temple of the greedy and ungodly? Jesus cracked a whip, yelled, scattered coins, overturned tables and drove all the fools & animals out. No one even dared attempt to stop him; in fact, the religious leaders responded with **fear** and the bystanders with **amazement** (Mark 11:15-18). Are these the actions of a milksop? Would a weak doormat inspire fear or amazement and provoke arrogant leaders to plot murder? Of course not. Although this type of extreme behavior was not the norm, **the incident appears in all four Gospel accounts**. In other words, this is clearly a side of the Messiah our heavenly Father wants us to grasp.

If you're a believer and ever deal with a situation involving demonic spirits, just remember that **the very name of Jesus Christ provokes them to shriek in horror and beg for mercy**! This explains something James pointed out:

> **You say you have faith, for you believe that there is one God. Good for you! Even the demons believe this, <u>and they tremble in terror</u>.**
> **James 2:19** (NLT)

Speaking of dealing with situations that involve evils spirts, let's look at...

---

[47] See, for example, Matthew 7:28-29, 14:26, Mark 1:27, 2:10-12, 4:37-41, 7:37, Luke 5:8-11, 7:14-16, 20:20-26, 20:40 and John 2:13-17.

Chapter 16

Exorcism and the Believer's Authority

I'd like to take a different approach with this chapter by examining a relatively recent film based on a true story. We'll flesh out its biblical themes and use it as a bridge to *our* dealings with cases of demonic oppression or possession.

The Exorcism of Anneliese Michel

Released in 2005, *The Exorcism of Emily Rose* was loosely based on the real story of a 23 year-old German girl, Anneliese Michel, who died while a priest was trying to exorcize her of demons in the late 70s. He was then put on trial for neglectful homicide.

In the movie, Erin Bruner (Laura Linney) is the agnostic lawyer who defends the priest (Tom Wilkinson), while the prosecutor (Campbell Scott) is a non-Catholic believer. I'm sure you see the conundrums of the situation: How can an agnostic defend a minister who performs a supernatural operation that ends in the death of a young woman? How can a genuine believer prosecute another believer who was simply fulfilling his calling and performing a service for a congregant?

The prosecution argues that the woman was physically & mentally ill with symptoms of epilepsy, psychosis and schizophrenia; and that the attempted exorcism was just a bunch of witch doctor hooey. The defense, on the other hand, argues that such physical/mental manifestations were the *result of* diabolical spiritual possession. In other words, the girl's possession produced the symptoms of epilepsy, psychosis and schizophrenia. It's the proverbial chicken or egg question.

Observations

In the Bible, didn't Jesus deliver people from demons who *induced* insanity, deafness, muteness and infirmity? See Mark 5:1-20, 9:17-29 and Luke 13:10-16. It's clear from the Scriptural evidence that being possessed (or oppressed) by an evil spirit can induce mental or physical ailments. Such demons are "spirits of infirmities," which we'll address momentarily.

Another point of the defense in the movie is that a powerful drug that Emily was prescribed prevented the exorcism from being successful because it physiologically trapped her in a mode that was resistant to exorcism and the corresponding freedom.

All of this provokes many questions: How many people in our mental institutions are being drugged up and essentially imprisoned for the rest of their lives when what they really need is exorcized of dark spiritual entities that have possessed them to one degree or another? Don't get me wrong here, I'm not against these kinds of asylums and realize that we, as a society, are just doing what we have to for such ailing people; that is, what we can.

Yet, what if someone of Jesus Christ' stature were around, someone who had the authority, faith and courage to rebuke demons and send them fleeing with their tails between their legs, so to speak? The first chapter of the gospel of Mark shows the Messiah exorcizing demons from numerous people and this is merely one chapter of the New Testament! (See verses 25-26, 34 and 39).

A Real-Life Experience with Demonic Possession

I know of one person who was seriously mentally ill all her life but the best professionals medical science had to offer couldn't deliver her. The best they could do was sedate her, try this or that (including shock treatments) and help her cope. Some of this is good to an extent, but *they could not set her free*. She lived and died with this severe illness. I'm convinced that these symptoms were the result of some type of demonic possession/oppression. Others who were close to the situation have drawn the same conclusion. The signs pointed to a *partial* possession, which we'll look at shortly. If only I knew then what I know now and was the person I am now, I would have exorcized her of this spiritual subjugation without a second thought, as long as she was willing (which is necessary since God will never heal or deliver people against their will).

Am I suggesting that we should let loose a bunch of religious kooks into our mental institutions to supposedly exorcize the severely ill of their (very possible) literal demons? No, but *if* some people show evidence of the power and boldness Jesus Christ walked in, shouldn't we? Didn't Jesus come to "set the captives free," "heal the sick and brokenhearted" and "release the prisoners from the darkness"? (See Luke 4:16-21 and Isaiah 42:5-9).

The fact that so few believers are walking in this authority, power, faith and boldness is a shame to the modern Church in general. It's also testimony to the powerless nature of so many counterfeit sects and "believers" who "have a form of godliness but deny its power" (2 Timothy 3:1-5). Not that all the believers within these camps are counterfeits, not at all. But their leaders are ignorant, disingenuous or spiritually blind. And didn't Jesus say, "If a blind man follows a blind man they will *both* fall into a pit"? (Matthew 15:14).

One of the purposes of this book is to reveal the reality of dark spiritual entities, how their attacks manifest, and how to effectively combat them by faith.

Further Commentary on the Film

The Exorcism of Emily Rose works beyond the courtroom drama where the theological questions are hammered and tested; it works as a simple horror film, based on a true story. The movie successfully shows the reality of dark spiritual malevolence. It drives home the reality of unseen menace and literally scares the hell out of the viewer, but only unbelievers and immature Christians. Strong believers, by contrast, laugh at evil spirits and simply command 'em to shut up, like Christ did (more on this momentarily). You must understand that believers have authority over evil spirits and thus we have no reason to fear them (Luke 10:18-20). I don't.

And yet, thankfully, the film is somehow affirming of life, love, hope and faith.

I only have one theological criticism introduced late in the story, the idea that Emily only had one of two options: To physically perish and go home to be with the Lord or stay in the body and suffer further as a supposed testimony to the world of the reality of the spirit realm and the dark powers thereof. This implies that God allowed Emily's possession for the purpose of showing the world the unseen truth. The obvious problem with this is that Jesus was Immanuel, aka "God with us," and He never hesitated to exorcize demons from the afflicted. In other words, **it's *always* God's will to deliver the demon-possessed, as long as the person wants free**. Such deliverances are not only a testimony to the realm of the spirit, but of the victory of light over darkness.

Although I wouldn't call the film a masterpiece it's effective in many ways. It provokes important questions: How many of our mentally ill—perpetually drugged-up and confined—are suffering from demonic possession? The drugs and confinement can only sedate them and help them cope (which helps those nearest them, of course); they *cannot* set them free. Only exorcism can do that, which is ***deliverance***.

The Believer's Authority

Where is the church of Jesus Christ, the "called-out" ones who are called out of the darkness of this world? Why is the church so inert and seemingly powerless when it comes to dealing with victims of demonic possession or oppression? I know there are a few "radicals" or "extremists" who function in this capacity, but what of the general body of Christ? I'm not talking about young, immature or erratic Christians, but rather seasoned *believers* who know the Lord & His Word and function in the body as deacons, elders, praise & worship warriors, teachers, pastors and prophets.

Let's not forget the incredible authority Jesus gave believers:

> **"I saw Satan fall like lightning from heaven. [19] <u>I have given you authority to trample on snakes and scorpions and to overcome all the power of the enemy</u>; nothing will harm you. [20] However do not rejoice that <u>the spirits submit to you</u>, but rejoice that your names are written in heaven."**
>
> **Luke 10:18-20**

"Snakes and scorpions" are figurative of the devil and demonic spirits. Jesus gave his disciples authority to trample them under their feet, that is, overcome their power. Hence, filthy spirits *had* to submit to them and the disciples were understandably elated (see verse 17). They delivered people from demonic oppression and possession; they healed the sick and brokenhearted; they set the captives free *because they had the authority and power to do so*. Authority is the right to rule whereas power is the ability to rule.

If Jesus' disciples—who weren't even spiritually regenerated at the time—had authority to overcome the powers of darkness, how much more so Christians who have been spiritually *born* of the imperishable seed of Christ?

Get a hold of this fact: If you're a believer **YOU have authority over the kingdom of darkness! All the spiritual forces of evil are under your feet! They don't have the authority to overcome you;** *you* **have the authority to overcome them!**

As stressed in **Chapter 4**, words have the power of life and death (Proverbs 18:21), so make this powerful positive confession:

I [state your name] ***have the authority to trample on snakes and scorpions and to overcome all the power of the devil and his wicked angels. Nothing will harm me. I have the victory in Jesus Christ — Hallelujah!!***

Make Biblical statements like this your regular confession. Speak them with fervor! Never speak disempowering words of doubt, defeat, fear or grumbling. Cast such things off on the LORD in prayer, which is venting (Psalm 55:22 & 1 Peter 5:7). When you spend quality time praising, adoring and communing with the Most High the very light of his presence will squelch emotional waste like doubt, fear and worry. Do this regularly. God is the Fountain of Life and in his light we see light (Psalm 36:9); darkness naturally vanishes!

Jesus Christ is the Genuine "Lion" while Satan is a Counterfeit

The devil may prowl around like a roaring lion trying to frighten people immobile with his intimidating roar, but for the believer who walks in faith he's a toothless, clawless, sinew-less lion. More than that, the Bible describes Jesus Christ as the *genuine* Lion of Judah. In other words, Jesus is the real deal, while the devil is just a counterfeit—a fake—who prowls around *like* a roaring lion. Oh, sure, he can attack since he's "the god of this world" and we're invading his turf, but the Bible says that all we have to do is "submit to God and resist the devil" "standing firm in the faith" and the enemy will literally "flee" from us (James 4:7 & 1 Peter 5:8-10).

This is what the apostle Paul called fighting "the good fight of faith" (1 Timothy 6:12). When we stand in faith with our spiritual armor on and swing our spiritual swords the forces of evil have no recourse but to "flee." One minister I heard said the imagery in the original language paints the picture of a dog running away with his tail between his legs— *"Yipe, yipe, yipe yipe!!"* Picture that the next time you take a stand in faith against the enemy—including exorcisms—and have yourself a knee-slapping victorious laugh.

Walking in the Amazing Authority of Jesus Christ

As *The Exorcism of Emily Rose* illustrates, we live in a generation that idolizes reason and science above all. These are the only criteria for determining reality to the unspiritual man, and understandably so. Thus anyone who looks to the Holy Scriptures for truth and has the audacity to act accordingly is viewed with disdain and ridicule. Which explains why the church is so powerless and timid when it comes to dealing with demonic possession or oppression: **We fear the scorn of the world.**

This reminds me of a Pentecostal pastor who told me about a prophet he had at his church for a series of services. The prophet ministered to the people and apparently dealt with a couple cases of demonic oppression or possession. The pastor said he was uncomfortable with the man's ministry because it was sometimes awkward and even shocking. But, let me tell you, dealing with filthy spirits can get ugly! Yelling, vomiting, screaming, wiggling on the floor, etc. come with the territory. We'll look at examples from the Scriptures in a moment. The pastor said that the experience made him "gun shy" of demonic deliverance and everything that goes with it. Unfortunately, he threw the baby out with the proverbial bathwater because his church had the most sterile atmosphere of any I've experienced, and it was "Pentecostal"!

I realize we have to "become all things to all people that by all possible means we might save some" (1 Corinthians 9:22). Hence, we have to "locate" where people are and act accordingly, otherwise we'll scare 'em off with things they simply can't handle, at least not presently. We need to do this to reach people, but let's not do it to the extent that we become as spiritually powerless as the world. We are the "light of the world" (Matthew 5:14), meaning that the Church is the light that inspires those lost in the darkness of this world. Those in the darkness "who have ears to hear and eyes to see" will naturally be drawn to the light and ultimately delivered; and the closer they get to *The* Light the freer they'll be (John 8:12,31-32). This is the way it's supposed to be.

But something's wrong when the church allows the darkness of the world to squelch our light to the point that we're impotent and ineffective, all because we fear the world's contempt and ridicule! Needless to say, this is an example of allowing the world to mold us into its form; something the Bible instructs us *not* to do (Romans 12:2).

One of the things that drew people to the Mighty Christ was the genuine authority he walked in, which shouldn't be confused with pompous authoritarianism. This made his ministry—his service—effective, including demonic deliverance. Observe:

> They went to Capernaum, and when the Sabbath came, Jesus went into the synagogue and began to teach. <u>²² The people were amazed at his teaching because he taught them as one who had authority</u>, not as the teachers of the law. ²³ Just then a man in their synagogue who was possessed by an evil spirit cried out, ²⁴ "What do you want with us, Jesus of Nazareth? Have you come to destroy us? I know who you are – the Holy One of God!"
> <u>²⁵ "Be quiet!" said Jesus sternly. "Come out of him!"</u> ²⁶ <u>The evil spirit shook the man violently and came out of him with a shriek</u>.
> ²⁷ The people were all so <u>amazed</u> that they asked each other, "What is this? A new teaching – and <u>with authority! He even gives orders to evil spirits and they obey him</u>." ²⁸ News about him spread quickly over the whole region of Galilee.
> **Mark 1:21-28**

Verse 22 shows that the people were *amazed* at the aura of authority Jesus displayed merely with his public teaching. This was something the religious leaders of that day didn't have, like the Pharisees and the Sadducees. The people were even more amazed when he proceeded to **command evil spirits to shut up and come out of people**, as shown in verse 27. Unsurprisingly, news then spread about him throughout the region (verse 28).

Speaking of commanding demons to shut up, Christ typically did this when encountering possessed people (Mark 1:24-25 & Luke 4:35,41). Why? Because evil spirits are liars who have ages of experience duping even the brightest of people. In light of this, never talk with demons; just tell 'em to shut up and exorcize the individual, presuming the person is willing.

A pastor I know testified of his first encounter with a demon-possessed man. The wicked spirit started a conversation with him that went on for a couple of hours (!) whereupon the pastor's head was spinning, so to speak. Then a seasoned fellow-minister, who just happened to be visiting from out of state, entered the room and immediately discerned what has happening. He didn't talk with the foul spirit at all, but simply said *"loose"* and that was the end of it.

Rise Up and Walk in Your Authority!

Unlike 1st century Israel where Christ ministered, I realize most reading this live in irreligious cultures of the post-Christian Western world (or, at least, Western-influenced). As such, we have to be careful how we minister and make sure we're led of the Holy Spirit. Regardless, you can be sure that if we boldly rise up and walk in our authority and people start getting miraculously healed and freed from life-dominating sin and demonic oppression or possession nothing will keep the news from spreading. It will light a spiritual fire in this dark, dying world and those who long for healing and freedom will literally come running for deliverance! Make no mistake, Jesus plainly said that "anyone who has faith" will do the works he did. In fact, he said such people would do even *greater* works (John 14:12)! Please note that he said "***anyone*** who has faith;" this means "anyone" who simply ***believes****!*

Do you sometimes struggle with faith? All believers are *believers* precisely because they have "a *measure* of faith" (Romans 12:3). The wonderful thing is that this is merely the starting point of the faith walk because *faith can grow*. Faith grows three ways:

1. Getting closer to God, who is the Fountain of Life and therefore He gushes life, light, power and belief into whoever gets close to Him (Psalm 36:9).
2. Through regular *feeding* on God's Word, as shown in Romans 10:17 and Matthew 4:4. Whatever element of the Word you feed

on is where your faith will grow. For instance, if you want strong faith in regards to the believer's authority, spiritual warfare and exorcism then I encourage you to master the material in this chapter as well as **Chapter 19** and **20**.

3. By praying in the Holy Spirit, as shown in Jude 20 (see also Ephesians 6:18, 1 Corinthians 14:14-15 and 2 Timothy 1:6-7).[48]

A pastor I know, Rick, testified to something he experienced when he was in Bible college: He attended a big service where the Charismatic leader was ministering and Rick happened to be standing in the front row. The minister was not far from him when fear suddenly seized Rick and he felt paralyzed. The minister looked at him, but seemed to be focusing on something unseen over Rick's shoulder. He simply pointed to this *thing* and waved his hand, as if to say "Go," and the fear immediately left the brother.

This minister was obviously walking in the gift of discerning of spirits (1 Corinthians 12:1-11), which is the ability to perceive what's happening in the spiritual realm. (Contrary to what some think, discerning of spirits is *not* the gift of carnal judgment and gossip & slander). We saw an Old Testament example of this spiritual gift in **Chapter 2** wherein Elisha's assistant was suddenly able to see into the spirit realm (2 Kings 6:15-17).[49]

Don't you want to walk in the gifting and authority that this minister functioned in when he delivered this brother seized by a spirit of fear? Of course you do; I do too. The material in this book is a good starting point.

---

[48] For details, see the seventh piece of the armor & arms of God in **Chapter 19**.

[49] Since Paul, by the Spirit, didn't elaborate on the gift of the discerning of spirits there must be a biblical precedent to define it. While the gifts of the Spirit are a New Testament phenomenon, Old Testament prophets obviously functioned in these gifts, as the Spirit willed.

Dealing with "Spirits of Infirmities"

At the beginning of this chapter it was pointed out that Christ delivered people from demons which *induced* infirmities of one sort or another, including mental illness. Here are two biblical examples:

1. **Deafness and muteness:** Mark 9:17-29.
2. **Crippling:** Luke 13:10-16.

Let's look at both cases, starting with the first:

> A man in the crowd answered, "Teacher, I brought you my son, <u>who is possessed by a spirit that has robbed him of speech.</u> [18] <u>Whenever it seizes him, it throws him to the ground. He foams at the mouth, gnashes his teeth and becomes rigid.</u> I asked your disciples to drive out the spirit, but they could not."
> [19] "You unbelieving generation," Jesus replied, "how long shall I stay with you? How long shall I put up with you? Bring the boy to me."
> [20] So they brought him. When <u>the spirit</u> saw Jesus, <u>it immediately threw the boy into a convulsion. He fell to the ground and rolled around, foaming at the mouth.</u>
> [21] Jesus asked the boy's father, "How long has he been like this?"
> "From childhood," he answered. [22] "<u>It has often thrown him into fire or water to kill him</u>. But if you can do anything, take pity on us and help us."
> [23] "'If you can'?" said Jesus. "Everything is possible for one who believes."
> [24] Immediately the boy's father exclaimed, "I do believe; help me overcome my unbelief!"
> [25] When Jesus saw that a crowd was running to the scene, <u>he rebuked the impure spirit. "You deaf

and mute spirit," he said, "**I command you, come out of him and never enter him again.**"

²⁶ **The spirit shrieked, convulsed him violently and came out**. The boy looked so much like a corpse that many said, "He's dead." ²⁷ But Jesus took him by the hand and lifted him to his feet, and he stood up.

²⁸ After Jesus had gone indoors, his disciples asked him privately, "Why couldn't we drive it out?"

²⁹ He replied, "**This kind can come out only by prayer**."

Mark 9:17-29

This passage reveals several insights:

- As you can see, this evil spirit *induced* muteness and deafness (verses 17 & 25).
- While the muteness and deafness were presumably constant conditions, the demon only seized the child on occasions, not 100% of the time (verse 18). Luke's account verifies that the spirit would leave him on occasion (Luke 9:39), which indicates a **partial possession**. (This was the situation with the person in my life, shared earlier this chapter). In this particular case of *partial possession* there was only one demon involved whereas in the example of *total possession* with the man from the Gerasenes there were hundreds, perhaps thousands, of demons involved (Mark 5:1-20).
- Speaking of partial possession, it's clear that the infamous serial killer Ted Bundy was demonically influenced to commit his atrocious crimes; and the evidence points to partial possession: When he was his normal self he was affable and charismatic, which explains the inexplicable loyalty of several naïve people close to him, not to mention his mounting fan club (!). Many remained loyal *during* his eleven years of imprisonment before his execution. Even the judge who sentenced him noted how likable and gifted he was. Yet his myriad wicked murders and subsequent abuse of the corpses indicated a wholly sinister side. An investigator who visited Bundy's cell in Florida witnessed

firsthand his satanic mood swings: During an ordinary conversation the murderer abruptly metamorphosed before his very eyes wherein Bundy's body & countenance weirdly altered and the investigator perceived an odor. He described the situation as extremely intense during this dispositional change, which lasted about 20 minutes.

- Getting back to Mark 9:17-29, when the demon took control of the boy it threw him to the ground where he foamed at the mouth, gnashed his teeth and became rigid. Needless to say, it helps to recognize these characteristics of demon-possession (verse 20).
- The demon **drove the boy to self-harm** by often trying to kill him, throwing him into fire or water (verse 22). We addressed this demon-influenced tendency in **Chapter 9**.
- Christ rebuked the demon, calling it a "deaf and mute spirit," which simply means it was a demon that had the ability to bring about deafness and muteness (verse 25).
- Jesus *commanded* the wicked spirit to **come out of the boy**, adding "**and never enter him again**" (verse 25). It's an important addition.
- The spirit shrieked and convulsed the lad violently during the exorcism (verse 26). These are further characteristics we need to recognize when exorcizing demons.
- Explaining why the disciples couldn't cast out this particular wicked spirit, Jesus said "This kind can come out only by prayer" (verse 29).[50] Since prayer is communion with God this indicates that a close relationship with the LORD and the corresponding increased spiritual sensitivity & anointing are required to operate in the authority necessary to deliver people from demons of this magnitude. Obviously some evil spirits are more powerful and obstinate and hence are more resistant to exorcism.

---

[50] While some translations say "prayer *and fasting*" (e.g. the KJV), the earliest (and therefore most reliable) manuscripts omit "fasting." It was likely added by an overzealous scribe at some point.

Now let's look at the other passage and cull insights from it as well:

> On a Sabbath Jesus was teaching in one of the synagogues, [11] and <u>a woman was there who had been crippled by a spirit for eighteen years. She was bent over and could not straighten up at all</u>. [12] When Jesus saw her, he called her forward and said to her, "<u>Woman, you are set free from your infirmity.</u>" [13] <u>Then he put his hands on her</u>, and <u>immediately she straightened up</u> and praised God.
>
> [14] Indignant because Jesus had healed on the Sabbath, the synagogue leader said to the people, "There are six days for work. So come and be healed on those days, not on the Sabbath."
>
> [15] The Lord answered him, "You hypocrites! Doesn't each of you on the Sabbath untie your ox or donkey from the stall and lead it out to give it water? [16] Then should not this woman, a daughter of Abraham, <u>whom Satan has kept bound for eighteen long years</u>, be set free on the Sabbath day from what bound her?"
>
> **Luke 13:10-16**

- The woman's crippled condition was *caused by* a demon (verse 11). This shows that evil spirits have spiritual powers that can negatively affect those in the physical world. Medical science has, of course, discovered various other causes of ailments, whether physical or mental, but this does not discount the effect the spiritual has on the physical. Furthermore, could it not be possible—even likely—that these spirits induced these "causes," as pointed out earlier this chapter?
- Unlike with the spirit that induced muteness and deafness, Christ did not rebuke the demon or command it to leave (at least Luke didn't cite this in his account). Jesus simply said, "Woman, you are set free from your infirmity," followed by laying his hands on her, and she was both delivered from the spirit and healed

(verses 12-13). This shows a correlation between the two—being delivered from demonic oppression and receiving healing. Comparing the two accounts also shows that **1.** exorcizing demons and healing people are not one dimensional in nature as there are various methods we can employ, which grant the same result, and **2.** we should rely on the Holy Spirit's distinctive leading in each case.

➢ On a side note, this passage shows that legalists like the Pharisees—i.e. lifeless religionists—are prone to *opposing* genuine ministerial works, such as exorcism and healing. Big surprise, huh?

Of course, not every infirmity is directly caused by evil spirits, so you have to have spiritual discernment in order to effectively minister in these situations. And the only way you can do this, again, is to have genuine spiritual sensitivity, which comes by drawing closer to the LORD, as well as eagerly *desiring* gifts of the Spirit rather than eagerly *denying* them (1 Corinthians 12:1,31 & 14:1,39). If you're not sure if a malady was induced by a demon, you can simply rebuke the ailment itself, as Jesus did here:

> **Now Simon's mother-in-law was suffering from a high fever, and they asked Jesus to help her. ³⁹ So he bent over her and <u>rebuked the fever</u>, <u>and it left her</u>. <u>She got up at once</u> and began to wait on them.**
>
> **Luke 4:38-39**

As a believer and co-heir in Christ you have the authority to do the works the Messiah did (John 14:12). We'll look at this further in **Chapter 20**.

Chapter 17

How to Deflect Demonic Spirits

In **Chapter 9** we briefly touched on how *not* to be oppressed or possessed by demons. Let's now go into more detail on how to keep these malevolent beings at bay and deactivate them in your life.

A basic understanding of human nature is necessary to grasp how evil spirits negatively influence people and destroy their lives. This will help you to understand the simple measures we need to take in order to prevent them from doing this. I want to stress that these are *simple* actions and they're easy as pie to master.

So let's first establish the essentials of human nature and then observe some key passages that show how malicious spirits negatively sway people.

Human Nature and Spiritual Influence

Human beings are made up of three basic parts: **spirit**, **mind** and **flesh**. Your mind is the center of your being and it's flanked by two opposing natures—spirit and flesh. Your spirit is your higher nature whereas your flesh is your lower nature. Put another way, your spirit is your godly nature while your flesh is the sinful nature. Your spirit is the part of you that inclines toward what is positive, productive and godly whereas your flesh is the part of you that veers toward what is negative, destructive and *un*godly.

These two natures regularly transmit impulses, images and desires to your mind. The mind is the center of your being; it's the part of you that thinks (intellect), feels (emotion) and decides (volition). Your mind is caught between these opposing natures (Galatians 5:17). In other words, you regularly experience the *conflict* of these two natures in your mind. This diagram helps picture all this:

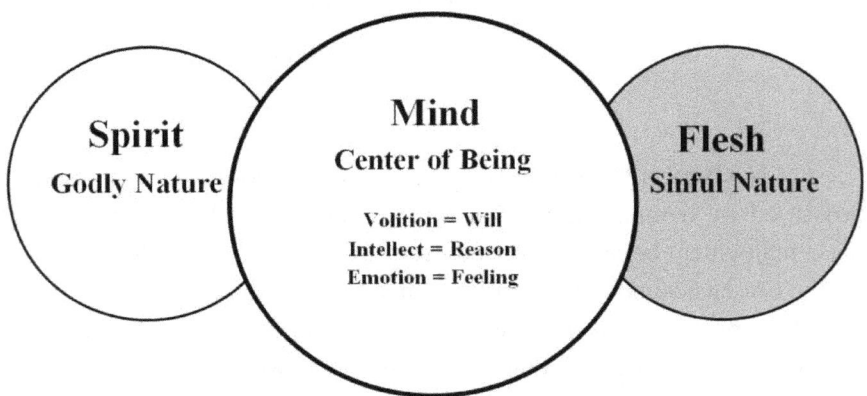

While it's not fun being caught in a conflict between two opposing natures, there's good news: Because your mind possesses volition—*will*—you have the God-given **power of decision** and therefore the ability to **DECIDE** which nature you're going to receive from and follow—your godly nature (spirit) or your sinful nature (flesh).

Assuming you're a believer, the Holy Spirit gave birth to your new regenerated spirit (John 3:6), which was "created to be like God in true righteousness and holiness" (Ephesians 4:24). On top of this, you are a temple of the Holy Spirit—a **temple of God**—because the Spirit of God resides *in* you. Exactly what part of your being does the Holy Spirit inhabit? Your spirit, of course, since your spirit was made holy through regeneration (Ephesians 3:16). In fact, it's only *because* your spirit has been reborn **holy** that the *Holy* Spirit is able to indwell you! With this understanding, your spirit—your "new self"—is indwelt and led by the Holy Spirit. So when you follow the impulses of your regenerated human spirit you are simultaneously following the leading of the Holy Spirit.

By contrast, if you follow the impulses of the flesh—the sinful nature—you are automatically following the leading of the devil and filthy spirits because the flesh *is* the sinful nature, which is the satanic nature. In other words, all a person has to do in order to fulfill the devil's will in his or her life is to live according to his/her fleshly impulses.

What I'm getting to is this: **The Holy Spirit (God) works with you through your spirit—your godly nature—while demonic spirits work with through your flesh—the sinful nature.**

In light of this, it's imperative that you learn to distinguish spiritual thoughts from fleshly ones. Both types of thoughts will be transmitted to your mind on a regular basis. Once you can distinguish these two kinds of thoughts you simply need to learn to discard the negatives impulses and feed positive proclivities.

Doing so naturally keeps demonic spirits from being attracted to you and setting up house, so to speak. How so? Because, remember, demons are *impure* spirits and are therefore attracted to what is morally filthy. So keeping moral filth far from your "house"—your mind & body—naturally keeps filthy spirits away.

How to Distinguish Spiritual Thoughts from Fleshly Thoughts

To accomplish this you'll have to learn to differentiate thoughts that originate from your godly nature from impulses that proceed from your sinful nature. The former are positive and productive whereas the latter are negative and destructive. Distinguishing the two is easy.

The Bible offers fairly detailed descriptions of what these conflicting natures produce:

> **The acts of the flesh** are obvious: sexual immorality, impurity and debauchery; [20] idolatry and witchcraft; hatred, discord, jealousy, fits of rage, selfish ambition, dissensions, factions [21] and envy; drunkenness, orgies, and the like. I warn you, as I did before, that those who live like this will not inherit the kingdom of God.
>
> [22] But **the fruit of the spirit** is love, joy, peace, forbearance, kindness, goodness, faith-fulness, [23] gentleness and self-control. Against such things there is no law.
>
> **Galatians 5:19-23**

Every believer has to learn to recognize and throw off thoughts that stem from the flesh, like sexual immorality, hatred, discord, jealousy, rage, selfishness, envy and other obvious carnal traits, such as arrogance, deceit and slander (Proverbs 6:16-19). Don't feed these types of thoughts. Instead feed thoughts that stem from your spirit, your higher nature, which is why Paul said:

> Finally, brothers and sisters, **whatever is true**, whatever is **noble**, whatever is **right**, whatever is **pure**, whatever is **lovely**, whatever is **admirable** — if anything is **excellent** or **praiseworthy** — **think about such things**. [9] Whatever you have learned or received or heard from me, or seen in me — put it into practice. And the God of peace will be with you.
>
> **Philippians 4:8-9**

The more you "feed" positive, productive thoughts like these, the more you'll live out of your higher nature. It's simple. The Bible puts it like this:

> **Those who live according to <u>the flesh</u> set <u>their minds</u> on the things of <u>the flesh</u>; but those who live according to <u>the spirit</u>[51] set <u>their minds</u> on the things of <u>the spirit</u>.**
>
> **Romans 8:5**

So learning to set your mind on things of the spirit rather than things of the flesh is key to walking free of the satanic nature and the influence of evil spirits.

Also, as verse 9 of the previous passage instructs, get in the habit of observing genuinely spiritual believers (not religious people) and put into practice the positive things you observe. When you practice these two things, notice what results: "and the God of peace will be with you." Needless to say, filthy spirits will *not* be attracted to you when you do this (which is *not* to say that they won't attack you for righteousness' sake when permitted, as explained in **Chapter 6** and **20**).

Managing the Soil of Your Heart

It helps to understand the biblical concept of **the heart** and how it fits into the model of human nature.

"Heart" is *kardia (kar-DEE-ah)* in the Greek, which is where we get the English 'cardiac.' Like the English word 'heart,' *kardia* literally refers to the blood-pumping organ but figuratively to the **core thoughts or feelings of a person's being or mind** (Strong 39). Greek scholar E.W. Bullinger describes the heart as "**the seat and center** of man's personal life in which the distinctive **character** of the human manifests itself" (362). The heart could therefore be described as the core of the

---

[51] Since there is no capitalization in the biblical Greek, translators must determine if "spirit" should be capitalized in reference to the Holy Spirit or not capitalized in reference to the human spirit. Many translations capitalize "spirit" in these passages and some do not (for example The New English Bible). I believe these passages (and other such passages) are plainly referring to the human spirit and therefore "spirit" should not be capitalized because the context is contrasting the conflicting parts of human nature (e.g. Matthew 26:41). In a way it makes no significant difference since our born-again human spirit is **indwelt and led by the Holy Spirit** (Ephesians 3:16).

mind. It is *part* of the mind, but specifically refers to the deepest, most central part; that is, **the core**.

What dwells in your heart is determined by which nature you have *decided* to live by, whether spirit or flesh (Romans 8:5-6). Jesus said, "The good man brings good things out of the good stored up in his heart, and the evil man brings evil things out of the evil stored up in his heart" (Luke 6:45). What's this mean? Simple: If you, in your mind, *decide* to dwell on carnal thoughts, then carnal, negative, destructive things will naturally store up in your heart over time. If, on the other hand, you *choose* to focus on spiritual thoughts, then good, positive, productive things will store up in your heart. Whatever's in your heart then determines your actions and therefore the course of your very life. This is why the book of wisdom says: **"Be careful what you think for your thoughts run your life"** (Proverbs 4:23 NCV). Take heed—truer words have never been spoken!

Here's our diagram of human nature with the heart added:

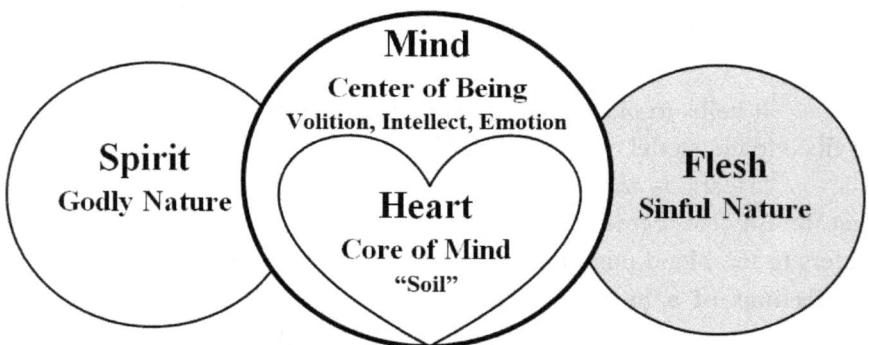

Notice that the heart is the core of your mind and is figuratively called "soil." Why? Because the Bible likens the heart to **soil** (Luke 8:15). Soil in the natural is a neutral substance that grows whatever seed is planted in it. This is the way it is with the soil of your heart, except that it grows non-physical "seeds," whether spiritual or *un*spiritual. By "seeds" I mean thoughts, impulses, desires, images or impressions. Dwelling on these "seeds" waters them, so to speak, and thus enables them to grow. In other words, your meditation *feeds* them; and that is how they grow. And whatever grows in your heart is what eventually fills your heart and produces the desires thereof. These desires of your heart then determine your actions, good or bad.

Has someone ever offended you and you dwelt on it so much that you made more of it than what it was? When the issue was finally resolved you realized you made a mountain out of a mole hill. How did this happen? Simple: You fed the offense with your thought life and thus it grew. As you kept thinking about it, the bigger it got. This principle goes into motion with any impulse you choose to focus on and give life to, whether of the spirit or the flesh.

In regards to fleshly impulses, the Bible details the scenario like so:

> **but each person is tempted when they are dragged away <u>by their own evil desire</u> and enticed. ¹⁵ Then, after desire has conceived, it gives birth to sin; and sin, when it is full-grown, gives birth to death.**
>
> **James 1:14-15**

People are tempted by evil desires that stem from their flesh, the sinful nature. Once they grab ahold of the bad impulse and feed it with their thought life, desire is conceived in the soil of their hearts, which eventually gives birth to the action, the sin itself.

Demons Work with People through their Flesh

The reason I'm going into detail about human nature is so you'll grasp how **the Holy Spirit (God) works with you through your spirit, your higher nature, whereas evil spirits work to destroy you (and those linked to you) through your flesh, the sinful nature**.

Because the flesh is the satanic nature all a person has to do in order to be "of the devil" is to habitually live out of his/her sinful nature. For instance, envy, jealousy, rivalry, hatred and strife are works of the flesh. If a person regularly lives out of these fleshly impulses he or she will automatically carry out the Devil's will in whatever environment s/he operates.

Take a woman at a church assembly who embraces thoughts of envy and jealousy. This naturally gives birth to rivalry and hostility toward the people with whom she's envious and jealous. Hostility *is* hatred. There are degrees of hostility, of course, but—whatever the degree—hatred always eventually morphs into unjust attacks, starting with malevolent gossip, which is slander. This of course poisons people's minds against their maligned brother or sister, which then produces discord in the assembly and robs the fellowship of peace and unity. Every Christian assembly on Earth has experienced this scenario and the root problem can always be traced to an individual who gave-in to the fleshly impulses of envy, jealousy & rivalry and then spread the resulting hostility to others.

Or consider the example of a married Christian man who meets an alluring woman on the job and it stirs up fleshly interest. The more he *thinks* about her the more desire grows in his heart until it manifests into adultery when the opportunity presents itself.

In both of these cases neither the woman who gossiped and created strife in her assembly nor the man who committed adultery were possessed by evil spirits. They simply ignored the leading of their higher nature (and the corresponding guidance of the Spirit) and surrendered to their fleshly desires by feeding them with their thought life, which made the corresponding desire grow in the soil of their hearts. And then they eventually acted on these desires.

Allow me to point out that the word 'spirit' does not always refer to a spiritual entity; it can simply refer to a person's character, as in Joshua had "a different spirit" than other Hebrews and thus served the LORD wholeheartedly (Numbers 14:24). Neither the woman who engaged in hostile gossip and created strife in her fellowship nor the man who committed adultery was possessed by demons to do what they did. They simply gave their hearts over to the destructive impulses of their flesh, fed those desires, which then grew in their hearts, and ultimately acted on them. As such, the woman had a spirit of gossip and strife—a *character* of gossip and strife; and the man had a spirit of adultery—a *character* of adultery. But neither was possessed by a demon to do what they did. They have no one to blame but themselves for their foolish decisions. Remember, we all have **the power of decision** and therefore we *decide* which nature we're going to live out of, whether flesh or spirit, sinful nature or godly nature. It's our choice every day.

However, this is not to say that demonic spirits didn't "whisper in their ears," so to speak (which we'll look at momentarily). Not to mention, once they started engaging in their particular sin it no doubt attracted evil spirits because filthy spirits are drawn to that which is morally impure, much like flies are attracted to dog excrement and rats to garbage.

I shared in **Chapter 9** how an anointed minister picked up a stench in the spirit when practicing homosexuals came up for prayer as he was ministering. I also shared how a boy, my nephew, smelled vomit when he was around a practicing witch who married into the family. People who take paths that are morally filthy like these—homosexuality and witchcraft—naturally attract filthy spirits. This results in demonic bondage to the sin, at best; and demonic possession, at worst. I'm not saying this with Pharisaical condescension or condemnation, but rather godly compassion and the desire to see people set free, whatever their transgression is, whether homosexuality, witchcraft, adultery, gossip/slander, religious legalism, drunkard-ness or what have you.

Needless to say, don't entertain impulses of the flesh. Learn to put into motion the law of displacement by focusing on impulses of your higher nature (Ephesians 4:22-24). Concentrating on spiritual thoughts naturally displaces carnal desires. This keeps evils spirits at bay because they're not attracted to that which is pure, godly and spiritual. And when they observe that a person is stubbornly single-minded they'll give-up and seek easier prey. Remember: sloth is a trait of the satanic nature and so impure spirits are lazy by nature.

How Does Satan "fill a Person's Heart"?

All of the above helps us to interpret a couple cases in the Bible where it says that Satan filled a person's heart.

Let's start with the case of Ananias from Acts 5:1-11. This was the era of the early church where believers were selling land and extra houses to provide money for the needy in the church (Acts 4:32-37).

Ananias followed suit by selling a piece of property and giving the proceeds to the church, but he kept a good chunk for himself. There was nothing wrong with this and Peter even said so (Acts 5:4). It was Ananias' property and his money; and he could do whatever he wanted with it, as led of the Spirit. The problem was that Ananias and his wife deceptively said they gave *all* the proceeds to the church, evidently to appear exceptionally generous and spiritual. Thus Peter asks: "Ananias, how is it that Satan has so filled your heart that you have lied to the Holy Spirit and have kept for yourself some of the money you received for the land?" (verse 3).

How did Satan fill Ananias' heart? Did he literally possess him? No, he filled his heart in the sense that Ananias gave his mind over to the fleshly impulses of the sinful nature, which is the satanic nature. Ananias wanted to impress others by appearing more generous than he actually was, so he lied about giving all the profit of his sale when he only gave part.

This is the typical way the devil fills a person's heart, which we observed in the examples from the previous section: Satan filled the heart of the woman who succumbed to envy and hostility, which resulted in gossip and produced strife in the assembly. The married man surrendered to his carnal lust for a flirtatious woman at work and allowed desire to build in his heart until it manifested in adultery. The devil "filled their hearts" in the sense that they gave themselves over to the cravings of the satanic nature, but they weren't possessed by Satan or demons.

How did Satan fill Judas' Heart?

The case of Judas Iscariot shows that Satan or demons can fill people's hearts more literally. Judas, of course, was the fake disciple who betrayed Christ for 30 pieces of silver. This reveals that his main problem was greed (that is, his main problem beyond not actually *knowing* the Lord). The Bible blatantly describes him as a thief who regularly pilfered from the treasury of Jesus' ministry (John 12:6). The Lord knew what was going on, of course, because he functioned in the gifts of the Spirit, one being the word of knowledge (1 Corinthians 12:4-11). Thus Jesus indirectly referred to Judas as "a devil" well before this incident (John 6:70-71). Why? Not because Judas was literally possessed by an evil spirit at the time, but because he walked in the flesh without repentance and therefore wasn't a genuine follower of Christ. Anyone who chooses to live out of their flesh will automatically perform the will of the devil because the flesh is the sinful nature, the satanic nature. This is why Jesus called Judas "a devil"—his allegiance was clearly with the devil, even though he wasn't likely aware of it.

Yet a couple other passages reveal that Satan literally possessed Judas on two separate occasions over a year later:

> **Then Satan entered Judas, called Iscariot, one of the Twelve.**
> **Luke 22:3**

> **As soon as Judas took the bread, Satan entered into him.**
> **So Jesus told him, "What you are about to do, do quickly."**
> **John 13:27**

The verse from Luke is talking about when Judas skulked away to the chief priests to agree to betray Jesus for a monetary reward. The verse from John takes place over a day later during the Last Supper, which is when Christ discharged Judas from the celebratory meal to betray him.

The texts do not contradict one another because John acknowledges the first occasion where Judas was possessed in verse 2 of the same chapter: "The evening meal was in progress, and **the devil had already prompted Judas**, the son of Simon Iscariot, to betray Jesus." This refers to the events of the Luke passage.

We can glean a few important facts from both verses:

1. Satan possessed Judas not once, but twice
2. There was an interim period between the two possessions where Judas was not possessed. This indicates a *partial* possession, as detailed last chapter.

3. Even though Judas' will was not under the direct control of the devil during the interim he did not repent or seek to undo Christ's unjust arrest which he had set in motion.

No doubt the Sovereign LORD insisted on the interim so that Iscariot had time to reflect on what he had done, graciously providing him the opportunity to repent.[52] Since Judas didn't have a change of heart, however, he was without excuse. In other words, Judas couldn't justify his actions on the grounds that "the devil made him do it."

A fourth point is something noted in **Chapter 9**: This kind of demonic possession does not come out of nowhere. A person isn't just morally heading one way one day and is suddenly possessed by a demon and proceeds to go in a totally different direction. No, possession of this nature occurs when a person has *already* given in to the sinful nature and is therefore *already* habitually fulfilling the devil's will, which naturally attracts wicked spirits. If the person is eventually possessed by a demon or demons he or she simply goes deeper down the same fleshly path s/he was going.

We see this with Judas: He was *already* habitually stealing from the treasury because of his greed. Jesus knew this early on due to the word of knowledge and thus thoroughly interceded for the thief. Christ even made it known that he was on to him outright (John 6:70-71). Unfortunately, Judas remained unrepentant. His eventual succumbing to the temptation of blood money for Christ's arrest & murder was simply deeper down the same dark road. *It wasn't until **then** that Satan possessed him.*

Of course, Judas' possession was a special case that warranted the devil's direct involvement. When Satan possesses the Antichrist during the future Tribulation it's likewise a special occasion (2 Thessalonians 2:9 & Revelation 13:2). In the vast majority of cases, however, Satan prefers to kick back and allow his filthy underlings to perform hands-on work like this (i.e. possess people).

---

[52] God reigns supreme, which includes reigning over the devil who's the temporary "god of this world" (2 Corinthians 4:4). Thus even Satan has to have permission to carry out his wicked attacks, as shown in Job 1:6-12 and 2:1-7. That said, this is a general truth and it's uncertain how far and detailed it extends concerning any given satanic strategy and the target(s) thereof.

It's important to distinguish between demonic possession that occurs due to increasing immoral activity (as was the case with Judas) and demonic possession by a spirit of infirmity, which results in some kind of mental/physical malady. The latter type of possession may have nothing to do with a person participating in immorality. For instance, the boy who had a mute, deaf spirit (Mark 9:17-29) and the woman with the crippling demon (Luke 13:10-16), both addressed at the end of the last chapter. There's zero indication that either of them suffered possession and the corresponding maladies due to increasing, unrepentant immorality.

This shows that living a morally blameless life (which, of course, requires keeping in repentance as necessary[53]) is not enough to walk free of demonic possession as far as spirits of infirmities are concerned. Having a close relationship with God is not enough either. Why? Because these kinds of spirits prey upon **the ignorant**. The only antidote to ignorance is knowledge; and knowledge is power, assuming it is implemented (Proverbs 24:5). Any believer who knows and practices the Scriptural truths detailed in **Chapter 19** and **20** will protect themselves from spirits of infirmities.

This illustrates the difference between:

- The Person of God.
- The wisdom principles of His kingdom.

It's possible to genuinely know God, but be ignorant of the principles of His Kingdom, including spiritual warfare. Likewise, it's possible to grasp principles of godly wisdom and yet not know the LORD whatsoever. For instance, an atheist doesn't know God—and possibly hates God—but because he lives by the principle that "diligent hands will rule" (Proverbs 12:24) he prospers in his occupation.

The ideal, of course, is to walk in *both:* **1.** Develop a relationship with the Person of God and **2.** learn the wise principles of His kingdom.

Amen.

---

[53] Matthew & Luke 3:8. Keep in mind that *blameless* is not the same as *sinless*.

Can Believers be Possessed?

This brings up the question of whether or not genuine Christians can be possessed. The answer is no and yes. Let me explain…

True believers can never be *totally* possessed because they're already indwelt by the Holy Spirit (Romans 8:9). Of course, evil spirits are assigned to believers to try to oppress them and ruin their lives—the very opposite of what heavenly angels are commissioned to do (which is to serve people). This shows why learning and mastering spiritual warfare is vital as we grow in Christ.

Genuine believers cannot drink of the cup of the Lord and the cup of demons as well (1 Corinthians 10:21). To be *fully* possessed of a demon or demons, a believer would have to first fall away by denying Christ, whether literally or through incorrigibly wicked actions. For proof that a Christian can indeed fall away, see Hebrews 6:4-9, 2 Peter 2:20-21, 2 Timothy 2:11-13 and Titus 1:16. I want to emphasize that **God's Word supports the doctrine of eternal security 100%** and this is verified by Christ Himself in John 10:28-29. However, the Bible clearly does NOT support the doctrine of *unconditional* eternal security, as verified by these crystal clear passages and numerous others.[54]

Although genuine believers cannot be fully possessed, they can fall prey to *partial possession*, which was touched on last chapter (in the final section). Here are two types of partial possession observed in the Scriptures:

1. When a person suffers possession by a spirit of infirmity, which causes some type of ongoing physical disorder. In this scenario a spirit of infirmity induces a malady, but the person is otherwise uncontrolled by the spirit. The woman from Luke 13:10-16 whose crippling condition was caused by a demon and required exorcism is a good example. There's no evidence that she *wasn't* in control of her faculties. Thus the demon caused her crippling

---

[54] For details see **Chapter 20**'s *The Enemy WILL Attack these God-Given Blessings.* Also see the article *Once Saved Always Saved?* at the Fountain of Life website.

state, but it did not control her mind and will. It had power over her physically, but not mentally. It was thus a *partial* possession.
2. Another kind of partial possession is when a spirit takes control of a person's mental faculties one way or another, but **the spirit comes and goes** and thus it's not a perpetual condition. This was the case with the woman I personally knew discussed in the previous chapter. She was decidedly a Christian, but an evil spirit would come on her now and then, with two different manifestations—a depressed, worried state or a mean, stubborn state. Both of these manifestations were thoroughly demonic and she occasionally committed self-harm in one form or another. Yet she was her normal, pure, loving self about 50% of the time. Since the evil spirit came and went it wasn't a total possession, but rather a partial one. This is evidence that a true believer can suffer partial possession where a demon comes on him or her from time to time and wreaks havoc. It's not a total possession, but such people need exorcized nevertheless, like the boy in Mark 9:18 and Luke 9:39.

In cases where believers suffer partial possession the demon attacks their body or mind, but it cannot afflict their spirit because they are indwelt by the Holy Spirit (Ephesians 3:16).

Satanic Head Games

It was pointed out earlier that fallen angels are able to "whisper in a person's ear," that is, shoot thoughts into people's minds, obviously corresponding to the desires and weaknesses of their flesh. Consider Christ's temptation after the Spirit led him to fast in the wilderness for 40 days and nights:

> **Then Jesus was led by the Spirit into the wilderness to be tempted by the devil. [2] After fasting forty days and forty nights, he was hungry. [3] <u>The tempter came to him and said</u>, "If you are the Son of God, tell these stones to become bread."**

⁴ Jesus answered, "It is written: 'Man shall not live on bread alone, but on every word that comes from the mouth of God.' "

⁵ <u>Then the devil took him to the holy city and had him stand on the highest point of the temple.</u> ⁶ <u>"If you are the Son of God,"</u> he said, <u>"throw yourself down</u>. For it is written:

'He will command his angels concerning you,
    and they will lift you up in their hands,
    so that you will not strike your foot
    against a stone.' "

⁷ Jesus answered him, "It is also written: 'Do not put the Lord your God to the test.' "

⁸ Again, <u>the devil took him to a very high mountain and showed him all the kingdoms of the world and their splendor.</u> ⁹ <u>"All this I will give you,"</u> he said, <u>"if you will bow down and worship me."</u>

¹⁰ Jesus said to him, "Away from me, Satan! For it is written: 'Worship the Lord your God, and serve him only.' "

¹¹ Then the devil left him, and angels came and attended him.

Matthew 4:1-11

This occasion warranted Satan's direct involvement. He knew that the Mighty Christ came to destroy his work[55] so he personally tried to stop the Messiah by tempting him to succumb to the weaknesses of his flesh and therefore sin. This, of course, would've made Jesus unacceptable as a substitutionary curse for humanity since the sacrifice had to be innocent.

Notice that verse 3 says "The tempter came to him and said…". Did the devil actually *appear* to Jesus or did he come to him and

---

[55] See Hebrews 2:14, 1 John 3:8 and Acts 10:38.

'whisper in his ear,' so to speak? In other words, did he come to him invisibly and simply transmit the tempting words to his mind? The Greek word for "came to" doesn't necessarily mean appear visibly, but simply 'to come to, come near to, approach.' Since Satan is a spiritual being, not physical, it's more likely that he came to the Messiah spiritually and therefore invisibly, although Christ no doubt discerned his presence through the gift of discerning of spirits (1 Corinthians 12:4-11).

I'm not saying that Satan *didn't* appear to Jesus in some physical form, just that it's very possible they he simply came to him spiritually—invisibly—and spoke to him by shooting flesh-based suggestions into his head. This is how evil spirits try to negatively influence you and me, why wouldn't it be the same in this situation?

Someone might understandably argue that verses 5 & 8 show the devil taking Christ to the highest point of the Temple in Jerusalem and then to a high mountain, but Satan could've taken him there in a mental sense, relaying his temptation in thought form or perhaps a vision. After all, have you ever been tempted where an evil spirit *physically appeared* to you or *physically transported* you to the applicable environment or did you simply experience the temptation through thoughts, impulses and the imagery thereof? The latter, of course.

The Sword of the Spirit and the Law of Displacement

Christ counteracted these temptations by simply **speaking the truth**. On all three occasions Jesus responded with a quote from the Scriptures. This is what we need to do when we encounter temptation: When you experience an inner carnal impulse, perhaps combined with the corresponding imagery, recognize it for what it is—a negative, destructive, ungodly temptation rooted in the flesh. **Then** boldly speak the counteractive truth. Repeat as necessary until the temptation lifts. This is one of our God-given spiritual weapons; it's called **the sword of the spirit** (Ephesians 6:17). It's simply speaking the Word of God in bold faith as a defensive or offensive tool. Use it! This "sword" does you no good if you don't take advantage of it. It guarantees victory over temptation.

You'll notice in the second temptation that the devil quoted a Scripture verse. Please understand that Satan & evil spirits know the Scriptures and will sometimes use them to tempt people to take a wrong path, just as the devil did with Jesus here. The Messiah recognized that Satan's usage of this verse conflicted with other truths, of course, and so he cited *another* passage that gave balance to the matter, which is in line with the hermeneutical rule "Scripture interprets Scripture."

You can only do this *if* you're familiar with the Scriptures, so I encourage you to acquaint yourself with God's Word more and more by developing a daily reading program. Try different reading plans until you find one that fits your lifestyle and schedule. Change your plan every now and then so it doesn't get predictable and boring. Also switch translations from time to time; and consider reading plans based on topical studies. Always *pray for* knowledge, understanding and wisdom before you read and the LORD will bless you (Proverbs 2:1-7).

It's important as well to understand that the Enemy can tempt you **through a person or group** who cite Scripture (2 Corinthians 11:13-15). The Jehovah's False Witnesses are a good example. Yet such a temptation can very well come through people functioning under the tag of whatever camp you favor (Baptist, Evangelical, Charismatic, Reformed, Mainline, Pentecostal, Emergent, etc.). Thankfully, it's easy to recognize these fakes, if you know for what to look. Speaking of which…

Christ said that false prophets can be recognized **by their fruit** (Matthew 7:15-23). A false prophet is simply a minister who falsely speaks for God and you can identify them by the fruit they bear. Do they produce fruit of the spirit on a regular basis or works of the flesh? See Galatians 5:19-23. No one is perfect, of course, but what do they *habitually* produce? And are they willing to humbly 'fess up and apologize when they miss it (1 John 1:8-9). Do they have a spirit of love or a spirit of abuse? Do they build up or tear down? Genuine ministers are called to build up, not tear down (2 Corinthians 10:8 & 13:10). After giving appropriate correction, they build-up and encourage, not condemn. Needless to say, if you observe consistent bad fruit and an unwillingness to keep with repentance in a "minister" then **head for the hills** (Matthew 15:14).

One last thing on this matter: When you 'swing' your sword of the spirit by speaking the truth in bold faith, it doesn't have to be a word-for-word verse or even a Scripture text at all. It simply has to be **truth**, which is **the way it really is**. Say, for example, a wicked spirit whispers in your ear that you're a no-good piece of excrement who can't do anything right. You don't have to quote an *exact* Scripture to counteract this lie, just speak the truth: "I'm a child of God born of the seed of Christ by the power of the Holy Spirit; I was *born* righteous and can do all things through Him who strengthens me!" Those of you who know the Bible know that this is a personalized paraphrase of several verses.

But, again, you don't have to cite from Scripture at all to counteract a temptation—whether word-for-word or paraphrasing—as long as what you say is **the truth**. For instance, we earlier considered the example of a married man who was tempted by a coquettish "hottie" at work. All he has to say to thwart the temptation is the truth: "I am a *married* man of the Most High God! I *love* my wife and am faithful to her and God!"

When you do this you're putting into motion **the Law of Displacement**, which means that two things cannot occupy the same space at the same time. In this particular case it applies to your thought life. When you experience a tempting thought you counteract it by simply speaking (and thinking) the counteractive truth, which displaces the negative thought. Repeat as necessary. When you do this you're swinging your sword of the spirit and slicing down the lies of the Enemy.

Another thing you can do is sing praise & worship songs. Blast some music and have a praise & worship session; or, if you're musically inclined, do it yourself, like David did in the Psalms (e.g. Psalm 8 and 65). Praise & worship is a powerful spiritual weapon because praise ushers in God's manifest presence and there's fullness of joy in the presence of the LORD (Psalm 100:4 & 16:11).

Chapter 18

How to Deflect Demonic Spirits II

Continuing with *How to Deflect Demonic Spirits*, let's look at:

Examples of Demonic Head Games

The Bible repeatedly shows that the LORD *knows* our thoughts, which of course includes the Holy Spirit (1 Corinthians 2:11, Psalm 94:11 & Proverbs 20:27). But the devil and his loser minions have no such power. All they can do is determine your weaknesses by observing you and tempt you by shooting ideas into your mind corresponding to the weaknesses of the flesh, like lust, greed, pride, envy, jealousy, fear and doubt.

We know that angels are assigned to people to serve them. It's the same thing in the kingdom of darkness, except that demons *disservice* people through misleading, hindering, oppression or possession. In short, they want to ruin people's lives.

With this in mind, say a demon is assigned to a woman. This spirit cannot read her thoughts, but it can observe her actions and words day & night and so ascertain her fleshly weaknesses. The demon then transmits thoughts into her mind accordingly in the hope of ruining her one way or another. The spirit can also lure into her life the 'right' people to assist in the diabolic plot; that is, the *wrong* people. We saw this in **Chapter 6** with the teenage girl who embraced demonic thoughts and became convinced that she was going to be "taken" one day and her mother & sister would never see her again. Once the (presumed) evil spirit got her to use the power of her mind in conjunction with the power of her tongue the next step was to inspire the right psychopath to meet her at the wrong time and place. Thus she was apprehended, raped and tragically wiped off the face of the planet.

Now consider the hypothetical woman we talked about last chapter who caused strife in her fellowship due to her envies and jealousies. The demon (or demons) assigned to her would observe that she had issues with envy/jealousy/rivalry and so it would draw into her life the right person or persons who would stir up these fleshly impulses. Meeting these people would produce hostility in her—that is, hatred— and so she would start gossiping and slandering, which would in turn produce discord in the assembly, the precise opposite of what the Lord wants (Psalm 133).

It's the same thing with that hypothetical married man who was enticed by an alluring woman at work. The wicked spirit (or spirits) assigned to him would notice his penchant for a certain type of female and then lure into his environment the perfect candidate. The man would experience unwholesome impulses from his flesh, particularly when the woman flirts with him. The demon might assist in the temptation by transmitting thoughts into his mind. In other words, this spirit "whispers into his ear" corresponding to the evil desires of his flesh. Once he grabs ahold of the idea and feeds it with his thought life, desire is conceived in his heart and keeps growing as he feeds it. He eventually falls into adultery when the opportunity presents itself.

This is how evil spirits work behind-the-scenes in regards to any type of sin.

Two Real-Life Stories

Let me share a couple real-life examples that I've unfortunately witnessed.

I was a teacher at an assembly a decade ago where there was this fatherless preadolescence girl who started calling me her "spiritual father." She was a wonderful girl—bright, witty and fun. Carol & I never had a daughter so we enjoyed the honor of having a "spiritual daughter." I'll call her 'Melanie.'

Melanie had a somewhat sad situation, but she never let it bring her down in the least: Her father evidently molested her in the form of inappropriate touching a few years earlier and he was essentially no longer in the picture. But she thankfully had a loving, if overly looming, mother.

When Melanie was 13 a new family joined the assembly. The couple had three daughters and one of them was also 13. The two girls started a friendship that soon became problematic. They would gaze into each other's eyes in an unhealthy manner and walk together curiously close. It became so bad that visitors asked if they were "a couple." During this time Melanie morphed from a bright, joyful girl into a brooding, lifeless early teen. The dramatic change occurred in a matter of just a few months.

That summer my sister, Jen, visited from California. She knew Melanie from past visits where we enjoyed outings together. I didn't inform Jen about Melanie's new friend, their questionable relationship or Melanie's dark turn, but after sitting by Melanie during a service Jen asked me, "Who was that *evil* girl?" She was referring to Melanie's new friend who was hovering behind her the whole time with a grim visage (evidently jealous of Jen sitting by her).

It was eventually discovered why the new family left their former assembly: The daughter had developed the same type of questionable relationships with a couple of girls there and the family was eventually asked to leave when the parents failed to properly control their daughter.

The situation got so bad at our fellowship it was decided that Melanie and her friend were no longer allowed to spend the night at each other's houses; or even spend time alone together at all.

It goes without saying that any sense of closeness with our former "spiritual daughter" ceased as she fell under the spell of this girl. Shortly later the LORD called us out of this fellowship and four years passed before we received an email from Melanie. She was 18 by this point, on the verge of graduating high school and planning to go to art school. We met for coffee where she sadly confessed to being an atheist and explained away anything having to do with God or Christianity.

What went on "behind the scenes" in this sad situation? In light of the scriptural data we've covered, it's not hard to come up with a probable answer: Melanie was a threat to the Enemy's kingdom because she was genuinely fruit-bearing and on fire for the Lord. She spread joy to all the people she knew. She was overflowing with great potential. As such, the demonic spirit(s) assigned to her preyed upon her weaknesses. Her biological father had abused her and abandoned the family, but the LORD faithfully supplied my wife & me to help make up for it as her "spiritual parents." She was home-schooled and the church assembly was small, so she was hungry for a friend her age. Hence evil spirits inspired this family who were in need of a new fellowship to come into the fold where Melanie would meet this girl her age and start a relationship. The demon would 'whisper in Melanie's ear' according to her fleshly weaknesses. The friendship began and quickly descended into sullenness, unhealthy dependency, lesbianism and, ultimately, full-tilt atheism.

It's a sad story and we continue to intercede for Melanie to come back to the Lord one day. But it shows that *everyone* will be tested by the enemy, as permitted by the Sovereign LORD, even bright church girls full of fruit of the spirit.

Here's another real-life story: When I was a young man, shortly out of high school, I hooked up with this singer who was still in school for the purpose of starting a band. I'll call her Laura. We attended the same mega-church.

While the band thing didn't work out, I was impressed by Laura's devotion to God and her genuine evangelistic spirit. She told me several stories about being a witness for Christ at her school and so forth. After graduating high school she quickly went off to college and I fell out of touch with her. Unfortunately, her rock-solid Christian family experienced several serious blows within the course of a year, starting with her father, who was a respected deacon at the fellowship. He committed adultery and the marriage eventually fell apart. Around the same time Laura's younger sister, who was 17, died in a car wreck. On top of all this her first year at university didn't go well, to put it mildly. She was assaulted by the wave of ungodly humanism that secular colleges are known for and was date raped. She dropped out of college and came home, but she didn't return to her former assembly.

A close friend ran into Laura a couple years after these events and said she was palpably bitter. He brought up the Lord, but she didn't want anything to do with God or Christianity. That was three decades ago and I'm unaware of what happened to her from there.

Both of these sad tales show that no one is exempt from satanic attack. If you're a threat to the devil's kingdom you *will* be attacked. If you fail to take advantage of the armor & weaponry that God has faithfully provided and "fight the good fight of faith" the enemy will take you out, just like these two young women.

Forgive my frankness, but you can't half-buttocks it with the Lord. I've known several guys who got saved and went to church gatherings for a long season, but they never came to a point of taking the things of God seriously enough. They continued to flirt with the flesh and the world to some degree. I'm talking about things like boozing, porn, drugs, smoking, fornication and the like. They ended up losing their marriages, their jobs and basically becoming down-and-out. Three ended up in prison.

But—and this is an important "but"—I'm confident that this will not be the case with *you*. If you've come this far in this book then you obviously have a thirst for knowing the LORD and what God's Word says about angelic spirits, good and evil, and your responsibility in spiritual warfare as a New Covenant believer.

As insinuated, one of the keys to overcoming the enemy's attacks is to utilize God's armor & weaponry, which we'll go over next chapter. In the meantime let's address a couple of other demonic strategies. The Bible instructs us to be aware of the devil's schemes so that we're not outwitted (2 Corinthians 2:11).

How the Enemy Blinds People's Minds

The Scriptures show that the Enemy has the power to blind people's minds:

> And even if our gospel is <u>veiled</u>, it is <u>veiled</u> to those who are perishing. [4] <u>The god of this age has blinded the minds of unbelievers</u>, so that <u>they cannot see</u> the light of the gospel that displays the glory of Christ, who is the image of God.
> **2 Corinthians 4:3-4**

The devil & his loser minions don't want people to comprehend the awesome message of Christ because "it is the power of God that brings salvation" and sets them free (Romans 1:16). Evil spirits therefore veil it "to those who are perishing."

"Veil" means to hide, conceal or keep secret. How exactly do wicked spirits conceal the gospel to unbelievers? Do they unleash a spiritual fog around their minds? Not literally, but in a sense, yes. They blind people's minds by implanting an erroneous ideology, which is the result of embracing "deceiving spirits and things taught by demons" (1 Timothy 4:1). More traditional English versions refer to this as "doctrines of demons" or "doctrines of devils" (NASB & KJV). "Doctrines" is another word for teachings or instructions; so "doctrines of demons" simply means *teachings* or *instructions* of unclean spirits.

While these false teachings originate from a demon whispering error in someone's ear, so to speak, they are passed to others through a human agent—someone who's already blinded by the false indoctrination. The Bible describes such people as "hypocritical liars, whose consciences have been seared as with a hot iron" (1 Timothy 4:2). Although the context refers to false teachers in the Church, how much more so in the world? Libertine college professors are Exhibit A. As people give ear to these erroneous teachings they naturally develop an ideology; and this indoctrination—this perspective or mindset—blinds them to the good news of the gospel and the truths of the Word of God in general.

To understand how this works, let's look at...

Noémas—Mindsets, Ideologies

Notice what the Bible exhorts us to do:

> **We demolish arguments and every pretension that sets itself up against the knowledge of God, and we <u>take captive every thought to make it obedient to Christ</u>.**
> **2 Corinthians 10:5**

Christ is the living Word of God who is the truth (John 1:1 & 14:6). So we are to "take captive" thoughts and make sure that they comply with the truth. 'Truth' is *alétheia (ah-LAY-thee-ah)* in the Greek, which means "reality" or "the way it really is." So we are to take "thoughts" and make sure that they conform to **reality**. If they don't comply with the truth then they are 'weeds' of *un*reality and should be purged from the soil of our hearts.

The word 'thought' in this passage is *noéma* in the Greek *(NOH-ay-mah)*. While *noéma* can refer to thoughts, good or bad, it can also refer to **a person's perspective—mindset, attitude** or **ideology**—which is the result of indoctrination, good or bad. Indoctrination is naturally determined by the doctrine—the teaching or instruction—to which you are regularly exposed. For instance, if you sit under a secular humanist professor long enough and don't counteract what s/he teaches with the truth of the rightly-divided Word of God (or the truth *period*) you'll naturally develop a secular humanist ideology. You'll then start to live out of this mindset, to one degree or another. The doctrine or teaching you're exposed to on a regular basis determines your indoctrination, which is your mindset, good or bad. Such a mindset is a noéma.

The Greek word for "doctrine" is *didaskalia (did-as-kal-EE-ah)*. It means teaching or instruction and can be good or bad depending on how true it is or is not. The Bible speaks of sound doctrine (1 Timothy 4:6) and bad doctrine:

> **Now the Spirit expressly states that in later times some will abandon the faith to follow deceitful spirits and the <u>teachings</u>** *(didaskalia)* **of demons,**
> 1 Timothy 4:1 (ESV)

Obviously the teachings of demons aren't good because demons are *evil* spirits.

The point is that a person's mindset or ideology—noéma—is determined by the teachings to which he or she is regularly exposed. Noémas formulate over the course of time as a person is fed information. The longer it takes for a noéma to develop the more imbedded it is in the individual's psyche.

It is through negative noémas that the enemy "blinds the minds of unbelievers, so that they cannot see the light" (2 Corinthians 4:4). The devil has control of their minds—through demonic noémas—and the truth cannot penetrate the indoctrination. To help you visualize this, I went to the Facebook page of a Christian friend I hadn't seen for 25 years and was surprised by his cover pic. It was a skull with a red dragon wrapped around its head. No doubt he chose this pic because he thought it looked 'cool' or whatever, but it's actually an excellent illustration of how the enemy blinds people's minds: The red dragon represents the devil and he has control of the person's mind, which is depicted as a skull and symbolizing death, the natural result of Satan's misleading.

Notice how 2 Corinthians 10:5 (quoted above) says we are to "take captive" thoughts and mindsets. The Greek for 'take captive' literally means to "take captive as a prisoner and interrogate." The Bible is saying that we should take any perspective we have and honestly & thoroughly examine it, making sure it conforms to reality (the way it really is) rather than unreality (the way it really isn't). If we discover that the mindset does *not* comply with reality then we need to throw it out.

This can apply to any doctrine—*teaching*—you were taught during your formative years as a believer. Just because you were indoctrinated by a particular teaching in a relatively sound sect by a respected pastor doesn't make the doctrine true. So you need to "interrogate" it in light of reality. Does it comply with the rightly-divided Word of truth and the Spirit of truth (John 17:17 & 16:13)? If not, it needs to be thrown out in favor of whatever the truth is, which is reality.

As noted above, this applies to secular indoctrination as well, such as the godless humanism that's commonly taught at our secular colleges and universities. Generally speaking, the professors thereof teach that the idea of an intelligent Creator is absurd and thus life is meaningless and you're just an accident. There's nothing special about human beings, they say, and we're basically just animals. And, when ya die, that's it. The consequences of this kind of brainwashing are devastating—it produces moral rot and an attitude of no respect for life, including one's own; it encourages living with a temporal perspective (noéma) rather than an eternal one (noéma). Such a hedonistic philosophy can be summed up as: "Let us eat and drink, for tomorrow we die" (1 Corinthians 15:32).

One example of secular indoctrination is homosexuality. While homosexuality was still a crime in much of the USA as of the new millennium, that's all changed. Now homosexuality is taught to be innate and healthy in our secular culture and people are encouraged to experiment with it and embrace it as a legitimate alternative lifestyle. Our secular mentors are increasingly active homosexuals, like Ellen DeGeneres, Rachel Maddow and Anderson Cooper. Take the first two, for instance: Parents allow their children to sit under them where they're exposed to their smooth "gay" propaganda and then wonder why some of their offspring eventually embrace the homosexual lifestyle. Notable people who publicly "come out" are commended by celebrities and governing officials alike. Those who refuse to approve of homosexuality, by contrast, are considered evil bigots and punished severely, socially speaking. The truth about homosexuality, however, is that it's a damning sin and those who unrepentantly practice it will *not* inherit the kingdom of God. "Do not be deceived," the Bible warns (1 Corinthians 6:9-11).

A believer struggling with this kind of worldly indoctrination or same-sex attraction can take these noémas (mindsets) captive and interrogate them in light of the truth of Scripture and the leading of the Spirit of truth. Since these noémas don't comply with the truth they need to be purged out of one's mindset in favor of reality.

As you do this with every thought/impulse/attitude/mindset you purge your heart of falsity and unreality. This is "being made new in the attitude of your mind" (Ephesians 4:22-24).

How to Prevent Demonic Oppression and Possession

In **Chapter 9** we looked at the two main ways to deflect evil spirits. There are actually three and they're all taught in this passage:

> **Submit yourselves, then, to God. <u>Resist the devil, and he will flee from you</u>. ⁸<u>Come near to God and he will come near to you</u>. Wash your hands, you sinners, and <u>purify your hearts</u>, you double-minded.**
> **James 4:7-8**

The three ways to keep evil spirits at bay are:

1. Resist the devil and he will flee from you.
2. Draw near to God.
3. Purify your heart.

Let's look at all three:

Resist the Devil and he will Flee from You

As noted in **Chapter 9**, resisting "the devil" doesn't mean resisting Satan himself because the devil is, generally speaking, on his throne in the Underworld directing the activities of his dark kingdom. He only *personally* gets involved in matters that are of great magnitude to him, like tempting Christ to sin (Matthew 4:1-11) or moving Judas to betray Him (John 13:27). When James taught that we are to "resist the devil" he was speaking of the kingdom of darkness in terms of its leader much as historians speak of military aggression in relation to the aggressor nation's leader, like "Hitler invaded France," when, in fact, Hitler was nowhere near France. So resisting the devil means resisting the kingdom of darkness and, specifically, the evil spirits that are assigned to oppress you one way or another.

At the time that James wrote this passage he was addressing believers scattered across the nations, but his words apply to all believers scattered across the world throughout the Church Age. We're called to "resist" evil spirits and their oppression. This means we are to conduct spiritual warfare—confront and overcome enemy attacks by utilizing the armor & arms that God has faithfully supplied us, which we'll go over next chapter.

Draw Near to God

This simply means to constantly make an effort to come closer to the LORD and corresponds to the first and greatest command: "love the Lord your God with all your heart and with all your soul and with all your mind and with all your strength" (Mark 12:30).

More than anything else, to draw near to God refers to cultivating a close relationship. The gospel of Christ is called "the message of reconciliation" because it's all about *reconciling* to the Creator. To 'reconcile' means to turn from enmity to friendship. You must understand that God wants to be **your friend** (John 15:13-15). Of course, you can't have friendship without relationship; and relationship demands communion, which is genuine communication. So cultivating a close relationship with God requires developing a prayer life. Prayer is simply communion with God—talking with your Creator—and the foremost form of prayer is simple communion. This is observed in Jesus' outline for prayer:

> [9] "This, then, is how you should pray:
>
> '**Our Father in heaven,**
> **hallowed be your name,**
> [10] **your kingdom come, your will be done,**
> **on earth as it is in heaven.**
> [11] **Give us today our daily bread.**
> [12] **And forgive us our debts,**
> **as we also have forgiven our debtors.**
> [13] **And lead us not into temptation,**
> **but deliver us from the evil one.'** "
>
> **Matthew 6:9-13**

This is typically referred to as "the Lord's prayer" and people sometimes pray it word-for-word, particularly when the occasion calls for a brief scriptural prayer, like ceremonies. This is fine, but it's really not a prayer to be spoken by rote. It's actually an *outline* of different **types** of prayer. In other words, it's a prayer *skeleton* that needs to be filled in with the "flesh" of our spontaneous prayers according to our unique expressions, communion, needs or desires and the specific people or situations touching us.

The outline can be broken down as such:

- **Our Father in heaven** = Communion or fellowship with God.
- **Hallowed be your name** = Praise & worship.
- **Your kingdom come, your will be done on earth as it is in heaven** = Binding & loosing or intercession, that is, releasing God's will and kingdom into people's lives and situations on Earth, including your own (as explained in **Chapter 6**).
- **Give us today our daily bread** = Petition, that is, praying for your needs and righteous desires.
- **Forgive us our debts as we also have forgiven our debtors** = Repentance, venting, and forgiveness where applicable.
- **And lead us not into temptation, but deliver us from the evil one** = Armoring up, protection, watchfulness, speaking in faith, and deliverance.
- **For yours is the kingdom and the power and the glory forever. Amen** = Return to praise and close.

As you can see, each part of "the Lord's Prayer" refers to a specific type of prayer.

Let's consider the first two types, as they apply to our topic:

Our Father in Heaven refers to communion with God since the believer is addressing God as his or her "Father." 'Father' indicates *familial* relation and relationship requires communication, hence fellowship. Christianity at its core is a *relationship* with the Creator of the Universe, which is why the gospel is referred to as the *message of reconciliation* in 2 Corinthians 5:18-20. I encourage all believers to cultivate an intimate relationship with their heavenly Father where you're in constant communion throughout the day, even when you're in bed (Psalm 63:6). Paul referred to this as "praying without ceasing" (1 Thessalonians 5:17 KJV) and the "fellowship of the Holy Spirit" (2 Corinthians 13:14).

Please notice, by the way, that Jesus instructed us to pray *to the* Father, not to Him (Matthew 6:9). Praying to the Father in the name of Jesus is **prayer protocol** (John 16:23).

Hallowed be Your Name refers to praise & worship. To 'hallow' means to honor as holy and venerate, that is, treat with respect and reverence. God's name—YaHWeH—represents the Creator Himself so we are to hallow the Great "I Am" (Exodus 3:13-14). The only way you can accomplish this in prayer is by *telling* him. Praise is celebration and includes thanksgiving, raving and boasting, whereas worship is adoration. Praise naturally attracts God's presence and is in accordance with the law of respect: What you respect moves toward you while what you don't respect moves away from you. Worship, on the other hand, is adoration or awe, and is the response to being *in* God's presence. See Psalm 95:1-7 and Psalm 100 for verification.

We could further differentiate praise & worship as such: Praise celebrates God whereas worship humbly reveres Him; praise lifts God up while worship bows when He is lifted; praise dances before God whereas worship pulls off His shoes; praise extols God for what He's done while worship adores Him for who He is; praise says "Praise the Lord" whereas worship demonstrates that He is Lord; praise is thanksgiving for being a co-heir in Christ while worship lays the crown at His feet.

Every believer is called to deeper praise & worship. It will literally *revolutionize* your life, as it has mine and continues to do so.

It's no accident that **communion with God** and **praise & worship** are the first two kinds of prayer Jesus mentions in his outline (Matthew 6:9-13). They're simply the most important. After all, what does the average father or mother want to hear from their children, particularly as the children grow and develop? Not, "Gimme, gimme," but rather simple communion: "Hi Dad! How are you doing today? You're awesome!" "Do you have time? I'd like to just hang out with you." "Mother, I have something I've been thinking a lot about and I'd like to share it with you to see what you think." "Mom, you're so beautiful!" "Dad, tell me more about that project you're working on; it's lookin' great so far." Etcetera. If this is the kind of communion our earthly parents prefer, why would we think it's any different with our heavenly Father?

You can have these types of conversations with God throughout the day, every day—when you wake up in bed, when you're in the shower, when you're driving, when you're walking down the hall, in the evening, etc. As noted earlier, Paul referred to this as "praying without ceasing" and the "fellowship of the Holy Spirit."

We have to get away from the idea that we only encounter God when we go to church gatherings once or twice a week. This is an Old Testament mentality in the sense that the Israelites had to go to the Temple in order to meet with the LORD, as far as His presence on Earth goes. And, even then, He was hidden in the Holy of Holies where the Ark of the Covenant was located (see **Chapter 21** for details).

Purify Your Heart

As stressed in **Chapter 9**, demons are "unclean spirits" or "impure spirits," which means *filthy* spirits. As such, they're naturally attracted to that which is morally filthy. They are drawn to moral filth much as flies are attracted to excrement and rats to refuse. By contrast, the Holy Spirit and holy angels are attracted to that which is holy. "Holy" means absolutely purity, the natural result of being consecrated unto the absolutely pure Creator.[56]

This shows why the Bible instructs us to "get rid of all moral filth and the evil that is so prevalent and humbly accept the word planted

---

[56] I was at a church Bible study once where the associate pastor insisted that 'holy' doesn't refer to purity, but rather "consecrated unto God." I understandably asked: *So when God is worshipped by the seraphim and living creatures in Heaven as "Holy, holy holy is the LORD" (Isaiah 6:3 & Revelation 4:8) what these angels are really saying is "Consecrated unto God, Consecrated unto God, consecrated unto God is the LORD"?* This of course is nonsensical and the pastor had no answer; moreover he was upset that his definition of 'holy' was shown to be dubious.

in you, which can save you" (James 1:21). Doing this repels evils spirits because they're repelled by holiness and attracted to filthiness.

Yet notice that James didn't just say to get rid of the moral filth and evil, he also said to "humbly accept the word planted in you, which can save you." He was talking about the Word of God planted in believers through the teaching & preaching of Holy Scripture, which includes James' very epistle. Remember, in the 1st century they didn't have Bibles in book form available to every believer and so they relied on the teaching & preaching of the apostles, pastors and teachers who ministered to them. This included any epistles that might pass through their assemblies.

Why does James say "humbly accept" the Word planted in you? Because it "can save you." 'Save' is the Greek word *sozo (SOHD-zoh)*, which in this context means to rescue from the power of sin. James was teaching the "put off/put on" principle discussed in **Chapter 9**: Put off the moral filth and displace it with the truth. This corresponds to the law of displacement. As you do this you'll be transformed as you're "made new in the attitude of your mind":

> **You were taught, with regard to your former way of life, to <u>put off your old self</u>, which is being corrupted by its deceitful desires; ²³ to be <u>made new in the attitude of your minds</u>; ²⁴ and to <u>put on the new self</u>, created to be like God in true righteousness and holiness.**
> **Ephesians 4:22-24**

To "put off your old self" means to put off the sinful nature. The works of the flesh are obvious (Galatians 5:19-23). When you miss it, be quick to humbly 'fess up and the LORD will forgive you and cleanse you from all unrighteousness (1 John 1:8-9). John the Baptist called this "keeping with repentance" (Matthew & Luke 3:8). The repentance/forgiveness dynamic is fundamental to your walk with the Lord because it enables you to **1.** get back up when you fall, **2.** receive God's forgiveness, **3.** have your slate wiped clean, and **4.** continue to progress forward.

However, James' admonition to "get rid of all moral filth and the evil that is so prevalent" shows that putting off the old self is more than just repenting of sins committed, it's also a matter of **getting rid of anything that contributes to falling into sin, which includes anything that attracts filthy spirits**.

For instance, I've thrown away entire secular album collections because I sensed some of their dubious lyrics and imagery were holding me back. I was being led by the Holy Spirit to consecrate myself to the LORD further than I already was at the time. I've likewise thrown away movies for this same reason. I encourage believers to regularly take inventory of their possessions—the items to which they expose their eyes and ears—and purge as directed.

When I was a young Christian I had several posters on the wall of my bedroom at my parents' home that were 'sword & sorcery' in nature. I defended them on the grounds that the images were typically of warriors fighting demonic-type creatures. My brother-in-law, however, was visibly taken aback by them and argued that they could attract demonic spirits. While I didn't necessarily believe this—since they depicted mighty warriors *fighting* evil beings—I decided to take the dubious art down in favor of more agreeable and Christian-oriented works. I didn't regret the decision.

I know people who are essentially "stuck in a rut" of the past because they stubbornly refuse to move on from the art, music and accouterments with which they grew up. Please don't misunderstand me here because God's call on each person is different and the Lord often leads believers to stay within the culture or sub-culture with which they're familiar (1 Corinthians 7:17-24). Why? Because the best way to reach people in a culture is through believers *from* that culture who are familiar with it. They speak the same language and therefore people can more readily relate to them and hence receive from them. Nevertheless, if there are certain things that you sense are bogging *you* down spiritually you need to either remove them from your life or, at least, limit your exposure to them. Of course, if something's leading you into error or sin you need to get rid of it altogether.

In the early 2000s I read this book on ridding your home of spiritual darkness. The author argued that certain items can be cursed in the sense that impure spirits are attached to the articles and thus having such a cursed item in your house provides a door for that demon to oppress you one way or another. He didn't give much scriptural support and so I was skeptical—and still am—but *some* of it made sense in light of what we've gone over in these last two chapters, as well as **Chapter 9**: Demons seek places that are dry of God and are attracted to that which is morally filthy, including occult-oriented objects or items that support the occult. They're also attracted to objects of literal idolatry. In fact, the Bible says that demons are the entities *behind* the 'gods' that idols represent (1 Corinthians 10:19-22). Therefore those who worship idols are, in reality, worshipping demons! Needless to say, purge anything that has to do with idol worship from your household.

During the days of the early Church, articles that Paul touched, like handkerchiefs and aprons, "were taken to the sick, and their illnesses were cured and **the evil spirits left them**" (Acts 19:11-12). It was the same thing with Peter's shadow (Acts 5:15-16). These things had the anointing of God on them and thus physically or mentally ill people exposed to them **were healed and demons fled!** A good example from the Old Testament would be Elisha's bones (2 Kings 13:20-21). These various items were blessed as conduits of God's power. Could the inverse also be true? Could certain items be cursed with a demonic non-anointing? If the former is true with the kingdom of light, isn't it possible—even likely—that the reverse is also true with the kingdom of darkness? So don't take chances with dubious articles—purge yourself and your abode of anything questionable!

Let me share a couple of personal examples: In 2001 I purchased this wooden jungle mask while on vacation in Mexico and displayed it on our living room wall. Of course, I valued it as nothing more than an exotic piece of art, but I finally decided to discard it simply because I didn't want anything in my house to attract evil spirits, not that there was any evidence of the mask doing this. I just felt that biblically-oriented art would be more appropriate for my dwelling.

It was the same thing with these little elephant figurines that my sister innocently sent me from one of her trips abroad. My stepson informed us that they were actually idols in India, so I promptly threw 'em out. I realize that things like this come down to a person's heart and if the individual in question doesn't perceive the object in an occultist or idolatrous manner there's likely no problem. **But**, why even take the chance? As Paul said: "You cannot drink the cup of the Lord and the cup of demons too; you cannot have a part in both the Lord's table and the table of demons" (1 Corinthians 10:21).

Consider how Solomon decorating the Holy Temple in Jerusalem with godly art, like cherubim, (1 Kings 6:23-29). Fill your dwelling place with items that attract the Holy Spirit & holy angels and repel filthy spirits. Get rid of anything morally dubious. Amen?

Now relate this principle to the abode of your body & mind. YOU are a temple of God — a living, breathing *house* of God (1 Corinthians 3:16). What's 'decorating' the walls of your mind & heart? This offers additional insight to James' admonition to purify our hearts.

'You Kids Stay Off Drugs!'

Drugs played a vital role in ancient cults with their lifeless prayers to their gods—that is, demons—at pagan shrines and the magic empowered by these lying spirits. Sorcerers and witches used drugs in their spells, which explains something about the words "witchcraft" or "sorcery" used in Paul's list of the works of the flesh in Galatians 5:19-21. The original Greek term is *pharmakeia (far-mah-KIH-ah)* and is where we get the words pharmacy and pharmaceutical. It literally means "drugs" or "medication" and only refers to magic by extension due to witches and magicians using drugs in their spells. As a work of the flesh, *pharmakeia* concerns any and all drug-related sins, which includes drug experimentation, drug abuse, drug trafficking, etc.

Needless to say, we should shun drugs if we want to avoid demonic influence, oppression and possession. This includes doctor-approved meds that you don't really need, which doctors perpetually prescribe in order to keep the pharmaceutical biz thriving more than anything else.

The enemy uses witchcraft (including supposed "white" witchcraft), sorcery, séances, Ouija boards, and all occult-oriented activities to open a person up to demonic influence on a more personal basis, with partial or total possession being the goal.

Are there Spirits of Certain Sins, like Lust?

Christ said that some demons are more wicked than others (Matthew 12:45), but did he mean more wicked in general or more wicked in regard to a particular sin? I assume the former.

In any case, just as people are assigned heavenly angels (Matthew 18:10) so individuals are presumably assigned evils spirits on behalf of the kingdom of darkness. Just as angels are watchers, as detailed in **Chapter 1**, so demons are watchers. And it wouldn't take long for an evil spirit assigned to a person to discern what his/her fleshly weaknesses are, whether envy, jealousy, hatred, arrogance, strife, greed, lust, perversion, alcohol, drugs, sloth, fear, doubt, depression, etc. Once a demon determines the carnal proclivity, it then "works with" the person to get him or her to live according to their carnal weakness, whatever that is.

It must be stressed, again, that devils never *make* a person sin except in cases where someone is wholly possessed, which—as covered last chapter—is something that takes place down the road, after a person has *already* significantly conceded to the corrupt desires of the flesh. The Bible makes it clear that sin is the result of one's "own evil desire" and so no one can claim 'The devil made me do it' (James 1:14-15). Consider, for example, when Satan tempted Christ: The Enemy knew Jesus was weak & hungry from fasting so he slyly proposed that he turn the rocks into bread and partake, but the devil couldn't *make* Him do anything (Matthew 4:1-4). All evil spirits can do is *tempt*. The decision to commit evil or not comes down to the will of the individual.

If a demon successfully tempts a person and gets him/her into the habitual practice of sin it would eventually attract other evil spirits because filthy spirits are naturally drawn to that which is morally filthy. While these spirits may be attracted to the specific sin in question, they may just as well be attracted to sin in general. Whatever the case, a satanic bondage to the sin thus develops.

Thankfully, there's freedom in Christ (John 8:31-32), but it doesn't come through rebuking a demon of a particular sin, like a "spirit of alcohol" or a "spirit of gossip" or a "spirit of homosexuality." Although there's nothing wrong with authoritatively saying "Away from me, foul spirit" if you discern you're under severe temptation; after all, Jesus did this (Matthew 4:10). Freedom from sin comes through **1.** being spiritually regenerated (if the person isn't saved) and **2.** knowing and applying the relevant truths of God's Word, as detailed above—putting off the evil desires of the flesh and learning to live out of your new nature by the Holy Spirit, which includes renewing the mind (Ephesians 4:22-24).

Notice how the Lord said freedom is attained:

> **Then Jesus said to those who had believed in him, "<u>If</u> you <u>continue in my word</u>, you are truly my disciples;** [32] **and <u>you will know the truth</u>, and <u>the truth will make you free</u>."**
> **John 8:31-32 (NRSV)**

So acquiring the truth and putting it into practice is what sets people free, not verbally rebuking a demon of such-and-such sin. As the individual who is struggling with a particular sin acquires truth and puts it into practice any evil spirit oppressing him or her will eventually flee and seek easier game (James 4:7).[57] But the person has to be diligent with the things of the spirit because demons are going to fight tooth & nail to keep an individual in bondage to the sin in question. **Life's a fight, fight it.**

Of course, in cases where a person is partially or fully possessed he/she would have to *first* be exorcized of the demon(s), followed by the applicable 2-step process above.

In the previous chapter we saw that the word 'spirit' does not always mean a spiritual entity; it can simply refer to a person's character,

---

[57] This brings up a question: If a demon is assigned to an individual, where would it flee to if it leaves that particular person? We can only theorize based on the biblical data: Obviously demons aren't assigned to one individual and that's it. For instance, people eventually die and new people are born. Evil spirits are assigned to human candidates within a territory and they naturally go where their efforts are proving fruitful. The demoniac from the Gerasenes, for instance, had hundreds or thousands of demons in him. Also keep in mind that only a third of the angels fell with Satan, so there's a limit to their numbers.

as in Joshua had "a different spirit" than the other Hebrews (Numbers 14:24). So whereas I think it's unbiblical to say that a person has a spirit of a particular sin in reference to demonic spirits, you could say that s/he has a spirit of such-and such sin in regards to *their developed character*. For instance: "Mark has a spirit of lust," "Carrie has a spirit of lying," "Alex has a spirit of rage" or "Zach has a spirit of legalism." This simply means that they've developed the *character* of the sin in question due to habitually giving-in to the flesh in that particular area. This is true in regards to noémas (mindsets/ideologies) as well. For instance, someone can have a spirit of liberalism.

It *is* biblical, however, to rebuke a "spirit of infirmity" if you genuinely discern that a person's disability is induced by a demon or demons. Examples include a crippling problem (Luke 13:11,16), deafness and muteness (Mark 9:25) or mental illness (Mark 5:1-8). Of course, **not all infirmities are directly caused by evil spirits**, so you have to have spiritual discernment to effectively minister in these cases. And the only way you can do this is to have genuine spiritual sensitivity, which comes by drawing closer to the LORD, as well as eagerly *desiring* gifts of the Spirit rather than eagerly *denying* them (1 Corinthians 12:1,31 & 14:1,39). If you're not sure if a spirit is behind the infirmity in question, simply rebuke the ailment itself, as Jesus did (Luke 4:39). As a believer and co-heir in Christ you have the authority to do the works the Messiah did (John 14:12). So get in the habit of boldly declaring your authority in Christ, take charge over any sickness and command it to leave. We'll look at this further in the next two chapters.

For more details on dealing with spirits of infirmities see the final section of **Chapter 16**.

In these last two chapters we've explored how to deflect evil spirits, closing with the three simple yet effective ways to repel demons—**1.** resist their attacks, **2.** draw near to God and **3.** purify your heart. Actually, God has provided an easy, surefire means to achieve this. I'm talking about…

Chapter 19

The Armor & Weaponry of God

Anyone who regularly takes advantage of the armor & arms of God will automatically **1.** draw closer to God, **2.** activate angels on your behalf and **3.** deter evils spirits. Those who don't **won't**. Thus it's imperative to have a basic understanding of God's armor & weaponry.

We'll first look at what each piece of the armor & arms is and then observe how to use each of these spiritual tools throughout your day. I encourage you to utilize either of the two 7-item breakdowns as a checklist until you can "put on" the armor & weaponry without even referencing a list. I do this daily as soon as I wake.

Speaking of which, the armor & arms of God are not things you "put on" and that's it. They're obviously not literal pieces of armor & weaponry, but rather figurative of **spiritual things YOU DO, and continue to DO, throughout any given day**. Because of this, it's possible for a believer to be using the armor & arms of God without even knowing you're doing so. If this doesn't make sense, it will once you understand what each piece is.

You've no doubt heard sermons or read books/articles on this topic and that's great. But I encourage you not to limit your view of the armor & arms of God to the way you first heard it. I'm not saying that what you were taught was wrong, but simply encouraging you to be open to new insights. The armor & weaponry of God are instrumental to successful spiritual warfare and a proper understanding of them is vital to a victorious walk with the Lord.

Let's start by reading the relevant text:

> **Finally, be strong in the Lord and in his mighty power. [11] Put on <u>the full armor of God</u>, so that you can take your stand against the devil's schemes. [12] For our struggle is not against flesh and blood, but against the rulers, against the authorities, against the powers of this dark world and against <u>the spiritual forces of evil in the heavenly realms</u>. [13] Therefore put on <u>the full armor of God</u>, so that when <u>the day of evil</u> comes, you may be able to stand your ground, and after you have done everything, to stand.**
>
> **[14] Stand firm then, with <u>the belt of truth</u> buckled around your waist, with <u>the breastplate of righteousness</u> in place, [15] and <u>with your feet fitted with the readiness that comes from the gospel of peace</u>. [16] In addition to all this, take up <u>the shield of faith</u>, with which you can extinguish all the flaming arrows of the evil one. [17] Take <u>the helmet of salvation</u> and <u>the sword of the Spirit</u>, which is the word of God.**
>
> **[18] And <u>pray in the Spirit</u> on all occasions with all kinds of prayers and requests. With this in mind, be alert and always keep on praying for all the Lord's people.**
>
> **Ephesians 6:10-18**

The first paragraph is simply an introduction to God's armor & weaponry wherein several important points are stressed:

ANGELS

> ➤ **God *wants* you to be strong in Him and walk in his mighty power.** The way you do this is by putting on the armor of God and using the weapons he provides. Speaking of which…
> ➤ **Use the FULL armor.** Twice we're encouraged to put on the *full* armor, not part of it, which shows that every piece is necessary to effectively withstand the enemy's attacks.
> ➤ **The identity and nature of the enemy.** Your enemy is not flesh & blood—that is, people—but rather "the spiritual forces of evil in the heavenly realms." This refers to the evil spirits commissioned to assault you & yours.
> ➤ **Your *need* for God's armor & weaponry.** Since evil spirits are spiritual in nature, and therefore invisible, it requires intangible protection & arms to overcome them.
> ➤ **The "day of evil."** This refers to *when* you are attacked by the kingdom of darkness. You are not attacked every second of every day (although, of course, you have to constantly contend with the evil desires of the flesh, but that's a different issue). There are *specific times* when the enemy will assault you. This is the "day of evil." The Bible is warning every believer that the enemy will attack. It's not a question of *if* you will be attacked, but rather a matter of *when*.
> ➤ **The *purpose* of God's armor & weaponry: Your victory.** The LORD *wants* you to be victorious when the enemy attacks; He *wants* you to withstand the assault. This is the very reason he provides these defenses & arms. You must get it through your head that God is on *your* side: He's *for* you and *not* against you (Romans 8:31).

When Paul wrote the epistle to the Ephesians he was under house arrest in Rome and so there were Roman soldiers constantly in his vicinity. As such, he was able to get a good look at their armor & weaponry and drew parallels, by the Spirit, to the intangible armor & arms God provides for every believer, which includes YOU.

Here are the seven pieces of the armor & arms of God and an explanation of each:

1. **The Belt of Truth** (verse 14): This is the first piece of armor because truth is essential for victory in a world governed by the father of lies (John 8:44). Truth is *alétheia (ah-LAY-thee-ah)* in the Greek meaning "reality" or "the way it really is." The belt of truth is simply **devotion to seeking and finding the truth and living according to it, utilizing the sources of truth that God has provided**. The other pieces of the armor & weaponry of God are *dependent on* this piece of armor, which explains why it's the first one.

   There are two main sources of truth: **1. The Living Word**, who is truth (John 14:6), and **2. The written Word**, which is truth, assuming it's interpreted soundly, balancing out truth with truth (John 17:17). *Both* sources are essential: The first refers to seeking the Living Word so that you are led by the Spirit of truth (John 16:13) while the second refers to feeding from the written Word and acquiring truth through "rightly dividing" it (2 Timothy 2:15). The way you do the second is twofold—receiving from sound ministers of God (Ephesians 4:11-13) and receiving through personal study (1 John 2:27).

   Be careful to pursue the truth above loyalty to a particular sect. Otherwise you'll fall into the pitfall of sectarianism, which is a work of the flesh.[58]

2. **The Breastplate of Righteousness** (verse 14): This piece of armor refers to living out of your new nature—your spirit—because it was *born* righteous when you accepted the gospel and underwent spiritual regeneration. This is your "new self, which was ***created to be like God*** in true righteousness" (Ephesians 4:22-24). As you learn to walk according to this new nature with the help and guidance of the Holy Spirit you'll naturally walk in *practical* righteousness. So putting on your breastplate of righteousness is one-and-the-same as walking in the spirit (Galatians 5:16).

   Of course, as a human being with a flesh, you'll inevitably sin; this includes the more common sins like envy, jealousy, rivalry, hatred, gossip, lying, greed or lust. Those who

---

[58] See the footnote on page 111 for exposition on sectarianism.

have their "breastplate" on will humbly 'fess up and receive God's forgiveness, which "purifies you from all unrighteousness" (1 John 1:8-9). Doing this is "keeping with repentance" (Matthew & Luke 3:8). The repentance/forgiveness dynamic is essential to spiritual growth because it ensures God's grace continually flowing in your life and your ongoing progress. It keeps your spiritual arteries clear of the clog-up of unconfessed sin.[59]

A Roman soldier's breastplate guarded his heart and other vital organs. Just so, the breastplate of righteousness guards your figurative heart—your mind—and prevents it from being corrupted by things that would eventually destroy you (Proverbs 4:23).

3. **The Gospel of Peace Shoes** (verse 15): The "gospel of peace" refers to the message of Christ, which is the "message of reconciliation" (2 Corinthians 5:18-21). 'Reconciliation' means "to turn from enmity to friendship." It's through the gospel that you have *peace* with your Creator and are born His beloved son & daughter (1 John 3:2,9). It's through this gospel that you become Christ's friend (John 15:14-15).

The Roman soldier's footwear was designed for firm-footing, which was a life-or-death matter in combat. When you face spiritual attack, your peace with God is likewise a matter of life and death—success or victory. The text says that the gospel of peace shoes grant the believer "readiness." This is the Greek word *hetoimasia (het-oy-mas-EE-ah)*, which means "foundation" or "firm-footing" without which you won't be ready or prepared for battle.

Putting this all together, your *relationship* with the Lord is foundational to withstanding spiritual attack. **Having your gospel of peace shoes on means developing a close relationship with God and maintaining it.** Someone might say

---

[59] Incredibly, there's this widespread false teaching amongst Evangelicals today which suggests that believers never have to repent of anything, ever. Jesus must have been walking in gross error when he instructed the Ephesian Christians to repent in Revelation 2:5 (sarcasm).

that this sounds similar to the belt of truth, but the belt refers specifically to acquiring truth from both The Living Word and the written Word. The gospel of peace shoes, by contrast, are focused on your *relationship* with God period. In other words, the belt of truth concerns procuring the truth from the Living Word and the written Word whereas the gospel of peace shoes concern your *rapport* with the Person of God. The belt has to do with learning **the principles of God's kingdom** whereas the shoes have to do with knowing **the Person of God**.

Make no mistake, without this vital relationship the enemy will chew you up and spit you out, one way or another. One of the Enemy's favorite strategies is to mislead believers into the pit of sterile religiosity where they know *about* God, but don't *know* Him. People like this have "a form of godliness but deny its power" (2 Timothy 3:5). They're akin to the lifeless Pharisees.

If the gospel of peace shoes—that is, your relationship with God—is foundational to your spiritual walk, why isn't it the *first* piece of armor to put on? Why do truth (the belt of truth) and walking in the spirit (the breastplate of righteousness) take precedence? Because the gospel of peace shoes relate to communion with God and therefore worship. And Jesus said "God is spirit, and his worshipers must worship in the spirit and in truth" (John 4:24). Think about it: Without the belt of truth we can't worship God properly and our communion would be prone to error. Similarly, without the breastplate of righteousness we would fall into worshipping God out of our flesh rather than out of our spirit. So both the belt of truth and breastplate of righteousness come first.

4. **The Shield of Faith** (verse 16): The Roman soldier's shield was huge and would easily cover his whole body when he knelt behind it, protecting him from arrows, spears and the like. Just the same, the shield of faith protects the believer by "extinguishing all the flaming arrows of the evil one." *But* you have to put this faith shield up or you'll get hit. Think about it in terms of the space crafts on *Star Trek:* If the Enterprise doesn't have its invisible shields up, the opponent could destroy them

with phaser fire, photon torpedoes, etc. So it's imperative that you have your faith shield up to protect yourself from enemy attacks.

How do you do this? Simple: Regularly release your faith by speaking according to the promises of God in the five general areas of satanic attack. Remember, your tongue has the power of life and death (Proverbs 18:21). As you give voice to God's Word your angels will be employed to serve you accordingly. They'll erect a "hedge of protection" around you. What are these five areas of attack? As covered in **Chapter 6** and, particularly, **Chapter 20** they are **1.** physical ailments, **2.** mental maladies, **3.** defeat to human enemies, **4.** premature death and **5.** financial attack. Consider the first one as an example: If you use the power of your tongue to speak death by confessing something like "There's a flu bug going around so I'll probably get sick" you just threw your shield out the window and opened yourself up to attack. This foolishly prevents your angels from doing their job of protecting you. Instead, erect your shield and activate your guardian angels by saying "That virus that's going around is under my feet and has no authority on my body; by the torture of Christ, who redeemed me from all curses (Isaiah 53:5), I'm free of all sicknesses & diseases." If you do this and *believe*,[60] whatever virus that's going around will hit your invisible shield and not harm you whatsoever. *Never ever* talk sickness & disease. Speak health and blessing.

You must understand that every blessing in the New Covenant is *attained* and *maintained* by faith, including your salvation (Romans 10:9-10). What is faith? Faith is not belief in fantasies or fantastical things, like Leprechauns, but rather belief

---

[60] If you *don't* believe then you'll need to feed on the applicable Word of God, which is how faith comes (Romans 10:17), as well as pray in the spirit (Jude 20), which is the 7th piece of the armor. Every believer has a "measure of faith" when he or she comes to the Lord, but faith can grow (Romans 12:3) and these are two of the main ways to do it, as well as spending more time in God's presence, of course. Paul observed in 2 Thessalonians 1:3 that the faith of the Thessalonian believers was growing. Your faith can likewise increase, but it's dependent on YOU.

based on the knowledge of truth (reality) that you acquire; which is released through the power of your tongue.

How is this invisible "shield" erected and maintained around you as you walk in faith? By the angels assigned to you, who obey the voice of God's Word, as detailed in **Chapter 5**.

The text says that the shield of faith "can extinguish *all* the flaming arrows of the evil one." In other words, if you have your faith defenses up, no curse will be able to hit you. For instance, Carol & I always have our shields up concerning sickness & disease and so we're hardly ever hit. I say "hardly ever" because there are three kinds of exceptions, which we'll look at below when we cover the sword of the spirit.

5. **The Helmet of Salvation** (verse 17): The helmet protected the Roman soldier's head. Likewise, the helmet of salvation protects the believer's mind from distress when undergoing satanic attack. As you apply the wisdom principles of God's Word and "fight the good fight of faith" as led of the Holy Spirit (1 Timothy 6:12), it's guaranteed that the LORD will deliver you (2 Peter 2:9). This assurance grants you peace of mind that transcends understanding in the midst of attack. In short, the helmet of salvation prevents your mind from going squirrelly when experiencing demonic assault.

As an example, I underwent a serious attack last Fall, but I had peace of mind about it and therefore had the grace to endure the ramifications of the assault, which lasted exactly 40 days, the biblical number of perfection in testing or judgment.[61]

---

[61] For example, it rained on the Earth 40 days (Genesis 7:12), Moses fled to the desert to attend flocks for 40 years (Acts 7:30), Moses was on Mt. Sinai with God for 40 days (Exodus 24:18), Moses fasted & prayed for the Israelites for 40 days (Deuteronomy 9:18,25), the maximum lashes for a crime was 40 lashes (Deuteronomy 25:3), the 12 Hebrews reconnoitered the Promised Land for 40 days (Numbers 13:25), the Israelites wandered in the desert wilderness for 40 years (Deuteronomy 8:2-5), the Israelites suffered under the oppression of the Philistines for 40 years before God raised up Samson (Judges 13:1), Goliath balked at Saul's army for 40 days before David miraculously slew him (1 Samuel 17:16) and Elijah fled from Jezebel for 40 days to Mt. Horeb (1 Kings 19:8).

The helmet of salvation is the absolute assurance that God will deliver you when you suffer attack as you walk in faith & perseverance and don't give up.

This certainty of salvation includes the most important salvation—eternal salvation. Your eternal salvation is guaranteed as you continue in faith and endure (John 10:29 & Colossians 1:22-23).

The last two pieces of the armor of God are notable in that they're not solely defensive in nature, but offensive as well. That's because they're not actually armor, but rather **weaponry**...

6. **The Sword of the Spirit** (verse 17): This weapon is defined as "the word of God." How does this piece differ from the belt of truth, which refers to the truth of the rightly divided word of God? Simple: The sword of the spirit does not refer to the pursuit of truth, as does the belt of truth, but rather to the word of God spoken in bold faith as a weapon. To do this, of course, you have to first *acquire* the word of truth by "putting on" the belt. This shows that the belt of truth is a foundational piece of the armor & arms of God, which is why it's the first one you don.

    How does this differ from the shield of faith which is erected by speaking the word of God in faith? Simple: The shield is strictly designed for defense whereas the sword is intended for both defense and offense. Since believers are ambassadors of the kingdom of God and function on Earth as enemies in enemy territory it's necessary to have your shield of faith up at all times to protect yourself from unforeseen attacks. (Think of it in terms of potential sniper fire when soldiers are in war zones). The sword of the spirit, by contrast, isn't pulled from its figurative "scabbard" *until* there's evidence of enemy attack in one of the five general ways noted above, whether concerning you or someone for whom you're interceding. Similarly, Roman soldiers wouldn't pull out their swords until the enemy assaulted them or if they went to the enemy to attack them. Either way, the enemy must be in sight to use the sword.

Speaking of which, devils obviously won't manifest in your life in the form of red cartoony figures with pitchforks. When evil spirits attack it will manifest via one of the five general curses noted above—physical maladies, mental illnesses, unjust human attack, premature death and financial lack. We observe this in the Enemy's attacks on Job (Job 1-2). When one or more of these curses show up in your life you are under enemy assault and it's time to get your sword out and start swinging! If you don't, you'll be defeated. There are also five other kinds of enemy attack, which apply to spiritual things; they are detailed next chapter.

We'll further differentiate the sword of the spirit from the shield of faith below and elaborate on when and how to use both.

7. **Praying in the Spirit** (verses 18-20): Most ministers omit this last article when teaching on the armor of God, but it's a vital piece of spiritual weaponry. Paul instructed us to "pray in the Spirit on all occasions with all kinds of prayers and requests." What does it mean to "pray in the spirit"? Notice how the Bible defines it:

> **For if I <u>pray in a tongue</u>, <u>my spirit prays</u>, but my mind is unfruitful. ¹⁵ So what shall I do? I will <u>pray with my spirit</u>, but I will also <u>pray with my understanding</u>; I will sing with my spirit, but I will also sing with my understanding.**
> **1 Corinthians 14:14-15**

As you can see, God's Word defines praying in the spirit as praying in another tongue via your spirit by the Spirit. This is different than typical prayer, of course, which is to "pray with your understanding," meaning to pray with your mind using the language with which you're most familiar. In my case it would be English. Paul said he did both: He prayed (and sang) with his spirit and he also prayed (and sang) with his understanding. We need to do *both* as well; Paul was our example. And please notice that he lists praying in the spirit *before* praying with your understanding, which implies that it's at least *as* important.

Also observe that he instructs us to "pray in the Spirit on **all occasions** with *all kinds of prayers and requests.*" In other words, we should include praying in the spirit every time we pray; and with every *type* of prayer! We discussed the different types of prayer last chapter—communion, praise & worship, binding & loosing, intercession, petition, venting & forgiving. Get in the practice of praying in the spirit with all these different kinds of prayers on "all occasions."

Speaking of which, I encourage you to go on the offensive with this spiritual weapon. In other words, don't simply use it when you discern you're being attacked. Use this awesome gift on "all occasions" day and night. Evils spirits will run away screaming in all directions!

If you don't yet have the baptism of the Holy Spirit, then make it a priority to receive it. This awesome gift is available to *all* believers. Unfortunately, most of Christendom is either ignorant of this gift or is deceived about it, erroneously insisting that it "passed away" when the biblical canon was completed. Don't buy the lie. God's Word encourages us to eagerly *desire* spiritual gifts, not eagerly *deny* them (1 Corinthians 12:1,31 & 14:1,39). These gifts include the gift of personal tongues, otherwise known as glossolalia *(gloss-ah-LAY-lee-ah)*.

Paul didn't provide a metaphor for praying in the spirit as he did with the other pieces of God's armor, like "belt," "shield" and "sword." I suspect this was because there was no Roman armament that could compare to the weapon of praying in the spirit. I like to refer to it as *the missiles* of praying in the spirit because you can pray for people and situations on the other side of the planet; in fact, you can pray for situations you're not even cognizant of because when you pray in the spirit you bypass the limitations of your mind—your understanding— through your spirit with the help of the Holy Spirit.

For details on this awesome piece of weaponry and its benefits please see the teaching *Baptism of the Holy Spirit* at the Fountain of Life website.

Differentiating the Shield of Faith and Sword of the Spirit

Now that you understand what each piece of the armor & weaponry of God is, let's go into a little more detail on distinguishing the shield of faith from the sword of the spirit.

A question might have occurred to you: If the shield of faith "extinguishes *all* the flaming arrows of the evil one" why is the sword of the spirit necessary? In other words, how does a curse that's assaulting you get past your shield and require you to get out your sword? There are four possible reasons:

- If you don't have your belt of truth on your faith won't be effective as a shield because faith comes through first being exposed to the truth (Romans 10:17). In short, if you don't have the truth you won't have the faith. This, again, reveals why the belt of truth is the first piece of armor that you "put on."
- For one reason or another, your shield wasn't up. For instance, you canceled your shield by speaking doubt and unbelief. This, of course, deactivates your protective angels because angels are commissioned to obey the voice of God's Word, as covered in **Chapter 4** and **5**.
- You opened the door to the enemy through unrepentant disobedience, whether a sin of commission or sin of omission.[62]
- You're undergoing a **Maturing-Intended Trial** (MIT), which means that you're suffering attack for righteousness' sake. In this type of trial the LORD is permitting the assault for the purpose of testing your motivations and spurring growth through actively confronting challenges and working your faith muscles. Consider Job's trials detailed in Job 1-2: It is clearly established from the get-go that Job was blameless and upright so we know he didn't open the door to the Enemy through disobedience. Nowhere does

---

[62] A **sin of commission** is something you *do*, like slander someone through gossip, whereas a **sin of omission** is something you *didn't* do that you should've done, like give a poor person some money as the Spirit led you.

it state that Job opened the door to the devil through fear or disobedience; in fact, God praised Job to the devil as *blameless!* However, the LORD was compelled to allow Satan to attack Job to test his motivations: Was Job's piety a charade for the sake of acquiring God's blessings? Would Job curse the Almighty or deny God's existence if his many blessings were removed? Although the rest of the book of Job shows him struggling greatly and seriously venting to the LORD during his long trial (e.g. Job 10:1-3), Job didn't turn away from his Creator, but rather went directly *to* Him, which takes faith; not to mention he persevered. Job therefore passed the test and God restored him and doubly blessed him (Job 42:10).

When one or more of the five general curses manifests in your life you need to search your spirit and discern how it got past your shield (assuming your shield is up) and respond accordingly:

- If your words had no power when you spoke in faith because you failed to don your belt of truth, then put on your belt by going to God's Word and feeding on the truths relevant to your trial (Matthew 4:4). Then start speaking in bold faith accordingly.
- If you either failed to put up your faith shield in the first place or canceled out your shield by using your tongue to speak unbelief, you need to repent and do as above: Feed on God's Word in the relevant area and then speak it in authoritative faith. Remember: Your enemy is spiritual in nature, so defeating demonic assaults requires spiritual warfare, not physical. This and the previous point could be filed under **Self-Inflicted Trials** (SITs) because you're only being attacked due to your spiritual negligence or unbelief.
- If you are convicted of a sin immediately 'fess up and God will forgive you; and then start swinging your sword as necessary. This is a **Discipline-Intended Trial** (DIT) where you opened the door to the enemy through unrepentant sin (Ephesians 4:27). Hence the attack is a disciplinary measure on God's part. Just a few days ago Carol said she felt sickness trying to come on her at work and, upon searching her heart, she was convicted of

walking out of love with a contentious baby Christian (remember, "faith works in love," so if you walk out of love you walk out of faith). Carol swiftly repented and started swinging her sword and the sickness withdrew. By the time she arrived home there was zero evidence of sickness.

- If you *know* your shield was up and you're walking in obedience according to the terms of your Covenant—"faith working in love" (Galatians 5:6)—then you can be sure that you're undergoing a **Maturity-Intended Trial** (MIT). Simply resist in faith and the enemy will flee like a pathetic cur with his tail between his legs (James 4:7); in the meantime stand and endure. As was the case with Job, God will "restore you and make you strong, firm and steadfast" "**after** you have suffered a little while" (1 Peter 5:8-10). You will experience greater maturity and favor with God as a result, just as Job did.

Now, someone might complain that spiritual warfare is complicated by the fact that it requires you to determine if the malady is a disciplinary measure on God's part due to unrepentant disobedience or an attack from the kingdom of darkness for righteousness' sake, permitted by the Sovereign LORD. Well, that's just the way it is and it's this very factor that calls for an actual *relationship* with God through "the fellowship of the Holy Spirit" (2 Corinthians 13:14). Relationship is what true Christianity is about and this separates it from mere human religion. What do I mean? If a believer has a genuine relationship with God s/he will be able to discern fairly easily if the curse that's assaulting him/her is due to a **Self-Inflicted Trial** (SIT), a **Discipline-Intended Trial** (DIT) or a **Maturity-Intended Trial** (MIT). On the other hand, believers who fail to cultivate communion with God will have a harder time distinguishing SITs, DITs and MITs, particularly DITs and MITs (as SITs are always obvious). So this is a spur to go deeper in your walk with God, and that's what this book is all about.[63]

---

[63] See the final section of **Chapter 6** for a more thorough explanation of the three types of trials.

"Putting On" the Armor of God on Any Given Day

As noted earlier, the armor & arms of God are figurative of the spiritual tools the LORD has provided us in order to overcome spiritual attack. "Putting on" the armor is not something you do at the beginning of the day and that's the end of it. The armor & weaponry of God are spiritual principles to be practiced throughout your day and week. They empower you, shield you from satanic attack, activate your angels and guarantee victory.

I've gotten in the habit of going over the armor & arms in my prayer time when I wake up every morning (with the exception of a day of rest). It's basically a spiritual checklist that keeps me conscious of these seven vital articles and therefore regularly practicing them.

Let's succinctly rundown all seven pieces as you would practice them on any given day (since each is explained above I'm going to limit scriptural references to additional insights):

1. **The Belt of Truth:** Make a genuine effort to seek the truth—reality—through the two main sources of spiritual truth:
   - The Living Word via the Spirit of truth.
   - The written Word via the balanced teachings of sound ministers and your own studies in God's Word.
2. **The Breastplate of Righteousness:** Endeavor to live out of your new nature, which was "created to be like God in true righteousness." The Bible calls this "participating in the divine nature" (2 Peter 1:4). Cultivate a pliable, humble heart that's quick & willing to 'fess up if you succumb to the corrupt desires of the old nature. God is faithful to dismiss the sin and "purify you from all unrighteousness." Guard your heart as the wellspring of life by regularly rooting-out negative, destructive thoughts & desires (Proverbs 4:23).
3. **The Gospel of Peace Shoes:** Put on your gospel shoes by cultivating a prayer life, regularly communing with the LORD. Your relationship with God is foundational and offers you sure-footing when facing spiritual attack.

4. **The Shield of Faith:** Use the power of your tongue to erect a shield around you by speaking in faith concerning the blessings that are yours in Christ. Do not speak doubt & unbelief or you will cancel out your shield and deactivate your angels. Every blessing provided in your covenant comes through faith & perseverance. So never ever give up.
5. **The Helmet of Salvation:** Guard you mind by being conscious of God's promises of deliverance as you walk in faith & endurance. This assurance of salvation—including eternal salvation—will keep your mind from going batty during an attack.
6. **The Sword of the Spirit:** Use the Word of God as a defensive and offensive weapon by speaking it in bold faith when discerning an attack by the enemy on you or yours. Use it in intercession.
7. **Praying in the Spirit:** Pray in the spirit on all occasions with each type of prayer noted in the Lord's prayer outline (Matthew 6:9-11). This weapon is especially useful in situations where you don't know what to pray with your understanding or have limited knowledge concerning what to pray. Pray and sing in the spirit! Get in the habit of praying in the spirit full blast for five-ten minutes or so when you get up in the morning. It will get your day off to an awesome start.

The reason it's necessary to understand and utilize the armor & arms of God is because donning the armor and taking up your weapons empowers you by protecting you from evil spirits and their schemes; it activates angels on your behalf and guarantees your victory.

Someone might say, "But it's so simple." Yes, it is. Victory in Christ is easy as pie. That's the beauty and genius of it. There *is* a yoke and burden to serving the LORD, but the yoke is easy and the burden is light (Matthew 11:28-30). But religious people evidently want a hard yoke and heavy burden, speaking of which...

An Erroneous Reaction to the Armor & Arms of God

It boggles my mind when I come across sincere believers who respond negatively to the purpose of the armor & weaponry of God, as detailed above. Such people embrace the sickness, defeat, death & poverty gospel. They basically fight for their right to be downtrodden by curses, like physical maladies, mental illness, defeat to enemies, premature death and poverty/lack. They have a sick masochistic martyr complex.

I want to make it clear that **every believer will be attacked in these areas**. That's how the kingdom of darkness manifests, not as quaint red devils with pitchforks! Even if you have your shield up, which "extinguishes all the flaming arrows of the evil one," you'll have to get your sword out and fight the good fight of faith and persevere, as explained above. When this occurs, you're going to "suffer for a little while," as Peter put it, but the LORD *will* restore you and make you strong, firm and steadfast (1 Peter 5:8-10).

Consider the example of Paul, the great apostle, who undertook several missionary journeys to reach the world for Christ. Notice what he said:

> **I am not saying this because I am in need, for I have learned to be content whatever the circumstances.** [12] **<u>I know what it is to be in need</u>, and <u>I know what it is to have plenty</u>. I have learned the secret of being content in any and every situation, <u>whether well fed or hungry</u>, <u>whether living in plenty or in want</u>.** [13] **I can do all this through him who gives me strength.**
>
> **Philippians 4:11-13**

Paul starts off by insisting that he *wasn't* in need—a "positive confession" for sure—but admits that he experienced times of need in his ministry travels, as well as times of plenty. He then unveils his secret of contentment in every situation "whether well fed or hungry, whether living in plenty or in want": He can do all things through Christ who gives him strength. In short, Paul's resources—his finances, in essence—were assuredly attacked at times, but he endured in faith knowing that he was rich in Christ (2 Corinthians 8:9). As such, he knew the resources would come as he persevered in faith. **And they always did.** He could "do all things through Christ who strengthens him" (KJV). That's the secret to contentment during satanic attack and the suffering thereof.

You see Paul had his helmet of salvation on. He had his shield of faith up. He *didn't* cancel out his shield by giving-in to doubt and speaking unbelief, like "I don't think God's going to come through this time; I'm not going to make it." No, he held on in faith and endured; and the resources always came. Praise God!

A Personal Example

In the winter of 2013 my left knee swelled up and I could hardly bend it. Simply walking across the room or climbing stairs was painful. This was a malady that obviously got past my shield of faith. It was a Maturity-Intended Trial (MIT), an attack by the enemy for righteousness' sake. I needed surgery, but decided instead to claim healing and stand in faith. It took over three long months but my healing finally manifested and by Christmas time I was snow skiing. Needless to say, it wasn't fun during those 3½ months that I was suffering. Sometimes squirrelly thoughts would cross my mind, like *"Why are you allowing this to happen, God?! I'm seeking you and serving you more than ever!"* But I rejected the victim mentality and the corresponding verbiage. I refused to blow money on doctors, take meds and get surgery. I stood in faith, swinging my sword. Carol & I kept laying hands on my knee, praying and believing. And the healing eventually manifested! Before the year was over I was skiing down huge hills in New York! God is Good!

By the way, I'm not saying that you shouldn't go to the doctor. Do what you have the faith to do as led of the Holy Spirit. Luke was a physician and I encourage regular check-ups. During my trial I was simply led to receive healing from the Great Physician rather than blow time & money on earthly doctors. In order to do this you have to develop stubborn faith regarding the benefits that Christ bought for you. Speaking of which…

Chapter 20

Do You Know What You're Fighting For?

What good is it to know about the armor & arms of God if you don't know *when* the enemy is attacking you or someone else? I've said it before and I'll say it again, the devil & his loser minions aren't going to manifest as cartoony red characters with cloven hooves and pitch forks. They're *spiritual* beings and therefore invisible to the human eye. The way they attack is by trying to put one or more curses on you and those linked to you.

I don't mean "curse" like in those old horror flicks, e.g. *The Curse of the Mummy's Tomb*, but rather in a biblical sense. In this chapter we're going to define the five general curses of the Law that the enemy uses to attack believers. We're also going to look at five other curses which threaten believers' *spiritual* blessings, ten curses in all.

Let's first establish that…

Jesus Christ was *Your* Substitutionary Curse

Most believers know that Christ suffered substitutionary death for them. In other words, the Messiah died in our place—the innocent for the guilty—that we might have the benefit of eternal life. However, the majority of Christians don't know that Jesus was their **substitutionary curse** period. Notice what the Bible says on this point:

> **Christ redeemed us from the curse of the law by becoming a curse for us, for it is written: "Cursed is everyone who is hung on a pole."**
> **Galatians 3:13**

Christ *redeemed* us from the curse of the law. 'Redeem' means to release from the power of something through purchasing. What was the price for our redemption? The blood of Christ; that is, the very life of the Mighty Lord. In short, **Jesus suffered & died for you to be redeemed**.

How did Christ redeem us from the curses of the law? The text says "by becoming a curse for us"! In other words, he suffered being cursed so that we don't have to be cursed. How exactly was he cursed? Paul cites Deuteronomy 21:23 in reference to Christ's crucifixion: "Cursed is everyone who is hung on a pole." So when the Messiah suffered and died during his last 12 hours he became *our* substitutionary curse—an innocent human being cursed so that the guilty might be blessed. That's you & me and all people.

The Five General Curses of the Law

The text specifies that "Christ redeemed us from *the curse of the law*." What precisely is the curse of the Law? This phrase refers to the five general curses detailed in Deuteronomy 28:15-68: **1.** physical ailments, **2.** mental maladies, **3.** defeat to human enemies, **4.** premature death and **5.** financial lack. **Jesus suffered all these curses in his last hours so that you can be released from the power of them.** This is different than saying you won't be attacked by them, because the enemy *will* certainly try to oppress you with them.

Observe how the Anointed One suffered each of these curses:

1. **Christ suffered severe physical wounds to purchase health & healing for the believer:** "by his wounds you have been healed" (1 Peter 2:24 & Isaiah 53:5). Precisely what kind of wounds did the Messiah suffer? Read on…
2. **Christ suffered extreme mental anguish to redeem us from mental illness.** This suffering includes the psychological distress of the various tortures he experienced during his final hours on Earth: Severe scourging that ripped his flesh to pieces, unjust mocking & physical blows, a crown of thorns rammed on his head, his hands & feet literally nailed to a huge stake and the corresponding agony of crucifixion, which is arguably the most painful execution ever conceived and is where we get our term "excruciating." This form of execution, by the way, was reserved for the worst of criminals, as well as foreign enemies. On top of all this there was the mental anguish of being utterly separated from God wherein the Son cried out to the Father: "My God, my God, why have you *forsaken* me?" (Matthew 27:45-54). Lastly, the phrase "by his wounds you have been healed" refers to *both* physical and mental healing.
3. **Christ suffered defeat to his human enemies, which heretofore never happened.** While Jesus was attacked by people throughout his 3½ years of ministry on Earth, they were never victorious over him. He always eluded them or stumped them, one way or another; in other words, he was always ultimately triumphant. For instance, he refused to allow his opponents to unjustly apprehend and kill him on multiple occasions, as documented in Luke 4:28-30, John 7:30,44, 8:59 and 10:31,39. The only time he submitted his life to the hands of his enemies was when he was arrested in Gethsemane because it was God's will that he suffer and die for the redemption of humanity. We have to get away from this ludicrous religious idea that the Messiah was some kind of timid doormat when he was anything but (Mark 11:15-18).

4. **Christ suffered premature death by obediently dying at 33 years of age.** The Bible promises 70-80 years minimum (Psalm 90:10 & 2 Corinthians 1:20). The only God-approved exception to this promise is if a believer is called to martyrdom for the advancement of the kingdom of God, like Stephen (Acts 7:54-8:4). In such cases, the Spirit will reveal this to the believer and give him/her the grace to handle it, as was the case with Stephen. It should be stressed that even with this exception the believer has the victory, as shown in Philippians 1:21-23.
5. **Christ "*became* poor, so that you through his poverty might become rich"** (2 Corinthians 8:9). Christ wasn't poor during his lifetime on Earth; he was a carpenter who attracted business due to his honesty, diligence and superb craftsmanship (Proverbs 22:29). Nor was he poor during his 3½ years of ministry because his team had a treasury, which Judas regularly stole from without the disciples even detecting it (John 12:6). The Messiah only "became poor" during his last 12 hours when he was arrested, tortured, stripped of his very clothing and literally nailed to a huge stake, i.e. "cross," not to mention literally forsaken by the Father. This was the depth of poverty—physically, mentally and spiritually.

As you can see, "**Christ redeemed us from the curse of the law by becoming a curse for us**" (Galatians 3:13). He released us from the power of the five general curses by willfully suffering these curses in one form or another in our place. **He was our substitutionary curse.**

The "Hour When Darkness Reigns"

Those last horrible hours of Christ's life on Earth were when Satan & his devils were released to assault Him. Notice what they hit him with—all five of the general curses of the Law. Is it any wonder that Jesus referred to this time period as the "hour when darkness reigns" (Luke 22:53)?

What did he mean by that? Simply that it was the window of opportunity for the devil & his evil spirits to freely assault him, as permitted by the Sovereign LORD. And how did they attack him? **Through the five general curses of the Law.**

When Satan Attacks He Uses One of the Five General Curses

Let's now observe further scriptural evidence that the kingdom of darkness uses one or more of the five general curses of the Law when they attack a person. We just witnessed the example of Christ, so let's consider the examples of two righteous men from the Old and the New Testaments respectively, Job and Paul.

As covered in previous chapters, God was compelled to allow Satan to attack Job in order to test him and observe if he would forsake the LORD once the devil stripped him of his many blessings. Observe how Job suffered the five general curses of the Law when the devil was released to assault him:

- **Physical ailments:** Job was stricken with painful boils from head to toe (Job 2:7).
- **Mental illness:** Job was thrust into dire mental anguish after the satanic assaults to the point of craving death and hurling audacious accusations at the Almighty (Job 3, 10:1-3 & 30:31).
- **Human attack *and* defeat:** The neighboring Sabeans and Chaldeans, who up to that point lived peacefully by Job, unjustly attacked and killed almost all his employees and stole his wealth (Job 1:14-15 & 17). Keep in mind that this curse does not refer to simply human attack, but rather human attack *and* defeat, which is why I also describe it as 'defeat to human enemies.'
- **Premature death:** Job's ten children and nearly all his employees were killed (Job 1:14-19). Job's life was not at stake because the LORD wouldn't permit it (although in the second round God allowed his body to be attacked). So Satan struck down the next "best" thing—Job's offspring.
- **Financial attack:** Job's great wealth consisted of numerous employees and thousands of sheep, camels, oxen and donkeys;

all but four of his workers were killed and all his animals were stolen or destroyed (Job 1:14-17).

Job passed his great test because he turned *to* God rather than away from Him. He severely vented *to* God and accused Him of crimes against humanity based on his limited understanding of reality, but he never cursed his Creator or forsook Him.

Venting, by the way, is a healthy practice in which the Bible describes as "casting your cares on the Lord" (Psalm 55:22). We're instructed to do this because the LORD cares about us and doesn't want immaterial burdens to weigh us down or limit us, which will inevitably happen if we don't vent in some manner. To "cast all your anxiety on him" (1 Peter 5:7) means to literally **go to the LORD in prayer and hurl your burdens on him**. This is what Job did. The burdens you are to hurl on God include unjust offenses and the sense of violation & anger they produce, which can tempt you to become bitter. Why cast your cares on the LORD? Because we can't handle them. **Just as we must remove physical waste from our bodies so we must remove emotional waste.** Venting is as vital to our spiritual-mental health as the large intestine is to our physical health—the waste must be removed. No wonder venting is strongly encouraged in the Bible (Psalm 62:8) and we observe example after example of it (Psalm 142:1-3 & Jeremiah 20:7-18).

So Job passed his test and the LORD restored him and blessed him doubly (Job 42:10). Keep in mind that Job was presumably under the covenant of the Patriarchal Age,[64] which refers to the covenants the LORD made with Abraham, Isaac and Jacob (Acts 3:25 & Exodus 6:4-5). The terms of this covenant were obedience to God's revealed Law at the time, which included circumcision (Genesis 17:1-14,23) and, of course, keeping with repentance, which Job devoutly followed. This explains why God boasted of him as "blameless" (Job 1:8 and 2:3), which is not the same as sinless. The only sinless human being who ever lived was Jesus Christ.

Now let's consider Paul, who was under the New Covenant wherein the terms are **faith working in love** (Galatians 5:6):

---

[64] See Job 1:5, for instance.

- **Physical maladies:** Paul was stricken with some type of physical ailment according to Galatians 4:13, which provided the opportunity for him to preach the gospel to the Galatians. The word for "illness" in this text could also be translated as "weakness" as it does in Matthew 26:41, which reads: "The spirit is willing but the body is *weak*." If it does refer to physical weakness, some theorize that it could apply to Paul after he was stoned and left for dead in the Galatian city of Lystra (Acts 14:8-20). They speculate that Paul would surely need time for his body to fully heal from the abuse, which may be why he referred to the situation as a trial for the Galatian believers (Galatians 4:14). But this seems unlikely since Paul received an immediate healing and walked right back into the city (!), not to mention he left to preach in another city the very next day (!!). Other possibilities include malaria, which was common in the area, or an eye disease in light of Paul's statement, "If you could have done so, you would have torn out your eyes and given them to me" (verse 15), although this could simply be a figure of speech. Regardless of what Paul's physical problem was, he resisted the attack in faith & perseverance, received healing and lived over another decade to fulfill God's apostolic assignment from Jerusalem to Rome and all points between, not to mention write many other important epistles by the Spirit, like Romans and Ephesians, etc.
- **Mental ailments:** The apostles went through many hardships as they determined to advance the kingdom of God. Second Corinthians 11 details Paul's numerous sufferings, including being thrown into prison multiple times, severely flogged five times (typically 39 lashes!), beaten with rods three times, stoned and left for dead, shipwrecked three times, and more. Not to mention all his labor, sleepless nights and the pressure of all the churches he oversaw (verses 23-29). Facing such horrendous attacks, trials and pressures, Paul and the other ministers were understandably assaulted by negative emotions at times, like fear, doubt, frustration, anxiety and wanting to quit. This is why Paul said they were "sorrowful, yet always rejoicing" (2 Corinthians 6:10); he also mentioned "fears within" and being

"downcast" (2 Corinthians 7:5-6). But they never allowed such dark emotions to take root in their hearts and derail their faith and mission for God. There's no evidence of this in Scripture. They withstood in faith & patience and overcame. Take, for example, when Paul was about to be shipwrecked due to a great storm in Acts 27:21-26; instead of caving-in to the fear and despair of the situation—e.g. *"We're all gonna die!!"*—he received instruction from the LORD and boldly spoke in faith.

- **Human attack *and* defeat:** Paul was attacked by a man named Alexander the metalworker who caused him "a great deal of harm" (2 Timothy 4:14-15), but Paul overcame and wasn't defeated or dead. He was able to warn Timothy and believed that the Lord would pay Alexander back for what he had done. Another good example is from Acts 16:22-34 where we observe Paul and Silas being unjustly attacked in Philippi after exorcizing a demon from a slave girl. They were beaten, flogged and thrown in prison. This was a serious attack indeed, but Paul and Silas withstood in faith and perseverance. At midnight they were praying and singing hymns in their gloomy, smelly jail cell (!). They refused to be defeated. They refused to give-in to doubt, frustration and despair. They knew that victory was theirs no matter how bad the situation appeared. The next thing you know there was an earthquake and the cell doors flew open! God clearly responds to such stubborn, fervent faith. Not only did they escape, the jailer and his family were saved and baptized! Paul and Silas even stayed at their house that night and dined.

- **Premature death:** Paul healed a crippled man in Lystra, which was a powerful testimony to the people there, but some Jews came and stirred the crowd against him. As noted above, they stoned Paul and dragged him outside the city, supposing him to be dead. But Paul received an incredible healing after the disciples gathered around him and he went right back into the city! The next day he was well enough to leave for another town to preach, which indicates a total healing (Acts 14:8-20). Another example would be when Paul sailed to Rome as a captive in Acts 27. A great storm came and seriously threatened all their lives. Keep in mind that, according to Job 1:16,19, Satan has the ability to utilize nature for his own diabolic purposes. The devil didn't want Paul to fulfill his divine commission of carrying the gospel to gentile kings; hence, he tried to kill him on the open sea via the storm, but it didn't work because Paul received divine instruction and stood in faith (verses 21-26). Yet the devil didn't stop there. No sooner was Paul shipwrecked on the island of Malta then a deadly viper bit him (Acts 28:1-10). The islanders expected the apostle to drop dead at any moment but he withstood in faith—meaning he utilized his "sword of the spirit," which is the word of God spoken in bold faith—and ended up having a powerful healing revival!

- **Financial lack:** Paul pointed out in Philippians 4:12-13 that he knew what it was like to be in need and also to have plenty; he knew what it was like to be hungry and to be well fed. He also testified to his brushes with financial attack in 2 Corinthians 6:10. So we know Paul went through experiences where physical resources were seriously limited. Yet, in the Philippians passage he shared his secret of being content in any situation, whether living in plenty or in want: He said he could do all things through the Lord Jesus Christ who strengthened him. In other words, he stood in faith. He didn't give-in to worry or despair in times of need and cry, *"God has forsaken us—we're not gonna make it!"* Likewise, in the Corinthians passage he admitted to having nothing, but countered it with an expression of faith, "yet possessing everything." Consequently, he always made it through times of lack with a peaceful contentment. He fully understood that blessings come via faith & patience in our covenant, and faith works in love. Jehovah Jireh always eventually provided and Paul fulfilled his many missionary assignments. Late in his life, when Paul was in custody in Caesarea, Governor Felix frequently went to him hoping Paul would offer him a bribe (Acts 24:26). This indicates that even under house arrest Paul was financially blessed since wealthy politicians don't try to milk people who are impoverished and have no money.

A good example from the life of Christ would be when, out of nowhere, tax collectors required Peter and Jesus to pay the annual Temple tax, which amounted to about $500 each (Matthew 17:24-27). Jesus wasn't taken off guard and, interestingly, didn't even ask Judas to take the money from their ministry earnings. He had faith that God provides the power to get wealth (Deuteronomy 8:18) and knew precisely where to get the amount they needed by the Spirit. Hence, the LORD provided.

Christ, Job and Paul are *our* **examples**. When any of the five general curses of the Law show up in your life it means you are under satanic attack.

When this happens, the first thing you need to do is determine if the assault is a **Self-Inflicted Trial** (SIT), a **Discipline-Intended Trial** (DIT) or a **Maturity-Intended Trial** (MIT). These three types of trials were explained in the final section of **Chapter 6**, but here's a refresher:

SITs are obvious; the result of one's own folly.

A DIT means the curse is hitting you due to disobedience, whether a sin of commission or a sin of omission. If this is the case, immediately 'fess up and God will dismiss the charge (1 John 1:8-9); then take up your weapons and fight the good fight of faith until the curse departs.

An MIT means that the curse is striking you for righteousness' sake and the LORD is allowing the enemy to assault you in order to test your character and, once your character is proven, turn the negative situation around to your good (Romans 8:28). That's the genius of MITs: God takes something in which the enemy intends to destroy you with—or, at least, hinder you—and ultimately turns it around to your good, making you "strong, firm and steadfast" "after you have suffered for a little while" (1 Peter 5:8-10). Of course, this is providing you fulfill *your* role by fighting the good fight of faith and enduring. (Remember: the LORD is your "*helper*," not your do-everything-for-you-so-you-don't-have-to-do-anything-at-all-er). This is precisely what happened with Joseph (Genesis 50:20).

The reason this data is essential is so that you know with certainty *when* you're under satanic attack. After all, what good is the armor & arms of God if you can't even recognize when you're being assaulted?

This material is also essential so you don't mistake a satanic attack for "God's will." For instance, a genuine Christian woman was diagnosed with life-threatening cancer and concluded that, whether she lived or died from the cancer, it was God's will. No, **it's Satan's will to take out fruit-bearing believers prematurely**.

The obvious problem with this woman's type of fatalistic reasoning is that, if you *think* something's God's will, you won't fight it. You'll accept it and suffer the consequences. But if you recognize something as a satanic attack you'll fight it tenaciously.

Needless to say, ***don't*** **accept any curse of the Law on the mistaken grounds that it's "God's will"**! If a curse shows up in your life due to your own folly or rebellion, you're evidently undergoing an SIT or DIT; simply repent and proceed to fight the good fight of faith. The curse *will* flee from you as you persevere in faith.

If, however, you're walking blamelessly before the LORD, keeping with repentance, you're obviously undergoing an MIT. *Don't* embrace the curse as "God's will." Tenaciously fight the good fight of faith and don't give up. The curse will eventually depart and the LORD will turn around the negative situation for your good.

Handing an Unrepentant Believer Over to Satan

Speaking of Discipline-Intended Trials (DITs), this type of trial explains something curious Paul said to the Corinthian believers. It concerned an unrepentant man in their assembly who was having sexual relations with his father's wife. Paul instructed the church to "hand this man over to Satan" (1 Corinthians 5:5). What did he mean by this? Simply that the man must be excommunicated from the fellowship since he was unwilling to repent of his sin. The hope was that he'd be spurred to repentance whereupon he'd be forgiven and warmly welcomed back. Thankfully, this is precisely what panned out, as revealed in Paul's subsequent letter (2 Corinthians 2:6-11).

To explain, a dis-fellowshipped believer is removed from the protective covering of the church assembly and placed outside where the "god of this world" is at liberty to have his way with him/her, so to speak. The enemy will thus assault the individual with one or more of the curses of the Law because this is *how* Satan & evil spirits attack people. They don't manifest as spooky boogeymen, they attack through one or more of the curses of the Law.

Let me emphasize: the purpose for "handing a person over to Satan" is to win him/her back. Paul's goal was in line with God's love, in this case *tough* love. The hope was that banishment from the church community and suffering one or more of the curses of the Law would humble the man, provoke desperation, and ultimately shock him back to his spiritual senses, at which point he would be warmly welcomed back into the fellowship just like the prodigal son humbly returned to his father (Luke 15:11-32). So handing a person over to Satan is one-and-the-same as handing him/her over to a Discipline-Intended Trial.

God Motivates People *through* the Attraction of Blessings

The blessings of the Law are naturally the opposite of the curses of the Law; they are:

- Physical health.
- Mental health (e.g. peace of mind, faith, hope, love, etc.).
- Victory over human enemies and their unjust attacks.
- Long life.
- Financial provision.

Every sane person on Earth *wants* these five general blessings operating in his or her life. They're intrinsic to our spiritual/mental DNA. After all, no one wants sickness & disease, mental illness, defeat to enemies, premature death or poverty—*no one!* If someone says otherwise they're either a liar, a fool or cracked.

Is it any wonder, therefore, that the LORD used these blessings to motivate Israel to obey His Laws? Read Deuteronomy 28. It's a long chapter, but it establishes "the terms of the covenant" that God had with the Israelites (Deuteronomy 29:1,9). In modern lingo 'covenant' means *agreement* or *contract*. Every contract has terms. If you hire a company to provide a new roof for your abode the terms are *x* amount of money for a new leak-proof roof. The LORD's terms for the covenant (contract, agreement) that He had with the Israelites were: Blessings for obedience to the Law and curses for disobedience. In short, God used humanity's natural attraction to the five general blessings and our aversion to the five general curses to inspire compliance and discourage transgression.

Yet the entire Old Testament is testimony to the fact that the Israelites *couldn't* comply with these terms. Why? Because something was seriously wrong with their "spiritual DNA." The condition of spiritual death—which is the state of being dead to God—and their sinful natures rendered them incapable of fulfilling the simple terms of their covenant.

For Israel—and people in general—to fulfill such terms they would have to have a spiritual regeneration whereby they acquire a new spiritual nature that's united with God and, even more, indwelt, empowered and guided by the Holy Spirit. The attainment of eternal life is an awesome "fringe benefit." This is what the New Covenant is all about and explains why…

The New Covenant is *Superior* to the Old Covenant

As noted in **Chapter 3**, the New Covenant that believers have with God is superior to the Old Testament that the Israelites had. Notice what the Bible blatantly says on this point:

> **But in fact the ministry Jesus has received is as <u>superior</u> to theirs as <u>the covenant of which he is mediator is superior to the old one</u>, since <u>the new covenant is established on better promises</u>.**
> **⁷ For if there had been nothing wrong with that first covenant, no place would have been sought for another.**
> **Hebrews 8:6-7**

For the New Covenant to be superior to the Old Covenant it would have to contain all the benefits of the Old Covenant plus *more*. For instance, if I buy a new car that's superior to my old one it would have to have everything the old one had *plus* be new and likely have additional benefits, otherwise it wouldn't be superior. If the Old Testament promised the five blessings of the Law under the condition of obedience how could the New Testament be superior if it doesn't, *at least*, provide these blessings?

The New Covenant does provide them because the New Testament expressly assures us that "For no matter how many promises God has made, they are 'Yes' in Christ" (2 Corinthians 1:20). "In Christ" is a covenant phrase, meaning *in covenant* (in contract) with God through spiritual regeneration via the gospel of Christ. No matter how many promises God made in the Old Testament they are 'Yes' to those in covenant with God through Yeshua. In other words, a believer can claim any of the general blessings provided in the Old Covenant by faith.

For further proof, notice how the New Testament promises the five general blessings to believers:

1. **Physical health/healing:** 1 Peter 2:24 and 3 John 1:2
2. **Mental wellness:** John 14:27, Philippians 4:6-9 and 3 John 1:2
3. **Victory over unjust human attack:** 2 Timothy 4:17-18 & Luke 18:1-8
4. **Long life** (with the exception of cases where God calls the believer to martyrdom for the advancement of His Kingdom): 1 Peter 3:9-12[65]
5. **Financial blessing:** Mark 10:30, 2 Corinthians 8:9 & 9:11 and Philippians 4:19

While these blessings are promised to New Testament believers, the terms of our Covenant are different than the Old Covenant. The terms

---

[65] The Old Testament was more concerned with **long life on this Earth** (Deuteronomy 5:33, Psalm 91:16 & Proverbs 10:27) whereas the New Testament is more concerned with **acquiring eternal life period** (John 3:36, 11:26 & 1 John 5:11-12). Nevertheless, with the exception of Holy Spirit-directed martyrdom for the advancement of God's Kingdom, the New Testament promises long life with conditions.

are not obedience to the Old Testament Law because **1.** the dietary and ceremonial laws were fulfilled in Christ and are not applicable to New Testament believers (Colossians 2:16-17); and **2.** the moral laws—also fulfilled by Christ—are fulfilled in our lives by simply living according to our new nature, "created to be *like God* in true righteousness," with the help of the Holy Spirit (Ephesians 4:22-24). The terms of the New Covenant are **faith working in love** (Galatians 5:6), which the Amplified Bible reads as **faith being *activated* by love**. As such, anyone who fulfills the first and second greatest commands of the Law automatically fulfills *all* of the moral law (Matthew 22:36-40 & Romans 13:8-10). These two simple commands have three applications: LOVE GOD and LOVE PEOPLE as you LOVE YOURSELF.

Do you want these five general blessings supernaturally operating in your life on a regular basis? Of course you do. **They manifest through faith working in love—love for God and love for people as you love yourself.**

Yet you must understand that the kingdom of darkness is going to attack you through the five general curses of the Law, just as the enemy did with Job, Jesus and Paul, which is why it's necessary to learn how to "fight the good fight of faith" (1 Timothy 6:12). If there's a fight to faith that means there are enemies to faith. You must know your enemy and how assaults from your enemy will manifest in order to be victorious in your fight. That's one of the purposes of this book and this chapter specifically.

So you operate in the five blessings of the Law simply by walking in faith, which includes "fighting the good fight of faith." And faith is activated by love—**loving God** and **loving people** as you **love yourself**—which includes *tough* love when appropriate.

There are some things you need to keep in mind, however; let's start with...

Spiritual Laws Work in Conjunction *with* Natural Laws

Spiritual laws work in union *with* natural laws not in exemption from them. For instance, faith being activated by love is a spiritual law that works in conjunction with common sense principles. Consider these examples:

> ➤ The Bible promises physical health/healing, but if you consume unhealthy food on a regular basis, allow yourself to become obese or develop the habit of smoking, you'll naturally imperil your health.
> ➤ The Bible promises peace of mind, but this blessing will elude you if you choose to use your mind to dwell on negative, sinful things.
> ➤ The Bible promises deliverance from unjust attacks by enemies, but if you're an arrogant, contentious person who never prays for your enemies I wouldn't bank on it.
> ➤ The Bible promises long life but if you choose to be a careless daredevil or obstinate chain-smoker your life could be cut short.
> ➤ The Bible promises financial provision within the framework of your calling, season and environmental context, but if you're lazy (2 Thessalonians 3:10), stingy (2 Corinthians 9:6) or stubbornly unrepentant (Proverbs 28:13) don't count on it.

You see? Spiritual laws and parallel natural laws work in conjunction. It's a matter of simple wisdom.

You probably know unbelievers who operate in some of the five general blessings of the Law simply by observing the corresponding natural laws. For instance, someone could be a staunch atheist and yet prosper financially because he or she is diligent and rises to levels of authority in his/her occupation (Proverbs 12:24). Yet, without the Lord's guiding hand, there can be a price to such "success," like the loss of one's marriage or mental/physical breakdown. For those in covenant with God, however, "The blessing of the Lord makes one rich, And **He adds no sorrow with it**" (Proverbs 10:22 NKJV).

Financial Blessing is determined by Season, Calling & Environmental Context

Financial provision is the blessing that tends to upset some Christians, as if they want to fight for their right to be impoverished. While there have been problems with dubious ministers who essentially make Christianity out to be a get-rich-quick scheme or have used the gospel as a means to get rich (1 Timothy 6:9), we shouldn't throw out God's conditional promises of financial blessing with the proverbial bathwater. Disregarding the false teachings of greed-loving "ministers," the problem some believers have with the concept of financial blessing begins with an erroneous image of what it means to be financially blessed of God in a fallen world. Moreover, their criticisms do not take into account issues like **the season the believer's in**, **divine purpose** or **environmental context**. Let's look at these:

An erroneous image of financial blessing in a fallen world: Someone wrote to rebuke me in response to one of our teaching videos where he mistook my references to "the good life." He evidently envisioned it to mean living like Hugh Hefner, as if true prosperity is *all about* owning a huge mansion and sipping cocktails while lounging at an in-ground pool with myriad half-naked women prancing around, etc. (I'm not saying, by the way, that a believer *can't* own a mansion or have an in-ground pool). For one thing, this is a decidedly worldly image of "prosperity." Secondly, the video itself defined the "good life" as being hooked up with God's will and fulfilling the objectives He gives you, whatever they may be, which includes having the resources to carry out these objectives. An objective or purpose like this could be any number of things, including moving to a third-world country and being a missionary. God's objectives — His *courses* — for each believer are exciting and good because they're in line with your Creator's will who knows you inside out and therefore how you're "wired." Living in accordance with the LORD's purposes *is* "the good life," regardless of what that purpose is. There will be hardships and persecutions, of course, but God knows what you can handle and can't handle and will provide the grace to get through as you wisely fight the good fight of faith.

The Season You're In: You might be in God's perfect will and yet the season you're in will determine your prosperity to an extent. For instance, prosperity at 18 years-of-age is different than prosperity at 50. Consider the example of Joseph, who was a type of Christ: He was unjustly sold into slavery by his jealous brothers when he was 17 and became a slave, and then a prisoner, before eventually living in the palaces of Egypt many years later as second-in-command of the nation. This journey entailed about 13 years. When he was a slave in Potiphar's house the LORD blessed Joseph and he prospered in that context, but he was still a slave (Genesis 39:2-6). Obviously, there are limitations to how much you can prosper as a slave. Likewise Joseph prospered while an inmate in prison, but he was still a prisoner (39:21-23). You see? The season you are in determines the extent of your prosperity.

Your Divine Purpose: Your God-given calling will also determine the scope of your prosperity. This is similar to the previous one: Joseph was called to be a slave for a season, and then a prisoner, before becoming second-in-command of Egypt. He prospered as a slave and prisoner, but it certainly limited his prosperity. Why would God possibly call Joseph to be a slave and prisoner for so many years? Because Joseph was being groomed to be second-in-command of one of the most powerful nations on Earth at the time. The way up is down. People are more apt to be quality leaders if they have personally experienced humiliating circumstances, unjust suffering and corrupt non-leadership.

Your Environmental Context: A brother-in-the-Lord I know came from the more modest sections of Youngstown, Ohio, and as he became increasingly successful his fiancé wanted him to move to a better area before marrying. Yet he insisted that he was called to stay in that community to reach the people there. The LORD heavily put them on his heart. Whether he knew it or not, this corresponded to Paul's exhortation to the Corinthian believers: Generally speaking, they should remain in the situation they were in when they were called in order to reach the people thereof, as directed by the Holy Spirit (1 Corinthians 7:17-24). After all, who better to reach a group of people than those *from that* community and culture? This was a general instruction and not an ironclad law. Obviously if a person is led of the Spirit to move outside of such a context then that's what he or she should do. The brother who felt led to stay in a modest area of Youngstown would indeed prosper there, but it would be a different expression of prosperity than if he were called to, say, Hollywood or the jungles of the Amazon. What if your environmental context is a communistic country where the ruling elite ensure that everyone stays at an equally modest level (except for them, of course)? (What *hypocrisy*, by the way).

Obviously, there's some overlap between the season you're in, your divine calling and your geographical setting.

In any case, when you grasp these things, it helps set you free of envy and facilitates contentment in your God-given assignment.

What *is* "Prosperity" Anyway?

This all brings us to the definition of prosperity. What exactly is prosperity for the believer? It's having enough resources for your needs and righteous desires in order to fulfill your God-given calling, which depends on the season you're in, your specific assignment and the environment to which you're called. Righteous desires are, of course, not the same as *un*righteous desires, like greed, hedonism and pomposity.

People who lust after material things for the purpose of being greater than so-and-so (the proverbial Jones) and looking down on others are walking in eye-rolling carnality. Yet there's nothing wrong with having a spirit-of-excellence and wanting what you have to reflect the glory of God. I Praise the LORD for my neighbors who maintain a great home & yard rather than let things get rundown.

Nor is merely being rich evil, as Abraham, Job, Solomon and David were (or became) quite wealthy. When Paul instructed the young pastor Timothy on rich people in the congregation he didn't tell Timothy to rebuke them for being wealthy, he simply exhorted Timothy to tell them **not to be arrogant**, but to put their hope in God rather than their riches and "to be rich in good deeds and to **be generous** and **willing to share**" (1 Timothy 6:17-18). Why did Timothy have to tell them *not* to be arrogant? Because the attainment of material wealth tends to feed the fleshly ego and tempts people to look down on those with less. This is a form of greed, which Christ blatantly condemned (Luke 12:15); so is putting on airs to impress others. Needless to say, if you're wealthy don't let it go to your head. Instead, develop the spirit of a giver; giving is the antidote to greed (Romans 12:8). Yet don't become arrogant of your giving and look down on those you *presume* don't give as much and condemn them as not truly saved or what have you.

Lastly, it's not money that's the root of all evil, but rather the *love of* money (1 Timothy 6:10). It's fine to have money; it's just not fine for money to have you.

Objections to the Blessing of Health/Healing

It's astonishing, but there are genuine Christians who sincerely love the LORD who will fight tooth & nail for the right to be sick & diseased and prematurely perish. Yet a third of Jesus' earthly ministry was focused on physical health/healing:

> **Jesus went throughout Galilee, <u>teaching</u> in their synagogues, <u>proclaiming the good news</u> of the kingdom, and <u>healing every disease and sickness among the people</u>.**
> **Matthew 4:23**

> **Jesus went through all the towns and villages, <u>teaching</u> in their synagogues, <u>proclaiming the good news of the kingdom</u> and <u>healing every disease and sickness</u>.**
> **Matthew 9:35**

Christ's ministry was threefold: **1.** He taught the Word of God, **2.** He evangelized by preaching the Good News and **3.** He healed people of every disease and sickness. So His ministry consisted of **teaching, preaching & healing**. (Memorize that: **teaching, preaching & healing; teaching, preaching & healing; teaching, preaching & healing**).

One of the things he taught was that health/healing is a God-given right in covenant with the LORD. This explains how people whom Yeshua healed had the faith to be healed in reaction to his teaching & preaching (whether they heard the Word directly or indirectly):

> **Jesus turned and saw her. "Take heart, daughter," he said, "your faith has healed you." And the woman was healed at that moment.**
> **Matthew 9:22**

> **"Go," said Jesus, "your faith has healed you." Immediately he received his sight and followed Jesus along the road.**
> **Mark 10:52**

> **Then he said to him, "Rise and go; your faith has made you well."**
> **Luke 17:19**

These verses are from three different occasions taken from three different Gospel accounts. Christ regularly taught and preached the truth of health/healing and thus these people had the faith to receive healing, each from three different physical maladies—a bleeding problem, blindness, and a skin disease. Jesus was the conduit of God's power, but it was *their faith* that made them well. Everything in our covenant is by faith & perseverance, including salvation (Hebrews 6:12).[66]

By "conduit" I mean the channel through which God's power flows to an individual, or an article that inspires faith, or both. This could be a person, like Jesus or Paul (Acts 20:7-12), or a thing, like Peter's shadow (Acts 5:15-16), a handkerchief (Acts 19:11–12) or anointing oil (James 5:14-15). The LORD uses conduits like these because people obviously need them to inspire faith and it's their faith that ushers in healing via God's power. So it's not the conduit that heals the individual, but the power of God, which is appropriated through the believer's faith.

---

[66] Faith that gives up isn't true faith, only faith **that perseveres** (Colossians 1:22-23 & 1 Corinthians 15:2).

But you actually don't *need* a conduit to receive a healing or any miracle; you can receive directly from the LORD, as Jesus said: "Whatever you ask for in prayer, **believe** that you have received it, and it will be yours" (Mark 11:24). Of course, it takes spiritual growth to receive directly from God like this, which is one of the reasons Fountain of Life focuses on cultivating spiritual maturity (Ephesians 4:11-13).

"But Paul left a man sick in Miletus," someone might point out, based on 2 Timothy 4:20. Obviously this man didn't have the faith to receive healing at the time, despite Paul's teaching & preaching, which shows that the conduit itself doesn't heal. However, if the man kept drawing near to God and feeding on the message of faith & healing he would eventually have the faith to receive healing. We don't know if this ever happened because the Bible doesn't say.

If you want health/healing you're going to have to fight the good fight of faith for this God-given right in Christ. This is regardless of whether or not the problem is the result of simple wear & tear on your body, including age, or if it's demonic in nature (Luke 13:11,16). **Only a fool would fight for the right to be sick & diseased and die prematurely.**

Don't be Like Job's "Friends"!

None of this means, by the way, that we should negatively judge believers who are suffering some physical malady or any other curse, like Job's "friends" did with him (1 Corinthians 4:5). Rather, we should do our part to help hurting believers receive their healing or blessing, which *may* include walking in tough love by correcting a sin issue that, on some occasions, opened the door to the enemy (which would be a DIT—a Discipline-Intended Trial). For instance, Jesus saved an adulterous woman from the curse of premature death, yet he *also* corrected her sinful behavior which opened the door to this curse in the first place (John 8:1-11). True love corrects when appropriate, but don't presumptuously judge & condemn, like Job's "friends."

Many physical and mental maladies are passed down in one's family from generation to generation. The people suffering these ailments didn't do anything to incur it. But, if they want to walk free, they're going to have to learn to fight the good fight of faith; and fight it tooth & nail because the enemy is going to do everything in their power to keep a person bound up so as to not be a threat to their kingdom. This is *why* I'm sharing the material in this chapter and the previous one.

The Five Main Blessings of Your Covenant

Now that you understand the five general curses of the Law and the corresponding five blessings of the law, let's examine **the five main spiritual blessings** that are yours through Christ being your substitutionary curse:

1. **The apprehension of eternal life** (John 3:16 & 2 Timothy 1:10). The Son of God suffered the wages of sin—death—so that you might have eternal life (Romans 6:23).
2. **Reconciliation with God wherein you can have a *relationship* with your Creator** (2 Corinthians 5:18-20). 'Reconciliation' means to turn from enmity to friendship. Christ suffered separation from God on the cross so that you can be united with your Creator and have intimate fellowship (Matthew 27:46).
3. **Spiritual regeneration where you're *born* righteous in your spirit** (Ephesians 4:24). Jesus Christ never sinned when he was on Earth, but he suffered the curse of being "made sin" on the cross so that you "might *become* the righteousness of God" (2 Corinthians 5:21). 'Become' is translated from the Greek word *ginomai (GHIN-oh-may)*, which means to "come into being, to be born." This means that your spirit was made pure and in-right-standing with God when you came to Christ. And explains why God *sees* you as holy—because you *are* holy, spiritually speaking (Colossians 1:22).
4. **Freedom from bondage to sin.** This blessing is a natural outflow of the previous one: Since Christ suffered being made sin on your behalf so that you can be *born* righteous & holy in Christ, you can walk free of bondage to the flesh simply by learning to live out of your new nature. The Bible calls this walking in the spirit (Galatians 5:16-17) or "participating in the

divine nature" (2 Peter 1:4). Humbly "keeping with repentance" is a strategic key to maintaining this blessing (Matthew/Luke 3:8 & 1 John 1:8-9).
5. **A meaningful life with God-given purpose.** When Christ was forsaken by the Father on the cross he suffered the utter meaninglessness of life for the first time in his life so that you can have a meaningful life of Divine-purpose (Matthew 27:46).

The Blessing of a Meaningful Life with God-Given Purpose

Allow me to elaborate on that last blessing: The LORD provided for us an *entire book* in His Word to illustrate the curse of the meaninglessness of life. I'm talking about the book of Ecclesiastes, which isn't a long book so I encourage you to check it out if you're not familiar with it. Ecclesiastes happened to be the favorite book of an unbeliever I met who regularly read the Bible. Actually, this wasn't surprising because Ecclesiastes is the one book in Scripture that focuses on the *human perspective* "under the sun," a phrase repeatedly used in its twelve chapters.

This "under the sun" perspective refers to the mundane viewpoint, which is limited to the outlook perceived through the five physical senses. It's a viewpoint of life without the benefit of the divine, eternal perspective, which explains why Solomon—the writer—constantly laments the meaningless of life in Ecclesiastes. I've experienced this curse even after becoming a believer, yet only when I allowed myself to become distant from God for one reason or another, whether falling into sin or spiritual apathy. The good news is that Christ suffered this curse of mundane futility so that you can have the blessing of a purposeful life with God-given drive![67]

This blessing, along with knowing the LORD—that is, having an actual relationship with your Creator—will become the **driving force in**

---

[67] For a biblical 3-point plan on how to discern God's will for your life and fulfill His purposes see my teaching *How to Obtain Your Desires* and the corresponding video at the Fountain of Life website. Or check out Chapter 6 of my book *The Four Stages of Spiritual Growth*.

your life as you mature in Christ. Why is this important? Because these two blessings will enable you to endure the discomfort of the enemy's increasing attacks as you mature and increasingly engage in spiritual warfare (as they say: "Higher levels, bigger devils"). For instance, how was Paul possibly able to face the incredible satanic attacks on his life and endure? (See 2 Corinthians 11:23-29). Because **his main goal in life was not *mundane* peace, prosperity, pleasure and the avoidance of pain, but rather pleasing God through fulfilling the works He called him to fulfill**. Doing so produces far greater peace, riches and joy because they're spiritual in nature.

I should add that the LORD and His will should be our *first* priority, but not our *only* priority (Matthew 6:33).

Reflect on these things and the Spirit will give you insight.

The Enemy WILL Attack these God-Given Blessings

Just as the kingdom of darkness will try to stop the five blessings of the Law manifesting in your life by trying to put one or more of the five curses of the Law on you, evil spirits will attack these five spiritual blessings, whether in your life or in the lives of those for whom you're interceding:

1. The enemy will attack your eternal salvation (I'll show you *how* in a moment, don't freak out).
2. The enemy will attack your relationship with God.
3. The enemy will try to prevent you from living out of your new nature, which is righteous, and get you back into the flesh.
4. The enemy will try to get you stuck in life-dominating sin bondage.
5. The enemy will try to prevent you from fulfilling your God-given purpose(s).

Let me elaborate on each of these:

The enemy will attack your eternal salvation. The Bible certainly teaches that your salvation is secure (John 10:28-29), yet it's obviously contingent on *continuing* in faith (Colossians 1:22-23 & 1 Corinthians 15:2). Numerous passages clearly show that Christians can abort their salvation *if* they choose to neglect their faith (e.g. Hebrews 6:4-9, 2 Peter 2:20-21, 2 Timothy 2:11-13 and Titus 1:16). This is just common sense; after all, if it takes faith to be saved it naturally follows that people cannot be saved if they come to a point where they no longer believe. So the Bible supports the doctrine of eternal security, but not the doctrine of *unconditional* eternal security.

Since it takes faith to be saved (Ephesians 2:8) and **salvation is secure as one continues in faith**, the only way the enemy can successfully attack a believer's salvation is by deceiving him/her with doctrines of demons in an effort to get them to come to the point where they no longer believe. This is done through corrupt noémas—erroneous indoctrination—as explained in **Chapter 17** & **18**. Let me give you a recent example: A man I know, who was an evangelizing Christian for 25 years, foolishly read a book which championed atheism and he eventually publicly confessed that he no longer believed (!) and even encouraged people to read the book (!!). How did the enemy rob this man of his eternal salvation? Through false teachings that corrupted his mindset and therefore ripped off his faith.

Of course, this man's relationship with God must have been pretty feeble and his theology shallow for a mere atheistic book to derail his faith, but this just goes to show the importance of two pieces of the Armor of God—the gospel of peace shoes and the belt of truth, as covered last chapter. Without these vital pieces of armor the devil can rob you wholesale!

The enemy will attack your relationship with God. Did you notice that when the devil attacked Job his stated goal was to get him to curse the Almighty to His face? Make no mistake, the enemy's primary objective is to break the believer's relationship with God, with the first order of business being to break the fellowship. In short, evil spirits are obsessed with destroying your communion with the LORD.

The enemy will try to prevent you from living out of your new nature, which is righteous, and get you back into the flesh. Since any believer who learns to walk according to their new righteous nature will produce the fruit of the spirit—the very character traits of God—he or she naturally becomes a threat to the kingdom of darkness. As such, evil spirits will seek to keep believers from living according to their new nature, i.e. walking in the spirit.

The enemy will try to get you into the bondage of life-dominating sin. Since sin breaks fellowship with God and hinders believers from participating in the divine nature, the kingdom of darkness will do everything in their power to get believers in bondage to a particular sin wherein it becomes life-dominating. Some obvious examples include alcoholism, pharmakeia (drug-oriented sins), porn bondage, greed, fornication, homosexuality and pathological lying (1 Corinthians 6:9-11). When a person is captive to a particular sin—living it as *a lifestyle*—he or she is no threat to the devil's kingdom; in fact, s/he inadvertently supports it.

The enemy will try to prevent you from fulfilling your God-given purpose(s). Since any fulfillment of a God-given assignment is a direct threat to the kingdom of darkness, evil spirits will do everything they can to prevent believers from fulfilling their divine calling in whatever season they're in, however big or small.

Master the Ten Curses and Contrasting Blessings

Altogether there are ten curses and ten contrasting blessings— five curses of the Law and five spiritual curses; five blessings of the Law and five spiritual blessings.

- ➤ The five curses of the Law and the five blessings of the Law have to do with mundane things corresponding to your life on Earth.
- ➤ The five spiritual curses and the five spiritual blessings have to do with God, eternity and the things of the spirit (which, of course, affect your life on Earth).

This chapter was devoted to detailing these ten curses and ten blessings so that you'll readily recognize *when* you're under demonic attack and hence fight the good fight of faith accordingly. After all, how can you conduct spiritual warfare if you're not even aware you're being attacked? This goes for people you're interceding for as well.

You Must Fight the Good Fight of Faith for Your Rights!

The five blessings of the Law and the five spiritual blessings are *yours* **in Christ**. In other words, these ten blessings are *yours* **by right** in covenant (contract) with God through Christ. Remember, you are a co-heir in Christ through spiritual regeneration wherein you're *born* of the Messiah's seed, that is, the Anointed One's spiritual sperm (Romans 8:17 & 1 John 3:9).

Here, again, are the ten blessings:

The Five Blessings of the Law
1. Physical health/healing.
2. Mental health.
3. Victory over unjust human attack.
4. Long life till you're satisfied (minimum 70-80 years).
5. Financial provision/blessing (not a get-rich-quick scheme).

The Five Spiritual Blessings
6. Eternal life.
7. Reconciliation and relationship with the LORD.
8. Spiritual regeneration wherein you're spiritually *born* righteous and can live by this new nature.
9. Freedom from bondage to sin via walking in the spirit.
10. Meaningful life with God-given purpose.

These ten blessings are your rights ('10' is incidentally the number of completion in the Bible). *But* they are attained and maintained through faith & perseverance. This includes your eternal salvation, as explained above. Like I said earlier, faith that gives-up is not true faith. That's why faith *and* perseverance/patience/endurance are often spoken of in the same breath in the New Testament (e.g. Hebrews 6:12).

These ten blessings are *your* earthly "Promised Land." To explain, the Israelites were promised the land of Canaan and victory over the inhabitants thereof, which were their enemies; yet they still had to get their swords out and take the land. Similarly, these ten blessings are promised to you, the believer, but you must put your armor on, get your weapons out and fight the fight of faith in order to walk in them. Unlike with the Israelites, however, your enemies aren't flesh and blood (Ephesians 6:12). Your enemies are spiritual in nature and their attacks manifest through one (or more) of the ten curses above, which explains why it requires *spiritual* armor and *spiritual* weapons to overcome them.

I've heard Christians speak of the Promised Land as if it were a type of eternal life in the new Heavens and new Earth (typically referred to as "Heaven"). This is true as far as our *eternal* Promised Land is concerned. Even the Old Testament saints looked forward to the *eternal* Promised Land (Hebrews 11:10,16). Yet, just as they had an earthly Promised Land, so New Covenant believers have an earthly Promised Land, although it's not a piece of real estate. It's walking in the ten promised blessings above. This includes fulfilling whatever mission or dream the Lord gives you. In other words, the Hebrews' Promised Land is a type of your inheritance during your temporal life on this Earth.

The Hebrew's earthly Promised Land was Canaan where there were enemy nations that they had to conquer in order to obtain their Promised Land. Just as they had to put their armor on and take up their weapons in order to inhabit their Promised Land, we believers have to put on our armor and take up our weapons to inhabit ours.

Needless to say, get your armor on & your weapons out and fight the good fight of faith—conquer *your* Promised Land!

'What about Hebrews 11:39?'

Before closing this chapter we need to clear up an objection based on this passage:

> **These were all commended for their faith, <u>yet none of them received what had been promised</u>,**
> **Hebrews 11:39**

To properly interpret this passage both the hermeneutical laws **Context is King** and **Scripture interprets Scripture** must be applied. First, who is the subject of the text? Second, what specific promise(s) *didn't* they receive while on Earth? As far as the first goes, the writer is contextually referring to various Old Testament saints who, albeit flawed individuals, were commended for their faith as they endured great challenges and persecutions.

As far as the promise(s) they didn't receive on Earth goes, the context shows that it's referring to their *eternal* Promised Land:

> **By faith he [Abraham] made his home in the promised land like a stranger in a foreign country; he lived in tents, as did Isaac and Jacob, who were heirs with him <u>of the same promise.</u> ¹⁰ For <u>he was looking forward to the city with foundations, whose architect and builder is God.</u>** **Hebrews 11:9-10**

> **All these people were still living by faith when they died. <u>They did not receive the things promised; they only saw them and welcomed them from a distance</u>, admitting that they were foreigners and strangers on earth. ¹⁴ People who say such things show that they are looking for a country of their own. ¹⁵ If they had been thinking of the country they had left, they would have had opportunity to return. ¹⁶ Instead, <u>they were longing for a better country—a heavenly one</u>. Therefore God is not ashamed to be called their God, for <u>he has prepared a city for them</u>.** **Hebrews 11:13-16**

So the promise they didn't receive while on Earth is the new Jerusalem and, by extension, the new Heavens (Universe) and new Earth (2 Peter 3:13). The new Jerusalem is currently in Heaven but will "come down out of heaven from God" to rest on the new Earth in the eternal age to come (Revelation 3:12 & 21:2,10).

New Covenant believers are also looking forward to this promise and, like the Hebrews, will not receive it as long as we're on *this* Earth:

> **For here <u>we</u> do not have an enduring city, but <u>we</u> are looking for <u>the city that is to come</u>.**
> **Hebrews 13:14**

Someone might understandably point out that verse 13 (of Hebrews 11, above) infers more than one promise, as it says: "They did not receive *the things* promised; they only saw *them* and welcomed *them* from a distance." Answer: While the "promise" the Old Testament saints didn't receive on Earth mainly concerns the new Jerusalem and, by extension, the new Heavens and new Earth, it also naturally includes the foundational promises on which these future blessings are based: **1.** the promised prophet, Jesus Christ (Deuteronomy 18:15), and **2.** the New Covenant established through his death and resurrection (Jeremiah 31:31,33). Every Old Testament saint listed in the Hall of Faith Chapter of Hebrews 11 died before these promises came to pass.

Of course New Covenant believers have received these two promises, otherwise we wouldn't be New Covenant believers; and this ties into something noted in verse 40:

> **These were all commended for their faith, yet none of them received what had been promised, [40] since God had planned something better for us so that only <u>together with us</u> would <u>they</u> be <u>made perfect</u>.**
> **Hebrews 11:39-40**

This distinguishes the Old Testament saint from the New Testament saint. The spirits of New Covenant believers were "made perfect" through spiritual regeneration when they accepted the gospel of Christ (Hebrews 10:14, 12:23 & Ephesians 4:24). Yet deceased Old Testament saints won't receive this promise *until* their resurrection. At that time "together with us" they will "be made perfect."

Lastly, twice previously in the book of Hebrews believers are encouraged to walk in faith & patience to inherit their promised blessings (Hebrews 6:12 & 10:36) so Hebrews 11:39 *cannot* be interpreted to discourage this. Not to mention, we have the entire rest of the New Testament. Scripture interprets Scripture.

Chapter 21

Christ is *Our* Ark of the Covenant

I'd like to close our study on angels with a fascinating revelation about the Ark of the Covenant because it involves two angels and *The Angel* of the LORD, Jesus Christ.

The Ark of the Covenant

The Ark of the Covenant was a sacred chest during the Old Testament period (Exodus 25:10-22). If you've seen the popular movie *Raiders of the Lost Ark* then you're familiar with this chest. The "lost Ark" in that film is the Ark of the Covenant; a cinematic replica, that is.

The Ark was made of acacia wood overlaid with gold.
According to Hebrews 9:4 the Ark contained:

1. The **stone tablets** on which the Ten Commandments were written (Deuteronomy 10:2).
2. A pot of **manna**, the miraculous food that God provided for the Israelites in the wilderness after being rescued from slavery in Egypt (Exodus 16).
3. **Aaron's rod that budded** (Numbers 17).

The lid of the chest was made of pure gold and dubbed the "Mercy Seat," which will be explained in a moment. Two gold-sculptured cherubim—angels—were mounted on the Mercy Seat facing each other. And the **LORD's presence dwelt above the Mercy Seat** between the cherubim (Exodus 25:22). Here's an illustration:

The Ark was housed in the innermost chamber of the Temple (and, previously, the Tabernacle) known as the Holy of Holies.

Once a year, on the Day of Atonement, the High Priest entered the Holy of Holies and **sprinkled blood** on the Mercy Seat for the sins of the nation of Israel. But the blood of bulls and goats could only *cover* their transgressions year-to-year; it could not cleanse them of their sins. This reveals one of the many reasons the New Covenant is superior to the old one: Christ didn't offer the blood of animals on an earthly copy of the Ark, but rather offered his *own blood*, sprinkling it on the true Ark of the Covenant in Heaven (Hebrews 10:1-4 & 9:23-28).

This explains the name of the Mercy Seat: The spilling of innocent blood on the lid of the Ark would *cover* the Law of God contained *in* the Ark, represented by the tablets. This is important because the Law "kills" due to the fact that "the wages of sin is death" (2 Corinthians 3:6 & Romans 6:23). With the Law covered by the blood of a substitute the LORD's mercy was able to flow to those in covenant with God, the Israelites.

The Total Sinfulness of Humanity

Interestingly, the three articles in the Ark represented the total sinfulness of the human race before the Creator:

- **The Two Tablets** represented humanity's rejection of the Law of God (Exodus 32).
- **The Manna** represented humanity's rejection of God's provision (Numbers 11:4-6).
- **Aaron's Staff** represented humanity's rejection of God's human leadership (Numbers 16-17).

Since cherubim are associated with the presence of God as guardians and servants (Ezekiel 1 & Genesis 3:24), the two sculptured cherubs on the lid of the Ark flanked the presence of the Almighty. The Mercy Seat was made of pure gold and was comparable to God's throne on Earth during the Old Covenant since He literally dwelt above the Mercy Seat between the cherubim (Psalm 99:1). Since God is absolute righteousness and perfect justice and "the wages of sin is death," the sinfulness of humanity—wholly represented in the Ark—incurs the LORD's just penalty of death. This is why "the letter kills" and why all humanity is under a death sentence.

Thankfully, the blood of Christ was sprinkled on the Mercy Seat in Heaven by Christ Himself, as noted above, and so **mercy flows to those who approach God through the blood of Christ. They are saved from death and obtain eternal life**. As it is written:

> "For God so loved the world that he gave his one and only Son, that whoever believes in him <u>shall not perish</u> but <u>have eternal life</u>."
>
> **John 3:16**

> "Whoever believes in the Son has eternal life. <u>Whoever rejects the Son will not see life</u>. Instead, <u>the wrath of God remains on him</u>."
>
> John 3:36

The Christ Symbolism of the Ark

Just as interesting, every aspect of the Ark **pointed to the Messiah**, Jesus Christ, and his work:

- The **acacia wood** symbolized Jesus' humanity while the **gold** symbolized his deity.
- The **Ten Commandments** inside the ark symbolized the Law of God. Christ was/is the Living Word (John 1:1-3,14) and so perfectly obeyed the Law, the written Word.
- The **pot of manna** spoke of Yeshua as the Bread of Life, our life-sustainer (John 6:47-51).
- **Aaron's staff that budded** represented Christ's resurrection, as the rod was dead wood that miraculously came to life; it not only budded, it blossomed and produced almonds (Numbers 17:1-8).
- The **Mercy Seat** also pointed to the Messiah in that Jesus' blood was sprinkled on the heavenly Mercy Seat and, as such, believers **receive mercy** from the effects of the Law—*death*.

The Ark of the Covenant was Lost

The last time the Ark is mentioned in the Old Testament is 2 Chronicles 35:3, which was during righteous King Josiah's reign in Judah. Unfortunately, the subsequent kings led Israel back into utter apostasy and thus the LORD allowed Babylon to sack Jerusalem and take the apostate Hebrews into exile.

No one really knows what happened to the Ark, but there are theories, including:

- Many believe it was simply **destroyed** when the Temple was burned (2 Kings 24:13).
- Jewish tradition suggests that it was **hidden in a vault** underneath the Temple Mount.

Why isn't the Ark Mentioned in the New Testament?

There's interestingly no mention of the *earthly* Ark of the Covenant in the New Testament. Why? Simply because there was **no more need for the Ark**; Jesus fulfilled all that it stood for, as noted above.

This fact is pictured in an amazing verse that shows events shortly after Jesus' bodily resurrection. Mary Magdalene peaked into the tomb where Christ's body was laid to rest and notice what she sees:

> and [she] saw <u>**two angels**</u> in white, seated where Jesus' body had been, <u>**one at the head and the other at the foot**</u>.
>
> **John 20:12**

Is this not reminiscent of the Mercy Seat—two angels facing each other with the presence of the LORD between them? In other words, *this* is the New Testament Mercy Seat.

Why is this significant? Because the Ark was linked to the **presence of God** in the Old Covenant. As such, the Israelites *had* to go to the Temple (and, earlier, the Tabernacle) where the Ark was located in order to encounter God during Old Testament times.

In the New Testament, however, born-again believers *are* **the temple of God** and the Spirit of Christ dwells **within us**! (Romans 8:9).

And this explains the mystery of the gospel: "**Christ IN YOU, the hope of glory**" (Colossians 1:27). This doesn't just refer to the Holy Spirit indwelling you—as awesome as that is—it refers to the fact that your spirit has been born anew of the seed of Christ and is a "new creation" "created to be **like God** in true righteousness" (2 Corinthians 5:17 & Ephesians 4:22-24). Chew on that mind-blowing tidbit.

Closing Word & Benediction

You probably noticed that this is more than "just a book on angels." That's because angels—whether heavenly angels, fallen angels or *The* Angel of the LORD—are linked to the most important topics of Holy Scripture: creation, the fall of humanity, God's plan of redemption, satanic subterfuge, spiritual warfare, divine protection, behind-the-scenes events, your service for the Lord and even the very nature of God.

You perhaps saw as well that this book isn't just dry information on angels. That's because the focus is on *your responsibility* in activating angels on your behalf (and those for whom you intercede), as well as *de*activating fallen angels.

You also likely noticed that this is not a simple work. That's because angelology and demonology aren't simple topics; neither is Christology. Thus *ANGELS* is dense with info concerning celestial beings and connecting topics. There are "hidden gems" interspersed throughout. As such, the book will hopefully prove useful to you for years to come.

I'm sure you were surprised by some of the revelations, which I hope you found inspiring, one way or another. You may have even found some of these insights challenging. But that isn't necessarily a bad thing as the truth of God's Word is challenging by its very nature. It's *good* for the Word of God to ruffle our feathers now and then.

If you disagree with something, that's okay; seek it out in your studies, meditation and prayer time. Be patient and give it time; resist a kneejerk response. Don't presume that your pastor or sect is right about everything. Let the Word of God and Spirit of Christ be your final authority, not the word of man. If you still disagree, I'd like to hear from you. Who knows? What you say may influence a future revised edition.

May the LORD bless you as you seek & serve.

May His angels serve at your table and watch over your coming & going always.

May you effectively fight the good fight of faith *and* persevere.

May the enemy and corresponding curses flee from you & yours.

May you bear forth fruit as you fulfill all of God's purposes for each season in your life.

Amen.

Appendix A

Angels and Gender

The main question we want to answer in this appendix is: Are there male *and* female angels or are they all male? Or are they genderless? The topic is somewhat interesting, but essentially inconsequential and I didn't want to bog down **Chapter 1** with excess material. However, for those interested, let's see what the Bible says...

Angels are consistently referred to in the Bible in the masculine sense (he, him, his) rather than the feminine (she, her, hers). Actually, the Greek word for angel—*angeles (ANG-el-os)*—is masculine and there is no feminine form. There is one exception, however, where Zechariah sees two female spiritual beings with wings carrying out a service in a vision (Zechariah 5:5-11). While Ezekiel doesn't technically call them angels, what else are spiritual beings with wings conducting a service, if not angels? We'll examine this passage momentarily.

Another thing to consider is that on every occasion when angels appeared to people in human form they were male (Genesis 18:1-3,10,

16-17,22-23 & Ezekiel 9:1-2). This obviously includes the evil spirits—the "sons of God"—who transgressed when they adopted human garb to have intercourse with women, which gave birth to the legendary Nephilim (Genesis 6:1-4), as covered in **Chapter 10**.

Something else to consider is that the only three angels named in Scripture are male—Michael, Gabriel and Lucifer—as detailed in **Chapter 1**.

While all this is true, there are several things that need kept in mind on the gender of angels…

1. **Just because angels are shown appearing in human form as males doesn't mean an angel *couldn't* appear as female, particularly if the angel is female.** Consider, for example what the writer of Hebrews instructed believers:

> **Do not forget to show hospitality to strangers, for by so doing some people have shown hospitality to angels without knowing it.**
> **Hebrews 13:2**

This shows that angels can appear to believers in human form without us discerning that they're angels. The verse describes them as "strangers" and does not distinguish whether they're male or female. Notice that it *doesn't* add something to the effect of "But if the strangers are female they can't be angels because angels only appear as male." Actually, it's assumed that some of the "strangers" would be female.

Incidentally, the phrase "hospitality to strangers" is one word in the Greek—*philoxenia (fil-on-ex-EE-ah)*—which means "love to strangers; hospitality." It doesn't mean "love to strangers, but only male ones." It refers to hospitality to *people*, whether male or female.

I said above that there's no reason to assume that angels couldn't appear in human form as female, particularly *if* the angel is female, which suggests, of course, that some angels are female. This brings up the next two points…

2. **Christ said that people—male and female—would become *like* the angels at the time of their bodily resurrection.** Let's read the text:

> Jesus replied, "The people of this age marry and are given in marriage. ³⁵ But those who are considered worthy of taking part in the age to come and in the resurrection from the dead <u>will neither marry nor be given in marriage</u>, ³⁶ and <u>they can no longer die</u>; for <u>they are like the angels</u>. They are God's children, since they are children of the resurrection."
>
> **Luke 20:34-36**

This passage shows that people will become "like angels" at the resurrection in two ways: **A.** they "will neither marry nor be given in marriage" and **B.** "they can no longer die."

Concerning the first point, people—male and female—will become like the angels in the sense that they won't marry. This doesn't mean that they will become genderless or that females will morph into males. It just means that marriage as an institution shall cease, perhaps because we'll all be genuinely one in the Lord as the "bride of Christ" and so there will be no need to become "one flesh" with a person of the opposite sex.

The very fact that Jesus said believers—male and female—will become like angels in the sense that they won't marry presumes that some angels are female. Think about it. Christ did *not* say "neither will people marry… for they will be like the angels and will all be male in gender."

Regarding the second point, angels possess intrinsic immortality whereas unredeemed human beings do not. Immortality is only available to people through the gospel of Christ (2 Timothy 1:10 & Romans 2:7).

3. **In a vision Zechariah sees two female spiritual beings with wings carrying out a service, which suggests that they're angels.** Let's read the passage:

> Then the angel who was speaking to me came forward and said to me, "Look up and see what is appearing."
>
> ⁶ I asked, "What is it?"
>
> He replied, "It is a basket." And he added, "This is the iniquity of the people throughout the land."
>
> ⁷ Then the cover of lead was raised, and there in the basket sat a woman! ⁸ He said, "This is wickedness," and he pushed her back into the basket and pushed its lead cover down on it.
>
> ⁹ Then I looked up—and <u>there before me were two women, with the wind in their wings! They had wings like those of a stork</u>, and they lifted up the basket between heaven and earth.
>
> ¹⁰ "Where are they taking the basket?" I asked the angel who was speaking to me.
>
> ¹¹ He replied, "To the country of Babylonia to build a house for it. When the house is ready, the basket will be set there in its place."
>
> **Zechariah 5:5-11**

These two women with wings carrying a basket between Heaven and Earth are obviously angels because angels are spiritual beings, often described as having wings, who perform services for God, traveling back and forth from Heaven to Earth. The latter is reminiscent of Jacob's dream where he saw a stairway (or ladder) to Heaven with angels going back and forth from Heaven to Earth (Genesis 28:12). Thus Zechariah's vision suggests that angels can be female.

Some disagree on the grounds that **A.** they're not technically called angels, but rather "women," which is translated from the Hebrew term *ishshah (ish-SHAW)*, meaning "female" or "wife"; **B.** this is the same word used for the symbolic "woman" in the basket, which *isn't* a woman, but rather figurative of wickedness; **C.** this is contrasted by the "angel" whom Zechariah is actually talking to, which is the Hebrew word for angel, *malak (mal-AWK)*, and this angel is repeatedly referred as "he" (verses 6, 8 & 11); and, lastly, **D.** the two women with wings appear in a prophetic vision and visions do not necessarily illustrate actual beings or items; a good example is the "flying scroll" noted earlier in the same chapter of Zechariah (verses 1-2).

Response: **A.** this is a God-given vision imparted to one of the LORD's Old Testament prophets and is included in the Holy Scriptures; **B.** whether they're called angels by Zechariah or not, the two women carrying a basket *are* spiritual beings with wings performing a service "between heaven and earth," which implies that they *are* angels (after all, what else would they be?); **C.** God made a point to distinguish these two spiritual beings' gender as decidedly female; and **D.** Jesus himself gave a parable—which is a symbolic story, not reality—where he referenced the angels who carried a dead beggar's soul to Hades (Luke 16:22-23); while this parable is a fictional story containing symbolism[68] it presumes that these 'death angels' actually function in the spirit realm. Why would it be any different with Zechariah's vision?

A pastor who objected to the existence of female angels argued that the women with wings in Zechariah's vision are demons. Answer: Demons are fallen angels, so if there are female *fallen* angels there must also be female *heavenly* angels (unless Lucifer misled *all* the female angels, which isn't likely since he only misled a third of the angels anyway).

4. **The Hebrew term *adam* is used to describe the faces of cherubim in the Bible and this term can denote male or female.** This can be observed in Ezekiel's two visions where he describes the four faces of cherubs, one being that of a "man" (Ezekiel 1:6,10 & 10:14). This is translated from the Hebrew word *adam (aw-DAWM)*, which means "man" or "humankind" and *can* refer to male or female, as clearly shown here:

---

[68] See the teaching RICH MAN & LAZARUS: Fantastical Parable or Literal Account? at the Fountain of Life website for details. For even more details, see my book SHEOL KNOW.

> **So God created <u>mankind</u>** *(adam)* **in his own image,
> in the image of God he created <u>them</u>;
> <u>male and female he created them</u>.**
> **Genesis 1:27**

"Mankind" (or "man") refers to both male *and* female and were created in **the image of God**, which shows that the feminine nature originated with God.

5. **The Holy Spirit is referred to with masculine pronouns, but the Spirit's nature is decidedly feminine.** Before anyone cries *"HERETIC"* consider the obvious evidence:

God has a "feminine" side in that Scripture gives evidence of his softer traits (feminine), as well as his sterner side (masculine). Some good examples include Psalm 103:8, 1 John 4:8 and Matthew 11:28-30. Yet when it comes to Father, Son and Holy Spirit, which One especially suggests the feminine nature? (Please understand that this is not a question of sexuality, but of nature). Clearly not the Father or Son because, after all, they're the **Father** and **Son**—both obviously masculine.

The Holy Spirit, however, generally reflects the feminine nature. For instance, the symbol for the Holy Spirit is a dove, which suggests gentleness and harmlessness (Luke 3:22). Moreover, the Holy Spirit is referred to as a "Helper" of believers in John 14:16, 26 (also translated as "Comforter" and "Counselor"). This is significant in that one of Eve's main purposes was to be Adam's "helper" (Genesis 2:18, 20). In addition, the Holy Spirit is shown to be sensitive—easily grieved—in Ephesians 4:30 and Hebrews 10:29.

The most glaring evidence of the Holy Spirit's feminine nature can be observed in John 3:6 where Jesus pointed out that "Flesh gives birth to flesh, but the Spirit **gives birth to** spirit." Jesus was comparing human birth with spiritual regeneration. Just as a woman gives birth to a child ("flesh gives birth to flesh") so the Holy Spirit gives re-birth to a person's spirit when he or she turns to God. Giving birth clearly bespeaks of the feminine nature.

By contrast, in 1 Peter 1:23 believers are said to be "born again" of the imperishable **seed** of the living Word of God, who is Jesus

Christ. This is also conveyed in 1 John 3:9 where "seed" in the Greek is *sperma,* which is (obviously) the Greek word for sperm. You see, believers are born-again of the sperm of Christ, but given spiritual re-birth by the Holy Spirit. One is masculine and the other feminine.

Furthermore, this may spur chuckles, but when the Messiah said, "Anyone who speaks a word against the Son of Man will be forgiven, but anyone who speaks against the Holy Spirit will not be forgiven, either in this age or in the age to come" (Matthew 12:32), I can't help but think of the way men get irate when someone says something insulting about their Momma.

It is true that the Holy Spirit is referred to by the pronoun "he" in the Bible (e.g. John 16:13), but the thrust of Scripture points to the Holy Spirit's feminine nature, as detailed above. Besides, God transcends quaint masculine and feminine associations and there is neither male nor female in Christ (Galatians 3:28).

This shows that just because angels are consistently referred to with masculine pronouns (he, him, his) it doesn't necessarily mean that there aren't feminine angels, which is pretty much proven by Zechariah 5:9.

6. **Jesus *is* the wisdom of God, as seen in 1 Corinthians 1:30, but wisdom is personified as a woman in Proverbs 8 and 9.** This isn't to suggest, of course, that Christ is womanly—far from it, as driven home in **Chapter 7**. It simply shows that, although the Son is decidedly masculine, Scripture is flexible in revealing one part of Him—wisdom—as feminine in a figurative sense.

7. **The universality of male & female living beings, which are created by the LORD.** Male and female are God-given genders. Both are blessed, yet they're different. Loony leftists, who claim that **A.** there's no such thing as gender and **B.** that a person has the right to reject his/her gender and therefore have their body mutilated to switch over to the other side, are blind fools. Enough said.

8. **A few times in Scripture a group of angels is referred to as "the sons of God" and it's obvious they're masculine in nature (Genesis 6:1-4, Job 1:6 & 2:1), yet all this shows is that these groups consisted of male angels; it doesn't prove that there aren't female angels.**

9. **In certain contexts "sons of God" obviously refer to *both* male *and* female.** This can be observed in Romans 8:14 where it says "For as many as are led by the Spirit of God, they are the sons of God" (KJV). While the original text literally says the "*sons* of God" (the Greek for 'son' being masculine[69]) the context is referring to believers led by the Spirit of God and therefore to both male *and* female Christians. This explains why the NIV translates "sons of God" in this verse as "children of God." Luke 20:36 is a similar example. Thus when Job 38:7 cites that "*all* the sons of God [i.e. angels] shouted for joy" when God created the Earth (KJV) it's not definitive proof that all angels are male. They could be, but more likely they're not in light of the overriding evidence. The usage of the phrase "sons of God" in the Bible to refer to both male and female simply reflects the patriarchal nature of Israel & surrounding regions during biblical times.

In light of all this, I don't see the problem with the idea that there are male *and* female angels, although male angels are the emphasis in Scripture and they clearly don't marry.

Nevertheless, the issue is trivial in the grand scheme of things and isn't worth arguing over, which is why I only include this info as an appendix.

---

[69] *huios (hwee-OS).*

Appendix B

Were Angels "Created in the Image of God"?

It has been pointed out several times in this book that human beings are "created in the likeness of God" or "created in God's image." What exactly does it mean to be created in the LORD's likeness or image? It has also been emphasized that people are the only *physical* beings created in God's image. Is it possible that angels are also created in the Creator's likeness? What's the Bible say on this intriguing topic?

Let's start by looking at the very first reference to people being created in God's image and likeness:

> Then God said, "Let <u>us</u> make mankind in <u>our image</u>, in <u>our likeness</u>, <u>so that they may rule over</u> the fish in the sea and the birds in the sky, over the livestock and all the wild animals, and over all the creatures that move along the ground."

> **²⁷ So God created mankind in his own <u>image</u>,
> in the <u>image</u> of God he created them;
> <u>male and female</u> he created them.**
>
> Genesis 1:26-27

As you can see, the LORD—Father, Son & Holy Spirit—decided to make humankind in their image and likeness and then did so. The Hebrew word for 'likeness' is *demuth (dem-OOTH)*, which means likeness or similitude—that is, something that *resembles* another; it's something that is a, *match* or *counterpart* to another. As such, human beings *resemble* the Almighty; you could say that we're God's *counterpart* in the physical realm.

The Hebrew for 'image' is *tselem (SEH-lem)*, which simply means image, representation, copy or duplicate. A scriptural example can be observed when the LORD instructed Moses to drive out the rejected inhabitants of the Promised Land and "destroy all their carved images *(tselem)* and their cast idols" (Numbers 33:52). The false Canaanite god Baal, for instance, was perceived as a man with the head and horns of a bull; and so the Canaanites' carved images depicted this—the carving (idol) was a physical *image* of the mental concept.

So humankind—male and female—is the physical image of God. This shows that, while "God is spirit" as Christ said (John 4:24), He's not some amorphous cloud entity in the spiritual realm. The LORD has a shape, similar to people, with a head, torso, arms and legs. It has been argued that God has no *physical* body, which is obvious, but the Creator certainly has a *spiritual* form or "body." For instance, the Bible says repeatedly that the LORD sits enthroned in Heaven (Psalm 47:8, 103:19 & Isaiah 40:22). Does this refer to a shapeless cloud being sitting on a throne in Heaven? No, the Creator has a central presence and spiritual form, similar to the body of human beings, who were created in God's image and likeness.

Verse 26 (above) provides further insight on what it means to be created in God's image and likeness: It means to possess authority of some sort, like humankind holds over the Earth and its creatures. This explains why people have zoos for animals and not vice versa.

Being created in God's likeness further means to possess volition, which is the power to consciously choose. It also means to understand and distinguish good and evil. Thus we have a conscience—an inward moral compass—and only those who foolishly harden their hearts are bereft of this sense. Animals, by contrast, are instinctual and do not comprehend such concepts.

Being created in the LORD's image also means having the ability to create in a *sophisticated* sense, like the Creator. Hence, human beings create cities, highways, languages, literature, art, music, movies, computer systems and so on. Animals, of course, lack such aptitude.

People are the only *physical* beings created in God's image, but what about angels? Are they *spiritual* beings created in God's likeness? The Bible doesn't expressly say it in these terms, but it could be argued that the Scriptures point to this conclusion. Consider the evidence:

1. **Angels are referred to as "the sons of God," which is *ben Elohim* in the Hebrew.** This can be observed in Job 38:7. The phrase is also used in Job 1:6 & 2:1 and Genesis 6:1-4, the latter of which refers to fallen angels. Needless to say, sons are created in the likeness of their father; they're "chips off the old block."

2. **When angels manifested physically they always appeared as people and not some other life form.** While fallen angels have been known to possess animals on occasion (Genesis 3:1 & Matthew 8:31-32), not to mention people, when angels actually manifested physically without possessing someone or something they always appeared as human beings (Genesis 18:1-3,10,16-17,22-23).

3. **When the "sons of God"—fallen angels—manifested in the physical realm to copulate with women and produce offspring they obviously had to be men in form.** To produce offspring you have to be the same basic species. For instance, a dog and a wolf can produce viable, fertile offspring, but two different species can't, like a giraffe and a lion or a human being and any animal. Since the coupling of these "sons of God" with women produced the legendary Nephilim they *had* to be a compatible species (Genesis 6:1-4), otherwise there would've been no offspring.

4. **The devil & his angels understood morality and possessed volition to make a choice for evil.** In other words, they weren't instinctual like animals; they comprehended good and evil and made a conscious decision for the latter.

5. **Christ said redeemed people would become "like the angels" at the First Resurrection (Luke 20:34-36).** He didn't say we would *become* angels, just that we'd become "*like* the angels" in two senses: **A.** We will never marry and **B.** we will no longer be able to die; in short, we'll attain intrinsic immortality at the bodily resurrection[70] (2 Timothy 1:10). Nevertheless, the fact that Jesus linked humans to angels reveals a degree of commonality, the main difference being that angels are decidedly spiritual in nature whereas people are created specifically to function in the physical realm. Yet neither of these is absolute since angels have been known to physically manifest and redeemed humans are shown functioning in the spiritual realm separate from their physical bodies (Revelation 6:9-11 & 7:9-15).

6. **Descriptions of angels in Scripture show them having the basic appearance and anatomy of people—head, human-like faces, torso, arms & legs—with the exception of their having wings.** True, Ezekiel described cherubs in two visions in terms of being covered with eyes and having four faces, including that of a man, but this is likely symbolic language, as detailed in **Chapter 1**; the same goes for John's descriptions of the living creatures in Revelation.

---

[70] Obtaining eternal life is a 2-stage affair: It begins with spiritual regeneration wherein the believer acquires eternal life *within*, that is, in his or her spirit (John 6:47 & Titus 3:5), which culminates with the bodily resurrection (1 Thessalonians 4:13-18 & Revelation 20:4-6). This explains the *seeming* conflict between passages that say believers *presently have* eternal life (John 3:36 & 1 John 5:13) and ones that say eternal life *will be granted in the future* (Titus 1:2, 3:7, Mark 10:29-30 & Jude 1:21).

7. **Jesus is *The* Son of God and *The* Angel of the LORD whereas angels are referred to as sons of God and angels.** Christ is Deity, of course—the Creator of all things, as detailed in **Chapter 7**—while angels are created beings created by the Creator, yet this terminology reveals some kind of affinity in likeness.

All this points to angels being created in the image of God, like human beings. However, I'm not going to give a definite "yes" because the Bible never technically describes angels as being created in God's image and likeness, which it repeatedly does with humans (aside from Genesis 1:26-27, there's also Genesis 5:1, 9:6, 1 Corinthians 11:7 and, arguably, Ephesians 4:24 & Colossians 3:10).

Besides, even *if* angels were created in the image of God they lack the privilege and position granted to people; that is, to be *co-heirs* with Christ, seated *with Him* at the right hand of the Father, as shown in these potent verses:

> **Now if we are children, then we are heirs—heirs of God and co-heirs with Christ, if indeed we share in his sufferings in order that we may also share in his glory.**
> **Romans 8:17**

> **To which of the angels did God ever say, "Sit at my right hand until I make your enemies a footstool for your feet"?**
> **Hebrews 1:13**

> **And God raised us up with Christ and seated us with him in the heavenly realms in Christ Jesus,**
> **Ephesians 2:6**

Reflect on these things; it's good stuff!

Conclusion: The idea that angels may be created in God's image is certainly an interesting topic, but it's not worth quarreling over.

Bibliography

NOTE: Just because a particular author appears in this bibliography it doesn't automatically mean that I embrace every jot & tittle of what they teach (with the exception of the LORD, of course); it simply means I "ate the meat and spit out the bones" (1 Thessalonians 5:21). I encourage you to do the same with *any* teacher of God's Word.

Archer, Gleason, and Gary Hill. *Helps Word-Studies Lexicon.* Retrieved from http://biblehub.com/, 1987, 2011

Barrier, Roger. *17 Things The Bible Tells Us About Angels.* Retrieved from http://www.godupdates.com/17-things-the-bible-tells-us-about-angels/ (no date)

Brown, Francis/Driver, S.R./Briggs, Charles A. *Brown-Driver-Briggs Lexicon.* Peabody: Hendrickson Publishers, 1994

Bullinger, Ethelbert W. *A Critical Lexicon and Concordance to the English and Greek New Testament.* Grand Rapids: Zondervan Publishing House, 1975

Cooper, James. *What the Bible says about Angels!* Retrieved from https://www.whyangels.com/, 2017

Dake, Finis Jennings. *Dake's Annotated Reference Bible.* Lawrenceville: Dake Bible Sales, Inc., 1991

Houdmann, S. Michael. *Got Questions?* Retrieved from https://www.gotquestions.org/, 2002-2017

Lindsey, Hal. *The Liberation of Planet Earth.* New York: HarperCollins, 1974

Lloyd, Majorie Lewis. *It Must Have Been An Angel.* Boise: Pacific Press, 1980

Kirkwood, David. *Your Best Year Yet!* Pittsburgh: Ethnos Press, 1996

LORD, The. *Douay-Rheims Bible.* Charlotte: Saint Benedict Press, 2000

LORD, The. *English Standard Version (ESV). Holy Bible.* Chicago: Crossway, 2001

LORD, The. *Holman Christian Standard Bible.* Nashville: Holman Bible Publishers, 2004

LORD, The. *King James Version. Holy Bible.* Iowa Falls: World Bible Publishers

LORD, The. *New American Standard Bible.* Nashville: Holman, 1977

LORD, The. *New International Version. Holy Bible.* Nashville: Holman, 1986

LORD, The. *New International Version (Revised). Holy Bible.* Nashville: Holman, 2011
LORD, The. *New King James Version Study Bible: Second Edition.* Nashville: Thomas Nelson, 2012
LORD, The. *New Living Translation. Holy Bible.* Carol Stream: Tyndale House Publishers, 2006
LORD, The. *The Amplified Bible.* Grand Rapids: Zondervan, 1987
LORD, The. *Quest Study Bible: New International Version.* Grand Rapids: Zondervan, 2003
LORD, The. *World English Bible (WEB).* Salt Lake City: Project Gutenberg, 2013
LORD, The. *Weymouth New Testament.* Ulan Press, 2012
LORD, The. *Young's Literal Translation (YLT). Holy Bible.* Grand Rapids: Baker Books, 1989
Luginbill, Robert D. *Judas Iscariot.* Retrieved from http://ichthys.com/mail-Judas.htm (no date)
Otnow Lewis, Dorothy. Cited in *Deseret News: Bundy Psychological Problems May have Started in his Infancy.* Retrieved from http://www.deseretnews.com/article/31997/BUNDY-PSYCHOLOGICAL-PROBLEMS-MAY-HAVE-STARTED-IN-HIS-INFANCY.html, 1989
Reagan, David. *Do pets go to Heaven?* Retrieved from http://christinprophecy.org/articles/do-pets-go-to-heaven/, 2017
Renner, Rick. *Seductive Spirits and Doctrines of Demons.* Tulsa: Rick Renner Ministries Inc. 1990
Servant, David. *God's Tests.* Pittsburgh: Ethnos Press, 1993
Servant, David. *Heaven Word Daily.* Pittsburgh: Ethnos Press, 2009
Strandberg, Todd. *Defending the Pre-Trib Rapture.* Retrieved from https://www.raptureready.com/rr-pre-trib-rapture.html, 2017
Strong, James. *Strong's Exhaustive Concordance.* Grand Rapids: Baker, 1991
Villanueva, Eric. *Territorial Spirits and Spiritual Warfare: A Biblical Perspective.* Christian Research Journal, Summer 1992
Vine, W.E. *Vine's Expository Dictionary of Biblical Words.* Cambridge: Nelson, 1985

Fountain of Life
Teaching Ministry
(Psalm 36:9)

The mission of Fountain of Life is to **set the captives FREE** by **reaching the world** with the **life-changing truths of God's Word**, the **power of the Holy Spirit** and the **Awesome News of the message of the Mighty Christ**.

**We're calling Warriors all over the earth
to partner with us on this mission!**

Books by Dirk Waren:

The Believer's Guide to Forgiveness & Warfare (2012)
Legalism Unmasked (2013)
HELL KNOW! (2014/2016)
SHEOL KNOW! (2015)
The Four Stages of Spiritual Growth (2015)
ANGELS: Their Purpose and Your Responsibility (2017)

www.ingramcontent.com/pod-product-compliance
Lightning Source LLC
Chambersburg PA
CBHW061630040426
42446CB00010B/1346